MY FA

D1342186

First published in 2009 by
Liberties Press
Guinness Enterprise Centre | Taylor's Lane | Dublin 8 | Ireland
www.LibertiesPress.com
info@LibertiesPress.com
+353 (1) 415 1286

Trade enquiries to CMD Distribution
55A Spruce Avenue | Stillorgan Industrial Park | Blackrock | County Dublin
Tel: +353 (1) 294 2560 | Fax: +353 (1) 294 2564

Distributed in the United States by
Dufour Editions
PO Box 7 | Chester Springs | Pennsylvania | 19425

and in Australia by
James Bennett Pty Limited | InBooks
3 Narabang Way | Belrose NSW 2085

A CIP record for this title is available from the British Library.

Cover design by Liam Furlong
Internal design by Sin É Design
Printed by ScandBook
Set in Garamond

MY FATHER, THE GENERAL
RICHARD MULCAHY AND THE MILITARY HISTORY
OF THE REVOLUTION

RISTEÁRD MULCAHY

Galway County Libraries

CONTENTS

ACKNOWLEDGEMENTS

I am grateful to Michael Laffan, Katie Drake, Déirdre McMahon, Anne Dolan and Maryann Valiulis for advice, and to Barbara Mulcahy for her secretarial assistance. Hugh Mulcahy undertook the major task of digitising my father's one hundred and sixty tape recordings and placing their contents on CD. Ulick O'Connor has always been generous in his encouragement of my writings. I am grateful to Séamus Helferty, Orna Somerville and the staff of the UCD Archives and to Commandant Victor Laing and staff of the Military Archives. I am particularly grateful to my editors, Seán O'Keeffe and Daniel Bolger of Liberties Press, for their patience and guidance, and to Peter O'Connell for his constant support. My wife, Louise, has been generously tolerant of my neglect during recent months.

INTRODUCTION

Richard Mulcahy played a major role as a military and political leader in the movement for national freedom during the early part of this century. He subsequently played an important part in the evolution of Ireland as a free and democratic nation. His biography was published by Maryann G. Valiulis in 1992.[1] He died in 1971 and I have been acting as his literary executor since his death. I assisted him in putting his large collection of War of Independence, Truce, Civil War and later personal and political papers in order, and to arrange for them to be transferred to the archives of University College Dublin. I also encouraged him to provide detailed information about his career, which is contained in the one hundred and sixty tape recordings he made and in his extensive critique of the Piaras Béaslaí biography of Michael Collins, published in 1926.[2] He did not release his papers until the year of his death and largely eschewed any reference to the revolutionary period during his active career in politics from 1924 until his retirement in 1961.

I am impelled to ensure that his contribution to Irish nationality and independence, and his wider contribution to the safeguarding of democracy, should be preserved in the national consciousness. His contemporaries and my own extended family were well aware of Mulcahy's seminal contribution to the revolutionary movement and to the subsequent formation of a stable and democratic state. He was described by his biographer as 'the forgotten hero'. Mulcahy's military reputation has been overshadowed by the increasing cult of Collins. In addition, his reputation has been tarnished by his perceived draconian conduct of the Civil War, and the difficulties he encountered in tackling the political, economic and social problems which existed after the foundation of the Free State – at a time when he was also faced with the demobilisation of the army after the Civil War, the Army Mutiny, and his own subsequent detachment from the army and from political and military power.

After his retirement, his conversations with others, his recollections, and particularly the patient archiving and annotating of his extensive collection of papers, fitted well with his orderly mind, and his tendency to take a systematic approach to things. I have used three documentary sources in writing about my father. They are his papers, lodged in the archives of University College Dublin, his three hundred an ten-page annotation of Béaslaí's biography of Michael Collins and his tape recordings, made between 1961 and 1969. I have also referred to his biography by Maryann Valiulis and to some other writers, all of whom I have acknowledged.

BACKGROUND AND FAMILY

Richard Mulcahy was born at 70 Manor Street, Waterford, on 10 May 1886. This is a large double-fronted building on one of the main streets leading to the west of the city. It is now a hostel housing students attending the Waterford Institute of Technology and is adorned by two plaques, one in Irish and the other in English, commemorating Mulcahy's role in the revolution. There were eight children in the family. He was the eldest boy and the second-eldest child. His father, Patrick, was a post office clerk in Waterford when he met and married Elizabeth Slattery, in whose house he was lodging. Although his father appeared to have a modest occupation, he was obviously a respected citizen if one is to judge by the size of his commodious residence and the fact that he was a burgess of the city. In 1901, Patrick Mulcahy was posted to Thurles in County Tipperary as postmaster, and he finally ended his career as postmaster in Ennis, County Clare. He died in 1923.

Richard Mulcahy attended the Christian Brothers School at Mount Sion in Waterford, the first school established by the founder of the Christian Brothers, Edmund Ignatius Rice. It was the forerunner of the many schools established widely at home, and later abroad, after Catholic Emancipation, and which had such a profound influence on the nationalist movement in Ireland and on education here and in the wider western world. He was greatly influenced by the education he received from the Brothers, and in later years he kept in close and sympathetic touch with his former teachers, including some who subsequently emigrated to as far away as western Canada and Chile.

Mulcahy's paternal grandfather was a tailor in Carrick-on-Suir, County Tipperary. His maternal grandmother was a Quaker named Maria Harris from Waterford, whose father, Samuel, was a wealthy merchant and an importer of wheat from the United States. The Harris family can be traced back to Thomas H. Harris, son of William Harris and his wife Hannah, who was born in 1663 in Parks Grove, County Kilkenny. (There is a family tree recorded in the Harris bible printed in the seventeenth century and now in the possession of the author's brother Padraig.) The family was well known and greatly respected in Waterford's business and social circles: they were members of every charitable board in the city.

Membership of the teaching profession was a strong feature of the Mulcahy family, going back several generations. It is therefore not surprising to find that four of my father's five sisters became secondary teachers or that, of the eight children, five became members of religious orders. Nonetheless, nothing in the history of the family would suggest that one member of the family would be chief of staff and later commander-in-chief of a revolutionary army.

Kitty, his sister, was the family's historian: her account of the family and their antecedents is lodged with the Mulcahy papers in the University Archives. Her reminiscences were recorded in 1965 on tape. She talks about the various in-laws and cousins named Slattery, Harris, O'Sullivan and Cremins, all from the south Munster area. She mentions her paternal great-grandfather, Richard Mulcahy, who was apparently a farmer in the Carrick-on-Suir region. However, unlike my mother's family in Wexford, whose lineage can be traced back to the early eighteenth century, the Mulcahy lineage goes no further back than Mulcahy's great-grandfather – except for the distaff Harris side. The Mulcahys clearly emerged from the poor Irish tenantry of the pre-Famine days, and there is little trace to be found of earlier generations.

It is also clear from conversations with my father and members of his family that they, like other Catholic middle-class families towards the end of the nineteenth century, were supporters of Home Rule but were otherwise not radical in their political views. Their nationalism did not conceive of the possibility of breaking with either England or the Crown. Mulcahy's participation in the 1916 Rising caused consternation in the family, particularly for his father, but this was changed to acceptance and later approval during his subsequent imprisonment and prominent involvement in the War of Independence. Unlike his children, whose sense of nationalism was kindled by Mulcahy's influence, his father did not approve of any separatist ideas. He said that he was grateful to Westminster for his appointment as postmaster.

While Mulcahy's five sisters went to university in Dublin and finished their third-level education, the three boys were not so favoured. Mulcahy had an excellent academic record with the Christian Brothers in Thurles, achieving at the age of fourteen one of the highest places in Ireland in what was then the Junior Grade examination. He describes in detail his days at school in Thurles, the boys he studied and played with, and the subsequent careers of a number of his contemporaries, some of whom distinguished themselves in the professions and in national affairs. He describes how he was unable to accept an offer of free education in Rockwell College after his Middle Grade because of the family's difficult financial position, and of his leaving school at the age of sixteen because the £20 exhibition money he had earned following the Junior Grade examination was needed to pay family debts. Despite the austerity of their lives in Thurles and the frugal circumstances under which they lived, the family always appeared to be in debt. It was therefore necessary for the three boys to finish their education early and to relieve the household of unnecessary expense. Further information about the Mulcahy family is recorded in Appendix 4.

Richard Mulcahy:
A Summary of his Career

Mulcahy left school at the age of sixteen in the autumn of 1902. He joined the post office as an unpaid learner in January 1903, when he spent his first six months with his father in Thurles before transferring to Tralee in County Kerry. Shortly after his arrival in Tralee, he was transferred to Bantry post office in west Cork, and his two years in Bantry were to play a seminal part in his social and cultural development. In Bantry, he went for long walks in the hills and valleys of that beautiful part of the country. He came into close contact with the local people and found in Ballingeary, some twelve miles from Bantry, the place which was to have the greatest impact on his early development. Ballingeary was, and still is, the centre of the West Cork Gaeltacht. There, Irish was the functional language at the time, and in the house of Siobhán an tSagairt he had the native Irish culture and traditions, and the native language, firmly implanted in his mind. He had already acquired a basic knowledge of Irish thanks to a teacher in Thurles who offered voluntary classes to boys who wished to learn the language. (At that time, Irish was not on the school curriculum.)

He called the house of Siobhán an tSagairt his 'university'. Here he met Irish poets and scholars, seanchaí and singers, teachers and language-revival enthusiasts. But most of all, he met Siobhán and the local Irish population, still unaffected by the insidious approach of materialism; they were generous, hospitable and modest in their needs, and living their days steeped in the native culture which was their heritage. Here he found the inspiration which was to bind him to the peasant culture of his native land.

Mulcahy left Bantry after two years but returned to his 'university' during his summer holidays until, in 1915, he attended the Irish Volunteers training camp in Coosan, close to Athlone. Afterwards, visits to Ballingeary were less frequent, though no less enjoyable. After the formation of the State, he maintained close contact with the gaelteachts in Kerry and, to a lesser extent, Connemara, and as chairman of the Gaelteacht Commission in 1925 he had welcome opportunities for indulging in his passion for the Irish language.

His stay in Bantry was also to introduce him to Irish nationalism and to the separatist movement. Here he read papers published by Denis McCullough and Bulmer Hobson, who established the Dungannon clubs in Northern Ireland and were leaders in nationalist thinking in the North in the early years of the century. Through his reading, he also learned about Arthur Griffith and his advocacy of a dual monarchy, and the still modest but more radical Sinn Féin movement. His interest in nationalism continued during his later time in Wexford but his active life as a nationalist and separatist only started when, after his arrival in Dublin to join the engineering section of the post office in 1907, he was introduced as a member to the Teeling branch of the Irish Republican Brotherhood. He found Wexford less inspiring than west Cork. The best he could say about it was that it was suitable for 'contemplation and work'! He spent his time there taking long walks in the countryside and attending Conradh na Gaeilge classes.

By the time he arrived in Dublin in 1907, he had become a fluent speaker of Irish. He prepared for a number of examinations at the newly established vocational schools to advance his career as an engineer in the post office. During his lifetime he continued his eclectic interests, as is evident from his extensive library, which includes books on history, philosophy, politics, economics, social affairs, personal health and self-help. In contrast to Wexford, he found Dublin a most exciting and vibrant city, and he took full advantage of the new third-level institutions which were becoming an important part of the city. His days were spent at work but his evenings were passed at the technical college in Bolton Street, where he continued his interest in languages and science, and where, among other interests, he learned shorthand, which was to prove to be of great value to him in his future political career. He recalled that he recorded de Valera's speech in support of constitutional change at the Sinn Féin meeting in October 1921.

Mulcahy's membership of the IRB from 1907 initially involved him in no political or military activities. He attended a monthly meeting but at best these were only roll-call meetings, where an occasional application for new members was processed and the monthly shilling subscription was collected. This inactivity came to an end when he and the other members of his branch were advised to join the Irish Volunteers when this organisation was established in November 1913. Mulcahy's orders from the IRB leaders were to join and 'obey his superior officers'; a precept which must have appealed to his orderly and disciplined mind. From November 1913 to the 1916 Rising, he trained with the Volunteers at weekends and at summer camp. Home Rule was finally approved by both houses of Parliament in Westminster in 1913 but the situation was complicated by the overt resistance to Home Rule of the Northern Unionists and the Ulster Volunteers, and the support they received from many prominent Tories and some sections of the British army. The enactment of Home Rule was postponed; the dilemma facing the British government was temporarily solved when the Great War started in August 1914. However, although the 1916 Rising was promulgated by a very small group of separatists, the Rising and its aftermath destroyed the Irish Parliamentary Party and made the very limited devolution enshrined in the Home Rule Bill unacceptable to a generation which was greatly influenced by the heroic sacrifice and radicalism of the 1916 leaders.

On joining the Volunteers, Mulcahy was appointed second lieutenant in the Third Battalion of the Dublin Brigade. Shortly before the Rising, he was elevated to the post of first lieutenant. However, he did not join his battalion during the Rising. He had successfully cut the telephone and telegraph lines to Belfast and England on the Great Northern railway line in north County Dublin on the instructions of Sean McDermott, the principal organiser of the Rising. Mulcahy was unable to get back to Dublin after he had completed his task because of roadblocks which had been erected by the British military. He therefore joined Thomas Ashe's Fingal Brigade in north County Dublin. There is a detailed description of this operation in his papers.[1]

The Ashbourne action was the only 'successful' action of a military nature mounted during the Rising but it has received little mention in subsequent recollections of 1916. Despite the Fingal Brigade's success at Ashbourne, where they fought and captured a large body of armed RIC men, they were obliged to surrender on the orders of Patrick Pearse. Soon, Mulcahy was sent to Knutsford Prison in Cheshire and, about six weeks later, to Frongoch in north Wales. His experience in these camps is described below.

Mulcahy returned to Dublin on Christmas Eve 1916 with the last batch of prisoners from Frongoch. The outlook for the returning prisoners seemed bleak, with little prospect of employment or assistance. He was appointed commandant of the Second Battalion of the Dublin Brigade on his return. The battalion was engaged in little activity at this time, however, and he spent the spring and early summer of 1917 fund-raising for the Gaelic League in Cork and Kerry. He then returned to Dublin to prepare for entry to the medical faculty of University College Dublin, apparently with financial assistance from the Volunteer Dependants Fund. He became involved with the other leaders in reorganising the Volunteers and was appointed commandant of the Dublin Brigade shortly after his return to the city. He owed this important military appointment to the reputation he had acquired as a military leader at Ashbourne, and to his role as the organiser of the funeral of Thomas Ashe (who died as a result of being force-fed while on hunger strike in September 1917).

Mulcahy greatly admired Ashe and, as commandant of the Dublin Brigade in September 1917, he was given the responsibility of organising his public funeral. Ashe's death, and his funeral, played an important part in advancing the separatist movement in Ireland. Dublin came to a standstill while vast crowds witnessed the orderly and punctual procession from the City Hall to Glasnevin Cemetery, with no intervention by the Castle forces. The event was to prove to be a reminder of Mulcahy's organisational skills – and an indication to Westminster that the remnants of the Volunteers were alive and well.

At the Volunteer Convention on 27 October 1917 a formal executive was set up, with Mulcahy as director of training. Six months later, in March 1918, just before the German Plot arrests and as the conscription crisis was looming, he was proposed by the other directors of the resident executive as chief of staff of the newly established general headquarters staff of the Volunteers. He and his colleagues on the staff were responsible for military policy during the subsequent three years before the Truce of July 1921, and it was GHQ which directed the War of Independence from January 1920 to July 1921.

Mulcahy became a member of the First Dáil after the 1918 general election and was minister for defence in the first Cabinet. However, when the Cabinet was reshuffled at the time of de Valera's return from Lincoln Jail in April 1919, Cathal Brugha became minister for defence; Mulcahy was assistant minister for defence while remaining military head of the army. However, he had little time for political activities because of his commitments to the army and to the organisation of GHQ. He remained head of the army during the Truce and until the ratification of the Treaty in January 1922. He retired as chief of staff when he was appointed minister for defence in the post-Treaty Dáil Cabinet. Prior to this, he played a symbolic political role: because of his prominence in the army, he was asked to second de Valera as President of the Republic in August 1921, he escorted the American delegates to the Peace Conference when they visited Ireland in the spring of 1919, and he was invited to comment on the Democratic Programme in the First Dáil.

Mulcahy spent the next five months after the ratification of the Treaty organising the Free State army with his successor as chief of staff, Eoin O'Duffy, and, with Collins, making strenuous efforts to avoid the split in the army, which was eventually to lead to civil war in June 1922. He returned to the army as chief of staff in June to lead the war on behalf of the Provisional Government, and he became commander-in-chief on 24 August 1922 after the death of Collins, who had returned to the army on 13 July 1922. Mulcahy finally retired from the army at the end of the Civil War in May 1923, when he was re-elected to the third Dáil, having decided to follow a career in politics. His role in leading the Free State army during the Civil War was endorsed by the electorate at this election, when he received a huge vote in his Dublin North constituency.

Mulcahy continued as minister for defence in the Free State Cabinet until

March 1924, when he resigned in protest at the sacking of the Army Council by the government at the time of the Army Mutiny in March 1924. He remained in the political wilderness from 1924 to 1927. He was reinstated to the Cabinet as minister for local government and public health after the first 1927 election and remained in this position until the advent of the Fianna Fáil Government in 1932. His reinstatement was against the wishes of William Cosgrave, who was obliged to yield to pressure from the rank and file of the Cumann na nGaedheal Party, and some of his ministers, including Kevin O'Higgins and Paddy Hogan, who with other Cabinet colleagues had been responsible for his resignation as minister for defence at the time of the Army Mutiny.[2]

Mulcahy remained out of the Cabinet until the first election of 1927. During these years, he continued to support the government and remained an active member of the Cumann na nGaedheal Party. He states in one of the tapes that, without his support, it would have been difficult for the government to survive. If this is true, it was probably because of the important segment of the pro-Treaty group which perceived him to have made a more important contribution than anyone else in the party to the country's independence and as the person with the most advanced national record and outlook. It was this element in the party which forced Cosgrave to reappoint him to the Cabinet in 1927. There is a lengthy transcription of a tape recording of his views about the national successes and failures of the Cumann na nGaedheal government during the period 1922-32.[3]

From 1932 to 1948, during the sixteen years of the Fianna Fáil administration, Mulcahy acted as the principal spokesman of his party and the Opposition. He was elected president of Fine Gael when William Cosgrave retired in 1944, and spent the next four years in a hectic reorganisation of Fine Gael, which was then at the lowest ebb in its history, with only thirty TDs. He also busied himself in the Herculean but successful attempt to organise an Inter-Party Government, in opposition to Fianna Fáil, after the 1948 election. Although he was head of the main opposition party, he agreed to have a neutral Taoiseach because of the numerous small parties involved in the coalition, some with political backgrounds and ideologies which were different from those of his own. These four years of reorganisation, followed by the change of government, were to mark the revival of the fortunes of the Fine Gael Party. He was minister for education in both Inter-Party Governments (1948-1951 and 1954-1957) and remained head of Fine Gael until 1959, when he resigned. He retired from politics before the 1961 election. He died in 1971.

THE YEARS 1916-1924

THE RISING

Like most of the other participants in the Rising, Mulcahy had no knowledge of the intentions of the organisers until a few days beforehand, and then only because, being an engineer in the post office, he was needed to carry out the crucial cutting of telephone and telegraph communication with the North and Britain. On this matter, he said:

> At the third training camp at Coosan, Athlone, in September 1915, I cannot recall any feeling of common gossip or common intention or expectation that a rising was in the air. We carried out our work there as a matter of pure training. We were very interested in it but all our comrade-like contact and the atmosphere that surrounded [it] was that of persons engaged at volunteer work in the same way as we might have been engaged at learning Irish in Ballingeary with the various trimmings that went with that – talks and meetings in houses and excursions, walks in the hills.
>
> On Saturday 15 April 1916, not only had I no idea that there was going to be a rising but that idea was so far from my mind that I had not the intention of being with the company on its manoeuvres on Easter Sunday, about which we got a rather important urging at the officers' meeting in Dawson Street that night from Pearse. It was my meeting with Sean McDermott at the Banba Hall after the officers' meeting that caused me to know that the Easter Sunday parade was in fact going to be a rising.[1]

Ashe appointed Mulcahy second-in-command of the Fingals when he arrived from the outskirts of Dublin after cutting the telephone and telegraphic communications with the North and Britain. According to his comrades in the Fingal Brigade, he played a major role in planning the strategy which led to the defeat and capture of a large force of the Royal Irish Constabulary in Ashbourne.

It was his record in the Ashbourne affair which established Mulcahy's reputation with his colleagues after 1916 and led to his appointment as head of the Dublin Brigade of the Volunteers six months after his return from prison. The Ashbourne action has been described in detail by the late Colonel Joseph Lawless, who was attached to the Fingal Brigade. Lawless had this to say about Mulcahy:

> Early in the week, however, we had the very good fortune to be joined by a few stragglers from a city battalion, amongst whom was Dick Mulcahy, known already to the other members of the staff. It was soon apparent to everyone that his was the mind necessary to plan and direct operations; cool, clear-headed and practical, and with a personality and tact that enabled him virtually to control the situation without in any way undermining Ashe's prestige as the commander.[2]
>
> . . . Ashe, who had a hurried consultation with Mulcahy. The last mentioned then turned to us and assured us that the police had not a chance of success, and that we were going to capture or rout the whole force. The quiet confidence with which he made this statement had a very good effect on the ranks, and I listened intently whilst he explained to me the general idea of our attack and what he wanted us to do. It was significant that Ashe, who was nominally the officer in charge, appeared to place himself in Mulcahy's hands.[3]

Lawless then proceeds to describe the plan of campaign which Mulcahy outlined and which eventually was instrumental in their capturing the large force of the Royal Irish Constabulary. There were fifty-seven members in the police contingent, according to official sources, and forty in the Ashe force. The latter number was somewhat inflated – to four hundred – according to a subsequent report in the *Constabulary Gazette*![4]

Several of the tape recordings deal with the Ashbourne action, and a further paper by Colonel Joe Lawless, who took part in the action, provides a graphic description of the battle and testifies to Mulcahy's cool leadership.[5]

During this action, the armed RIC suffered severe casualties, including several men killed, including the chief commissioner and his next in command. The rest were captured and disarmed.

There has been little reference to this sole military 'success' by historians dealing with the Rising, nor was it referred to as a significant action during the fiftieth and seventy-fifth celebrations of the Rising. I often wonder what my father – who in my perception was among the most religious and least violent and aggressive of men – thought of his participation in the deaths of so many innocent people who were merely carrying out their duty as protectors of the peace. Perhaps his conscience about the deaths of the policemen was assuaged by his commitment to the Rising and to the goal of achieving political independence for, and preserving the native culture of, the Irish people.

In discussing the justification of the Rising, I put it to my father that at the turn of the century the situation in Ireland presaged an early advance of democracy and of equality among the different Irish social classes. Such a social trend was also driven by the advance of the land question, the emergence of a Catholic middle class following Catholic emancipation in 1827, the huge contribution Catholic teaching orders were making to secondary education among Catholics, the National University Act of 1917, the Celtic Revival driven by Protestant and Catholic alike, and by the gradual takeover of local government by the Catholic majority. Home Rule had considerable support from Protestants as well as the great majority of Catholics. He responded to my comments:

> . . . the harshness of the Rising idea itself was smothered to a large extent, and the horror at the execution of the leaders was made more effective by the expounding and the growing understanding that the men who instigated the Rising were impelled by cultural, social and economic needs for the people, and had been deeply and variously active with regard to these.[6]

I comment elsewhere about my father's refusal to attend the ceremony in

1955 when the president, Seán T. O'Kelly, unveiled the large monument commemorating the Ashbourne action. I wondered if my father, as a man of peace and of strong religious feelings, felt sensitive about the deaths of nine innocent men who were simply doing their duty. His answer to my questions about the justification for the action was far from clear or convincing.

Mulcahy states that the Rising could not have been more politically successful, even if the whole country had risen and the arms had been successfully landed in Kerry. He said that the Rising, and the subsequent executions of the leaders, was the catalyst which was to lead to the final achievement of freedom for the Irish people to govern ourselves. It was clear that the instigators of the Rising knew that they could not defeat the British militarily and that their gesture was likely to be successful as a blood sacrifice. Michael Tierney, in his biography of Eoin MacNeill, writes:

> Early in 1918 the Volunteer staff conceived the not-very-wise idea of court-martialling officers and men who had not taken part in the rebellion.[7]

I have never heard Mulcahy refer to such a step, and he would have been firmly opposed to such an idea – although there is evidence that the IRB may have held an enquiry where Austin Stack was the subject of interrogation about the failure to land arms in Kerry in 1916.

Perhaps Cathal Brugha, as chairman of the Resident Executive, may have initiated this policy. There are several entries in the tapes, and annotation, where Mulcahy emphasises that there were no recriminations, and no justification for recriminations, among the 1916 veterans in relation to those who failed to turn out for the Rising. In particular, he comments on the lack of Volunteer action in Cork city and Limerick, and the failures associated with the landings of arms in Kerry. He deplores a few derogatory remarks on this subject made by a few companions in Frongoch, and he reminds us of the special care de Valera and others continued to take to honour Eoin MacNeill, who had tried to stop the Rising.

On the question of recriminations, he states:

> Nobody ever wanted to question anything about anybody's actions in

Easter week, and particularly all who knew anything of it maintained a generous and loyal silence.[8]

Of critical remarks contained in the Béaslaí biography about the failure of the Limerick men to take part in the Rising, he states:

But Limerick was very much affected by the Kerry situation, both as regards Casement and the Killorglin episode in which their own men were involved and the sentence about their inactivity etc is inexcusable.[9]

He also refers to the unfortunate criticism of the failure by the Cork people to take part in the Rising. Piaras Béaslaí was quoting Colivet on the subject, and my father showed his fondness for metaphor when he had this to say of Colivet: 'he was never anything but a bubble in the gas pipe'!

In a conversation about Easter week, my father, my mother and I talk about Tom Clarke and Sean McDermott, who were the organisers of the Rising, and Pearse, who was its inspiration (despite his earlier acceptance of Home Rule, which reflected the universally popular view before 1916). We talk about the failure of the arms landing in Kerry and the effect it had on McNeill's decision to stop the Rising. Mother recounts some of her experiences during the week, when, with her sister Phyllis, she visited the GPO every day until Thursday, and refers to the unusual gaiety of normally solemn people such as Tom Clarke. The tape finally comes to an end as we discuss the 'purifying' of the IRB – a process which was initiated by Denis McCullough, Tom Clarke and Sean McDermott in 1908. The 'purification' was aimed at restoring the morale and commitment of the IRB to its stated purpose of achieving freedom for Ireland.

The three of us discuss de Valera's performance in Boland's Mills and the possible cause of his nervous breakdown, as described by one of his senior officers, Simon Donnelly, to Dr Tom O'Higgins[i] in Ballykinlar Camp during the Truce. De Valera had a few days of mental detachment or confusion during the week but there was little mention by his companions of his reaction to the obvious stress of the fighting. Mulcahy discusses the week in Bolands Mills in considerable detail with Sam Erwin. Erwin was with de Valera in 1916 and talks about the rather futile instruction to burn down Westland Row Station: 'There was nothing to burn!' The conversation finishes with a final agreement

---

[i]Dr Thomas O'Higgins, brother of Kevin and later founder member of the medical corps of the Free State army. After the Civil War, he was appointed chief medical officer of County Meath and was a prominent member of the Fine Gael Party when he was elected to the Dáil.

that all the mistakes which occurred during the Rising were the result of inexperience and lack of professional training, and that everyone, including Dev, deserved perfect understanding!

We continue with a prolonged discussion of the attempted arms landing in Fenit, the background of its failure, and the decision not to proceed with the Rising; the American influence leading to the failure; and some interesting facts about Roger Casement, including his alleged intention to return to Ireland from Germany to stop the Rising. We talk about MacNeill's countermanding order and the fact that, if German troops had taken part in the Rising, it would have led to disaster and would have been inconsistent with the prime purpose of the Rising – which, according to Mulcahy, was always designed to be a symbolic action and was never thought likely to lead to a successful military outcome.

After the surrender on the Saturday of Easter week, Mulcahy was sent with his colleagues to prison in Knutsford, close to Manchester, and was later transferred to the prison camp in Frongoch in north Wales. He gives the following accounts of Knutsford and Frongoch at the beginning of his Béaslaí annotation.

KNUTSFORD

We arrived in Knutsford by daytime on Wednesday the third of May. It was a small jail, being used at that time for British soldiers who had been convicted of offences and were being punished there. They were down in the lower part of the prison; they appeared to have been very harshly treated; by daytime we sometimes saw them going through a kind of torture drill in one of the prison yards, very heavily laden with their equipment; at night we very often heard them screaming under apparently very heavy physical punishment.

The prison was built with a number of wings consisting of three storeys of cells. The cells were arranged along both sides of the wing; a railed balcony ran around, and the open space left by the balcony was covered over with heavy wire netting to prevent prisoners jumping over or throwing things over. A narrow high slit of a window lit the cell (I don't think there was artificial lighting arranged for in the cell), a small triangle of wood was inserted in the wall at a corner near the door to serve as a table for taking meals; a wooden bed consisting of three planks joined together and raised about four inches above the floor, together with one brown soldier's blanket and a chamber pot, was the only furniture in the place. Not only was there no mattress for the bed but there was no pillow. In the beginning, whatever leg you lay on 'went to sleep' and even lying on your back was no complete solution. The pillow problem was whether you were going to lie with your head flat on the board, or take off your boots and so tie them together with your boot strings as to make a kind of receptacle for your head, lifting it a couple of inches up. I used my boots as a pillow. Luckily I had leggings over short knee breeches and my feet therefore didn't suffer too much from the cold.

For about the first three weeks we were in solitary confinement for twenty-three and a half hours out of the day; we exercised for a half an hour a day by walking around in single file in a small circle around one of the prison yards; we just had the additional exercise of emptying our slops; and in an emergency we could ring a bell to get out. I am not sure if we could go for a shower bath once a week, but we did have shower baths now and then. On Sunday we had Mass in some kind of a prison church or large hall. When we stood up to leave after our first Sunday morning's Mass, some of the boys started to sing 'Faith of our Fathers'. The idea was taken up immediately and before a line or two had been sung, we were lifting the roof, until we finished the whole of the hymn through all its verses. I think we frightened the life out of the warders and soldiers who were in charge of us. We liked the idea so well that we continued with 'Hail Glorious Saint Patrick'. It was a real feast of defiance and it was adopted as the regular Sunday procedure after that.

We were as hungry as anything. We received our meals in a tin can into which an inverted cover fitted. For breakfast in the morning and tea in the evening, little more than a cup of tea was received in the tin can.

Galway County Libraries

It was dark brown and turned almost black if you didn't drink it quickly, and in the receptacle on top there was a small lump of bread. Either in the morning or in the evening, but only once a day, we got a small bit of margarine. This meal was taken on the little triangle of wood in the corner of the room. The approach to eating the bread was begun rather ravenously and it was only when the last bite or two remained that you remembered to chew it and chew it as much as you could, then you went around the table with a wet finger picking up the crumbs that had remained on the table. M 224,204

When we first entered our cells there were three books in them, one a Bible, the other a copy of Challenor's *Think Well of It*, and some other pious book. We were allowed no writing material, either paper or pen or pencil. I kept track of the day of the month by putting a pin-prick into the leather band of my hat. I had one pin. After a day or so, the door of my cell was pushed in very urgently and a soldier stood inside and shouted at me something that appeared like 'A.C.' I could do nothing but look at the fellow. He repeated several times but I couldn't make anything out of it. Finally I tumbled to the fact that he was asking me was I a Roman Catholic – an R.C. When I said I was, he stretched out his hand and made a glaum at the Bible and was taking it away with him when I pleaded with him to be left it – I felt that it was a real godsend for reading. But I was an R.C. and there were prison regulations and that was that. Off he went with the Bible.

Every week we were given a small octavo sheet of glazed paper upon which we might send one letter home. I don't recall how we were provided with a pen or a pencil for writing, that is in the early days of our solitary confinement, because my recollection of my row of pinpricks on the inside of my hat would show that I was dependent on the pin to mark the date for the greater part of the three weeks or so we were in solitary confinement. The hours of the day were indicated in various ways; those we were most interested in were indicated by the scurrying of feet on the ground floor, indicating that particular activity which brought us our breakfast, our lunch and our tea. In my cell after about noon, I had a kind of a sun dial formed by the split window where the sun traced a mark on that wall in which the cell door was. I had a particular interest in a particular spot down somewhat low to the left side of the door; it indicated that tea time was approaching. One of the Sunday afternoons there, I was watching it somewhat anxiously feeling that there was still a fair time to go before tea would arrive, when suddenly I was surprised by hearing the scurrying of feet that indicated that the tea movement was on. Right enough the tea came along. It was only some months afterwards that I realised that it was on that day that summer time was first introduced, so that tea arrived when the mark of the sun on the wall was an hour ahead of its normal point.

The problem of occupying the mind in relation to time was a very difficult one. The pros and cons of what had happened and what was likely to happen was in no way the occasion of any questioning of mind or cogitation of any kind. My mind was just in a state of waiting, it was looking for occupation and exercise. It very soon found that in a rather interesting and tantalising way. In the years 1913 and 1914 I had spent at least three weeks of the summer in Ballingeary. I had taken down from Siobhan an tSagairt a lot of pieces of poetry or rhyming, long and short. I had entered these carefully in a good notebook, and to some extent I had memorised some of them. Also in connection with the attempt to begin to write Irish, I had taken some lessons in French from Bertha Dumay, later to become the wife of Dick Browne of the ESB; and working somewhat on the lines of studying Irish, I had been collecting passages and memorising such things as a couple of Aesop's fables or something by Lamartine. I began therefore to occupy my time trying to recollect some of that kind of material that interested me.

I found it very absorbing and very tantalising. On the Irish side there was plenty of material to try and work on, like 'Maidean aoibhinn Fhómhair agus mé ag gabhall an róid tré choill' or 'Seán de Burca' or 'Nat an bHacaig' or 'Nat an Bhó'. It might be that in the case of something that had about four verses in it, I would recall a line in the third verse, then the job was to complete that particular verse. While trying unsuccessfully to do that, I might recall the opening of the first verse or a line in the first verse, but meantime I had no paper or pencil with which to write down what I had got in the third verse and perhaps I would have to forget all about that particular piece for a day or two and get on with something else. This kind of thing occupied days, changing from one Irish piece to another or from Irish to French. Material on the French side would include something from Aesop, *'Une chene un jour dit au roseau'* or the fable of *'Le Corbeau'* and *'Le Fromage'* or something from, I think, Lamartine's *'Un Nom'* – *'Il est un nom cache dans l'ombre de nom amer'* – or from, I think, Molière – *'L'esprit doit sur le coeur prendre le pas devant'*. It was a great occupational find.

Naturally there was a great sense of personal isolation, but it was accompanied by the feeling that there was a great mass of humanity of a sympathetic and intimate kind all round in the personnel of the prisoners. There was no possibility of any communication with them except such as could be given by a glance or a smile or a whispered word in the occasional moments in which we moved together either in the passages of the wing or going out towards the exercise ground; there was no suggestion of dejection of any kind in either the faces or the demeanour of the men; there was a fierce sense of hunger which was felt very much by the country boys, and the cold of the cells, particularly at night, was very trying. There was largely, because of the presence of British military prisoners in the jail and the impression we got of their treatment, a suggestion of brutality about the place; you hesitated very much to ring your bell lest you would bring some element of that down on yourself for giving trouble; but only on one occasion had I any trouble with one of the soldier warders, and that was when, for some reason or another, one of them in my cell threatened to beat the face off me as one of those bloody yankees who had come over here to create trouble.

The prison chaplain never made any impression on us except that of coldness. There was no sympathy between us. Different sections of the men exercised at different times of the morning. (One morning after about three weeks' solitary confinement we were allowed to exercise in one of the yards.) At certain times when they were exercising, we in our cells could hear numbers being called out. We weren't very sure what it could mean. It could mean that prisoners were being called out for returning home either for trial or for release. Up to that time I had been under the impression that there was a likelihood that I might be returned to Dublin for court martial; both detectives and military had searched our room at Richmond Barracks and surveyed all the men there in circumstances that could only mean that they were looking for the person who, on Ashe's behalf, had interviewed General Friend at GHQ on the Sunday. [Mulcahy was sent to interview Pearse in Kilmainham to receive confirmation of the surrender and was escorted there by British soldiers] When therefore after our 'lunch' I found myself summoned to the governor's office, I felt that the blow had at last fallen. I was utterly relieved when, on getting to the governor's office, I found that he had a number of people with him who appeared to be friends.

Some of the Irish in Manchester, with a Father Fogarty, had made up their minds that they would visit Knutsford and see if they could see any of the prisoners, bringing gifts. There were two girls by the name of Mulcahy on the party, and looking over the lists from Dublin they found the name Mulcahy, so they asked to see me. They were able to get their visit for the reason that instructions had just come that the conditions of our confinement were to be changed and that we were to be treated as internees, so that, if not from that night, at any rate from the following day, the cell doors were open except for bedtime, and, within limits, the prisoners had the run of the place and complete association with one another.

The visitors from Manchester had brought fruit, biscuits and cheese. These were all mightily welcome and in quantity and in value they appeared to be sevenfold multiplied by reason of what they signified. There were seven or eight in all of the Manchester people – Father Fogarty and a couple of men, and two Mulcahy girls. One of them afterwards married Sean King [I knew him in later years, too, as a shopkeeper in Clare Street], another Mary, who afterwards married Sean O'Muirthile [later to be Mulcahy's adjutant general in the Free State army during and after the Civil War, and to be sacked at the time of the Army Mutiny], and a couple of others. This visit of the Manchester people was to open a regular periodic connection between the Manchester people and ourselves in Knutsford and later on in Frongoch; it re-established our complete connection with the world outside as well as providing that satisfaction and help that came of complete mutual association among the prisoners themselves.

The general make-up of one of the prison wings, with its wire netting and its bars of various kinds, was such that on the following day when the full noise of intercommunication had got going, the prison became almost as intolerable as a monkey house, where all the animals had gone screeching mad. The noise and the clamour of talk and movement were almost unbearable. An interesting feature of this contact was the delight and surprise with which individual men met one another, very often very unexpectedly.

One of the earliest and most smilings that I got on our own landing almost immediately after the doors of the cells were open was from a young fellow who recalled the 'awful dance' that I had led them [on] a few Sundays before the Rising. On this Sunday morning, the Second Battalion were going out on manoeuvres against the Fingal men. Tom Hunter was the O/C in charge of the battalion that day. Somewhere beyond Whitehall he had halted his men, and he told me that he wanted me to take a party and go ahead on a reconnoitring expedition to find out the lie and the movement of the Fingal men. He marked off with his arm from one of the companies about twenty men; I was to take these. I said that, as I thought the work would be tough and might mean a lot of cross-country work, I thought it would be better to have volunteers; my idea was that we would want to have a group of men who were all fit. So volunteers were asked for and I started off at a rather quick pace. When we had got a fair distance away from our own main column, I started to move at a jog trot. It wasn't long until some of the men fell out and gave up. Then it wasn't long until in one way or another we got information that the Fingal men were not coming. So after moving into the fields a bit, we decided that we would turn ourselves into an ambush party and ambush our own column. My prisoner friend complained appreciatively that morning 'I went like a deer'.

At Knutsford we never had that type of organisation of ourselves for management that was an integral part of our internment camp conditions [in Frongoch]. We were all individual prisoners. I don't think that there was any particular person in charge of a wing or in charge of a row of cells, and if any work previously done by orderlies was now done by ourselves, such as the distribution of meals to the various cells, persons selected for this work were either self-selected or were appointed by agreement with the military people who had been responsible for the direction of that work before.

The conditions of our stay at Knutsford until the time we left for Frongoch were not such as to induce any sense of organisation or control, and there was no element of that relaxation which would induce quiet intimacies between individuals or among groups. We were something like six weeks in all at Knutsford, and [during] the last two or three [we] never got rid of the confusion of the first day of being released to internee conditions.

Father Fogarty became a regular visitor and heard confessions. The prison chaplain probably lost any work of that kind that he had. I don't think that razors were allowed, but it must have been by the assistance of some of the Manchester people and a safety razor that I got rid in time of a beautifully pointed red beard. A return to solitary-confinement conditions might help me to recall individual prisoners of that time, but at the moment I have no such clear recollections. I just have one picture of Pierce McCann standing with a group of others on the ground floor on the day he was preparing to go off to Frongoch, distributing some copies of Messengers of the Sacred Heart and some holy pictures. Pierce was one of those who were at the training camp at

Coosan, Athlone, in September 1915. He afterwards died under internment conditions in jail in England in 1919.

We probably left Knutsford for Frongoch on the same day. I don't know how many of us were in it. Denis McCullough [who later married Agnes Ryan, my mother's sister] has in his home two photographs I gave him. They are hanging up framed. One shows himself and myself and some others coming out of the main gate of Knutsford, the other shows the railway station before we embarked. We might find some familiar faces in the first photograph. That was on 17 June 1916. There are a number of letters available written by me at Knutsford. I don't think they contain any evidence at all of any thought upon what the future was going to suggest to me in the line of any outlook on Volunteer work or on political work. They would show that I was thinking of what kind of employment I might look for when release came and that that might be in some teaching work. I think they would suggest that I had a rather virgin outlook on a very virgin page suggesting that the future was entirely pathless by suggestion of any kind. But I think it will confirm that our minds were quite relaxed and unconcerned and waiting with a cheerful outlook for changes in the situation. There was nothing we could do about anything. We were all quite satisfied that something important had happened. We were all satisfied that there was a sufficient number of us in the position of prisoners to have a strength that could afford to feel quite peaceful, and there was a tremendous development of a feeling of satisfactory comradeship.

In Béaslaí's account of Frongoch, he speaks of timidity and divided counsels and distinguishes between fighting men and those who weren't fighting men. There was no element at all of that in any way in the atmosphere at Knutsford nor do I recall that there was any element of distress which spread itself in any way as a result of men with troubles about domestic responsibility at home.

FRONGOCH

In his commentary on Béaslaí's description of Frongoch, Mulcahy said:

> Béaslaí has no impression as to what life in the camp and the circumstances of its organisation and its direction were. The south camp consisted of a distillery in which there were three large floors used as dormitories. About two hundred men had sleeping accommodation in each of these three dormitories; North Camp consisted of about thirty huts capable of housing about twenty-five men each. In the south camp there was a camp commandant, Staines, and a couple of camp officers with him, and three officers in charge of a dormitory each. I was in charge of the dormitory at the top of the building. In the North Camp there was a camp commandant with one or two officers, and an officer in charge of each one of the thirty huts. Each officer was only responsible for the discipline and minor matters connected with his own room and his own men. During the time in the camp, Collins was rather a group man concerned with his own immediate colleagues, most of whom were apparently in his hut, and those who were refugees, that is, men from England who were liable to conscription if identified. Added to that, he was part of the Kimmage group in Dublin rather than of the Dublin Brigade. I had a greater position of responsibility and a greater sense of responsibility as far as the general camp position was concerned. That arose from my position in the Dublin Brigade, heightened by the Rising experiences and my contact with Staines. Collins didn't come much generally in the picture nor take any very obvious responsibility for the general camp arrangements or policy. Looking back, I would have to say that he probably confined himself, but very vigorously and attentively, to gathering together the threads of whatever IRB element there was in the camp, and preparing in this way to see that the IRB organisation and influence would be a very definite thing in the post-Rising political development in Ireland.

> It is important to get a correct picture of the control situation in Frongoch. We will find that prisoners first went to Frongoch on 9 June 1916. The batch from Knutsford arrived on 17th June. At that time it

is said there were about two hundred persons in the camp. It is further said that before the North Camp was set up, the number in the south camp had risen to about 1,100. A further date that has to be kept in mind is 26 June 1916, the date of the 'Camp Orders' by Commandant J. J. O'Connell, commanding Irish prisoners of war. W. J. Brennan-Whitmore is associated with the order as commandant and adjutant. He had arrived with us from Knutsford nine days before, that is on 17 June.

J. J. O'Connell[i] was one of the prisoners at Reading as recorded by Peadar [O'Donnell] on 12 July. The following description of O'Connell from Peadair is a translation from page 129 of his *Mar Mhaireas, Part One*: 'Ginger O'Connell is here also and is in great steam to direct everybody according to military ideas but he is not succeeding. He was the same way also in Richmond Barracks but he found it difficult to make headway there. But Ginger is sensible and he did not go too far. He was trying to get us to understand in Dublin that we were prisoners of war and that therefore we should show respect to the officers (British) who came around, but when the question was put to him about the way in which Maxwell was carrying on and whether his treatment of the commanding officers of our army had been in accordance with the treatment of prisoners of war, he had no answer except to say "if they break the rules of war we should not imitate them". A good enough answer but it was not accepted. He himself however used to show respect to every [British] officer that came to us. He was a soldier and he conducted himself accordingly. There is no officer here who wants to make a matter of argument of it with him.'

It is easy enough to understand how the first miscellaneous group of about two hundred prisoners with a man like John O'Mahony, no doubt the proprietor of O'Mahony's Hotel, Dublin, would set up an organisation based on messes and have a general council or civil government; and it is easy enough to understand that when people like [Michael] Staines, [Denis] McCullough, [Tomás] MacCurtain and [Terence] MacSwiney had arrived, that they would make use of a man

---

[i] J. J. O'Connell had been in the American army but returned to Ireland in 1914 when he joined the Irish Volunteers. He was on the GHQ staff in 1921, supported the Treaty and subsequently had a distinguished career in the Free State.

of whom they had such experience as O'Connell to set up a camp control on different lines. My earliest impression is that whatever kind of control there was within the first week or two of my being in Frongoch, there was a very placidly and generally accepted control, and that O'Connell was very active and very useful. He had been concerned with the original plans for the Rising in the Munster area, but in the circumstances of MacNeill's countermanding order and the non-arrival of the guns in Kerry, he had no part in the Rising. He could be regarded as being in the frustrated position that MacSwiney[i] and MacCurtain[ii] in Cork were.

I had no responsibility of any kind in the earlier fortnight or so but I was in frequent and cooperative touch with O'Connell. One of the things he said to me during that period was that I appeared to have had established a great ascendancy over the Fingal men. I have no conscious recollection of there being anything like 'civil government' or even a 'military staff'.

It is clear that the three weeks that elapsed between 26 June and 12 July, during which period apparently the North Camp was set up and M. W. O'Reilly appointed its commander, the military staff personnel had largely been removed to Reading [Jail], including O'Connell, and by 16 or 17 July, M. W. O'Reilly, commandant of the North Camp above, had gone there too. It would appear that Michael Staines was the camp leader for the whole of Frongoch after that. It would have been in relation to such changes that I became the officer in charge of dormitory number three, consisting of about two hundred-odd prisoners on the top floor of the distillery. I had plenty of work and responsibility to keep me going; the contacts and the acoustics of the camp were very good. I had the closest hour-to-hour personal contact with Staines and there were no matters to be discussed that had to be discussed at the level of anything like a military staff or a civil government's general council.

In the South Camp the whole working life of the place was directed to the dormitory leaders and the general plan and day-to-day direction

---

[i] Active in Volunteers, teacher and lord mayor of Cork. MacSwiney died on hunger strike in London. Mulcahy had been his best man when he was married while under house arrest in England in 1919.

[ii] Active in Volunteers, MacCurtain was lord mayor of Cork at the time of his murder by the Black and Tans in March 1920.

of particular matters was ordered by Staines in counsel if necessary with the dormitory O/Cs. There would have been a regular series of camp orders and the arrangement of companies for company drill. As far as the North Camp was concerned, each hut contained about twenty-five men and there was an officer in charge of each hut. I don't know who was the deputy in charge of it between the removal of M. W. O'Reilly to Reading about 15 July and the latter part of August, by which time it was shut down.

Mulcahy goes on to describe in some detail the organisation of the camp during the separate periods under different commanders and their 'military staffs'. He describes the movements of the men in and out of the camp, the early releases, and the persistent attempts by the British to identify those who might be subject to conscription into the British army. He describes the recurring complaints and strikes which occurred as a result of disagreements with the camp's governor and his staff, troubles which simmered right up to the release of the remaining prisoners on 23 December 1916. He differs strongly with Béaslaí, who inferred that a minority of the prisoners, who were seen to be fighting men and separatists, formed into a secret group to counteract the 'timid and divided counsels' of the others. He finishes his account with the following comments about Collins:

> The period involves a certain number of stories general and personal, and calls for further reflections and discussions on the Collins activity in the camp. There were very many groups of kindred spirits in the camp, but I have no recollection of any group that made itself assertive or critical in any way of the camp controller or general camp organisation or activities. Collins was no doubt a very important centre of such a group or companionship as such. Based on a west Cork and an IRB centre, a distinctive group or part of his grouping would be the internees who were liable for conscription and some of their immediate friends, but in addition, he was very consciously pulling the threads of the IRB men together with a view to the situation which would develop politically and organisationally when all the prisoners, including the

Lewes prisoners, were back at home and political life was beginning again in Ireland. The future politically in Ireland, as far as organisation of the Volunteers or of political parties was concerned, was not a matter that got my concentrated thought in any way at that time; it was something that the future alone could take care of. I had no special group contact with Collins or those he was associated with and I never had any purely IRB discussions. I was apparently always accepted as an IRB man but was never 'involved'.

I have in my possession a 'Universal' edition of the Works of William Shakespeare with three drawings dated 1916 by a T. McCartaigh. These drawings were done in Frongoch. They depict a Frongoch Siesta, three prisoners sleeping close together on the floor; a cell with a standing prisoner, described as a combined bedroom, dining room, sitting room and parlour; and a group of marching prisoners described as 'Forward the Ration Party, Frongoch Camp'. There are several signatures, including those of Tomás MacCurtain, Terence MacSwiney, Denis McCullough, J. J. (Ginger) O'Connell and Richard Mulcahy. The definitive history of Frongoch can be found in W. J. Whitmore's book entitled *With the Irish in Frongoch*.

RETURN FROM FRONGOCH AND ARMY LEADERSHIP

On his return from prison in Frongoch at Christmas 1916, Mulcahy undertook fund-raising for the Gaelic League in County Cork. He was there from March to August. He travelled the length and breadth of the county on his bicycle, including the Gaeltacht region of Ballingeary and Ballyvourney, with which he was so familiar. He was appointed commandant of the Second Battalion of the Dublin Brigade on his return from Frongoch, but there was little Volunteer activity during the early months of 1917. As has already been discussed, he was the principal organiser of Thomas Ashe's funeral in September 1917, immediately after which he was appointed the commandant of the reconstituted Dublin Brigade. In September 1917, a meeting was held in the Keating Branch of the Gaelic League to discuss the setting up of Sinn

Féin and Volunteer executives. A number of prominent nationalists and separatists were present, including Eamon de Valera, Arthur Griffith, Cathal Brugha, Sean McGarry, Michael Collins, Diarmuid O'Hegarty,[i] Michael Staines and Richard Mulcahy.

Shortly afterwards, on 17 October, Mulcahy became director of training in the newly established Volunteer executive. The Volunteer executive was formed the day after the Sinn Féin executive was elected. There was a national Volunteer executive, with twenty representatives drawn from the four provinces. De Valera was elected the nominal president. In addition, there was a smaller resident executive, with Cathal Brugha as chairman. Six members from Dublin were co-opted to strengthen the resident executive (including five responsible for military affairs). The six were:

- Michael Collins, organisation

- Rory O'Connor,[ii] engineering

- Michael Staines, supplies

- Richard Mulcahy, training

- Diarmuid Lynch, communications

- Sean McGarry, secretary of the resident group

In March 1918, at the time of the threat of conscription, the directors proposed the setting up of a general-headquarters staff. This proposal was approved by the national executive. Mulcahy was appointed chief of staff. The national and resident executives virtually ceased to function after the appointment of the GHQ staff. The formation and function of the volunteer executive is described by Mulcahy in some detail. He remained the military head of the army from March 1918 until the ratification of the Treaty in January 1922, and again from June 1922, at the beginning of the Civil War, to its end, in May 1923 (except for the period from 13 July to 22 August 1922, when Collins was commander-in-chief).

The original GHQ staff appointed in March 1918 had the following members:

---

[i] O'Hegarty had been prominent in the IRB and IRA during the War of Independence and was a senior civil servant after the foundation of the state. His family was well known to us later, when they lived in Brendan Road in Donnybrook.
[ii] Rory O'Connor, an engineer, was an intractable opponent of the Treaty. He was a leader of the Four Courts garrison before the Civil War and was one of the four Mountjoy prisoners executed on 8 December 1922.

- Richard Mulcahy, chief of staff

- Michael Collins, director of organisation and adjutant-general

- Sean McMahon, quartermaster general

- Rory O'Connor, director of engineering and O/C Britain

- Dick McKee, director of training

- Austin Stack,[i] deputy chief of staff (appointed but never acted)

By the Truce, in July 1921, the staff had increased in number to thirteen. They were as follows:

- Richard Mulcahy, chief of staff

- Michael Collins, director of intelligence

- Gearoid O'Sullivan, adjutant general

- Eamonn Price, director of organisation

- Rory O'Connor, director of engineering

- Eoin O'Duffy, deputy chief of staff

- Sean Russell, director of munitions

- Sean McMahon, quartermaster general

- J. J. (Ginger) O'Connell, assistant chief of staff

- Emmet Dalton, director of training

- Seamus O'Donovan, director of chemicals

- Liam Mellows,[ii] director of purchases

- Piaras Béaslaí, editor of An tOglach

O'Donovan and Béaslaí were appointed to the staff early in 1921. All the others, and Austin Stack, were named as being on the staff in the Cabinet minutes of 25 November 1920, but Stack's nomination was not agreed by the GHQ staff. This was one of the events which was symptomatic of the conflict

---

[i] Stack, who was born in Kerry and was a founder member of the Volunteers, was associated with the failed landing of arms in Kerry in 1916. He was subsequently minister for home affairs in the 1919-21 Sinn Féin Cabinet. He was strongly opposed to the Treaty but did not take part in the Civil War.

[ii] Mellows was born in England, and was a member of the Volunteers from 1913. He opposed the Treaty and was one of the four Mountjoy prisoners executed on 8 December 1922.

between Brugha and the leaders of the army. There are many references in the annotation and tapes to the personnel of GHQ during the period from the formation of the staff in March 1918 to the Truce in 1921,[1] but little was known about the personnel of GHQ from 1918-1921 until Mulcahy released his papers to the UCD archives in 1970.

In November 1920, on the night before Bloody Sunday, Dick McKee was killed when captured by the British. McKee had followed Mulcahy as commander of the Dublin Brigade and was on the GHQ staff. He was a particular loss during this crucial period of the war.

Béaslaí, in his biography of Collins, describes Mulcahy in several places as assistant chief of staff. Early in 1961, as I got more involved with Mulcahy's writings and recordings, I called on Béaslaí at the Catholic Commercial Club in O'Connell Street to question his reasons for describing Mulcahy as the assistant chief of staff. He replied that he thought that Cathal Brugha was the chief of staff – an error which oddly enough appears in some of Collins's earlier correspondence. Brugha was, of course, chairman of the resident executive of the Volunteers and was never on the staff, nor did he ever get involved in military activities after 1916. He acted as the link between Mulcahy and the political wing, Sinn Féin.

Although Béaslaí was the editor of *An tOglach*, the clandestine organ of the Irish army, and was a nominal member of GHQ, his connection was almost entirely with Collins and the Vaughan's Hotel group. This group was made up mostly of IRB members who were with Collins on the intelligence side and who formed 'the Squad', the active military wing under Collins's direction. Vaughan's Hotel, in Parnell Square, was a popular meeting place for Collins and his men. Many of the notices and articles which appeared in *An tOglach* under the name of the chief of staff were written by Ginger O'Connell, Rory O'Connor or Dick McKee. Béaslaí told me at our meeting that he had little contact with my father during the war. As O'Muirthile states in his memoirs, he too was originally part of the Collins group. When he ultimately came into closer contact with Mulcahy (as adjutant general and a member of the Army Council during the Civil War), he had this to say about Mulcahy and the Army Council:

The situation I stepped into then on 15 October 1922 was one of greater difficulty than I had expected – for the first time now I came into real association with two men I had never worked close to before, and outside of whose circle I had been up to then. I speak of General Mulcahy and General Sean McMahon. My school was that of Collins, O'Sullivan, Duggan, Boland, Tobin and others, and we were a happy, carefree lot, who in the hardest of times could be found carelessly congregated at one or other of our various haunts. Collins was the 'boss' of a merry collection of subordinates. There was no side nor no aloofness or ceremony. Of Mulcahy and McMahon and their work, I knew practically all there was to know, but I had come to regard them as stern, silent workers who scorned pleasure and frivolity and who had enslaved themselves to their respective tasks. My acquaintance with Mulcahy of course went back years, because through Gaelic League and Volunteer work we had occasion to associate. Sean McMahon I had known in more or less a distant way. Of the strenuous work he had been engaged in during the war with the British, when he so successfully received and delivered numerous consignments, large and small, of arms and ammunition at the Dublin docks, I was well acquainted.

As evidence of how false impressions and groundless opinions often lead to much mischief, I would like to say that had I remained in isolated and aloof subordination of these men, I might subsequently, as others did, regard them as a clique, and I too might have rebelled against their administration. In order to know men properly, you must live with them or work with them, and once I had begun to work and live within barrack walls with General Mulcahy and General McMahon, I realised the greatness of their outlook, their tireless devotion to their task, and their fairness to all within the limits of their responsibilities. Their unqualified ardency and resolve to prosecute the task begun by Collins was ever visible. I settled down to work with them and we went through busy days and nights together, directing our respective departments throughout the day and sitting in council throughout the night, framing policy and regulations for an unorganised army.[2]

Shortly after the Truce, my father and mother had afternoon tea in the Gresham Hotel. It was probably my father's first appearance in public after being on the run. At the next table, they recognised the painter Leo Whelan, who was with a priest. During the conversation with their two neighbours, my mother was inspired to suggest that Whelan should take the opportunity of painting the General Headquarters staff while the Truce lasted. Whelan apparently responded enthusiastically to the idea.

Mulcahy's appointment as chief of staff was proposed by the military directors who were members of the Volunteer executive. It was subsequently approved by Cathal Brugha, the chairman, and the other members of the Volunteer executive. Collins was the other nominee for the position but Mulcahy was preferred and the circumstances of the appointment were as described by Mulcahy, in his tape recordings and in his annotation of Béaslaí's book, as follows:

> When on the night before the Volunteer executive met to appoint the GHQ staff, the directors, about half a dozen of us, met at 46 Parnell Square to consider proposals to put before the executive, and when we had agreed that as between myself and Collins I would be the person recommended to the executive as chief of staff, McKee, as he came away from the meeting with me, expressed satisfaction and relief that Collins was not being recommended. The main reason for that was that in the light of what he knew of Collins's temperament, and the short period and the circumstances in which any information about him had been obtained, McKee – like the others – was a little bit wary of entrusting him with anything like complete control; in fact he did want time to disclose himself and his qualities, and even when so disclosed, he was in a better position to use his energies and capacities over a number of concentrated and very important fields by a certain greater freedom of action as a result of his not being chief of staff and by the fact that I, as chief of staff, was in a flanking position of protection for him and maintained complete and cooperative harmony in all our doings.[3]

There were five active members on the GHQ staff at the time of its inception but this number had increased to thirteen by the time of the Truce. Most of the new appointments were made towards the end of 1920 and the beginning of 1921, as the structure of the army became more formal, the control of countrywide Volunteer activity by GHQ increased, and the fighting became more intense. Other tapes and papers contain further details of the organisation and personnel of the GHQ staff from March 1918 until the end of the Civil War.[4]

During the War of Independence, decisions about the organisation and strategy of the Irish resistance were made by the GHQ staff. By the end of 1919, the Irish Volunteers had adopted a more aggressive role towards the British police and military and it was impossible for security reasons to hold formal meetings of the GHQ staff. Mulcahy met members of the staff individually or in groups of no more than three or four. His meetings with Collins provided the main focal point of army policy and organisation. In terms of policy, GHQ gave the lead but its policies were clearly influenced by the initiatives of the active Volunteers in the provinces.

Mulcahy talks about the role of the national and the resident executives of the Volunteers set up in October 1917, as the early body controlling the army and the subsequent role of GHQ:

> The fact is that, set up as the GHQ staff was, on the eve of the practical development of the conscription issue, the only work that had to be done on the Volunteer side was actual military organisation, and the preparation of the Volunteer mind. The attitude of the Volunteers to the work of actual conflict was what had to be clarified and strengthened. Not only the general executive but the resident executive of the Volunteers had no function [that is, after the appointment of the GHQ in March 1918]. On the military side, this was strengthened by the fact that certain important members of the resident and general executive were members of the GHQ staff occupying the principal positions on it. The analogy between the Cabinet and the GHQ Staff works the other way. Cathal as minister for defence, Collins as minister for finance and a member of the GHQ staff, and myself as assistant minister for defence and chief of staff, made it easier

at that responsible level to feel that, while the work of the Cabinet was entirely distinct from the work of the GHQ staff, the work of the GHQ staff would be completely harmonised and subservient to Cabinet outlook.[5]

He goes on to state:

From the time the GHQ staff was set up, I kept in close personal touch with Cathal Brugha, who was the chairman of the resident executive, in practically the same way as I did later when he was the minister for defence, namely, I kept in complete touch with the civil representative of the Volunteer organisation until the government was set up, and with the ministerial head after that. They were the same person.

And he continues:

I have suggested that from the time of the setting up of the General Headquarters staff, the general Volunteer executive had no particular function to discharge. The Volunteer responsibility to the executive was fully discharged by the contact that I kept with Cathal Brugha, the chairman of the executive [and subsequently minister for defence].

When the Dáil was established in January 1919 and a Cabinet set up, apart altogether from the dovetailing of the personnel of members of the GHQ staff and the Cabinet, and apart altogether from the fact that the minister for defence was the chairman of the executive of the Volunteers, and the head of the government the president of the Volunteer organisation [that is, de Valera], the spirit in which the whole work was being pursued was that the GHQ staff and the army generally accepted the fact of government, and the authority of the Cabinet and the expression of that authority through the minister.

The role of the Volunteer executive had largely atrophied following the setting up of the GHQ staff in March 1918. It was also likely that, for security reasons, meetings of the full general or resident executive would have been very undesirable following the Volunteers' change of policy to active aggression at the end of 1919. There was apparently one meeting of the resident executive in 1920 and a further meeting in 1921, which Mulcahy refers to as follows:

I have in my mind the elements of the picture of the scene, but it was really nothing more than a formal coming together and looking at one another as a recognition, when the circumstances of the Truce provided the opportunity, that there was such a thing as an executive of the Volunteer organisation. It had however completely atrophied, not only with regard to its function but with regard to any feeling that it existed; those who were active officers in the Volunteers throughout the country I'm sure never thought of it, and I'm sure that those who were not active Volunteers throughout the country had no particular wish to think of it. There was probably expressed at the meeting full satisfaction and agreement as to the administration of the oath to the Volunteers in accordance with the decision taken by the Dáil at its meeting on 20 August 1919.[6]

By April 1919, when Cathal Brugha was appointed minister for defence, the political function of the general and resident executives was vested in the ministry and in the Cabinet, such as it was. I have no information about the membership of either the Sinn Féin or the Volunteer executive at this stage. The failure of the latter to function is understandable, since GHQ had been formed. The Sinn Féin standing committee did meet regularly during this time but, according to the minute books in my possession, no business of any political or executive nature of importance was conducted by this body. The significance of the standing committee was lost in the shadow of the absent de Valera. (I presented the two volumes of the minute books in my possession to the UCD Archives.)

On the subject of the GHQ staff and Mulcahy's functions as chief of staff, the following paragraph, based on material in his annotation of Béaslaí's biography of Collins, was published by me in *An Cosantoir*.[7]

Each member of the GHQ staff had his own particular responsibilities of a full-time nature but it is clear that there was considerable overlapping in their work and in their contact with the army in the field. The circumstances of the time made it impossible to set up separate departments in a formal way, although by the spring of 1921 the different departments were clearly enough identified and demarcated to send in their own separate monthly accounts to the chief of staff's department. These accounts are now available in the University Archives. Mulcahy claims that the Volunteers were the hard core of the emerging political organisation of Sinn Féin, and he states that much of the organisation of the Volunteers in 1918 took place under cover of the by-elections of this time.

The War of Independence could not have been sustained without either the participation of the men in the field, Michael Collins and his intelligence activities and widespread contacts in the country, or the GHQ staff. They were the three points of the military tripod which supported the action against the British, and which led to the Truce in July 1921.

Firstly, the achievements, initiatives, courage and sacrifices of the fighters in the field, particularly in Dublin, most parts of Munster, Longford and, to a lesser extent, in a few other scattered places, were such that, without these active men, no effective resistance to the RIC and the British forces could have taken place.

Secondly, Collins, through his energy and talents, and assisted by his trusted men, provided an intelligence back-up and other essential services without which the central and peripheral units of the army could not have existed.

Thirdly, the GHQ staff, headed by Mulcahy and supported by such prominent figures as Rory O'Connor, Ginger O'Connell, Sean McMahon, Dick McKee, Gearoid O'Sullivan and others, provided a solid basis for an organisation which ensured progress towards a professional army with a good communications system, a structured command, a mature and ethical philosophy (which must have been unusual in an insurgent army) and a commitment to parliament and to the will of the people. The army's commitment to parliament was copper-fastened by virtue of the fact that many of the army leaders, including Mulcahy and Collins, were elected to the First and Second Dáils. Despite the work and influence of GHQ, as a body it maintained a low profile – which was probably essential for the survival of its members and which was maintained by my father's self-effacing personality and insistence on maximum security for his staff. This low profile is evident from the almost exclusive emphasis by the historians on Collins and the fighting men. It is understandable that Collins should dominate the history of the time from the historian's point of view because of his early death, his major political as well as his military role, his charismatic, flamboyant character, and the early publication of his biography by Béaslaí in 1926 – where virtually no mention is made of GHQ.

C. C. Trench, reviewing my father's biography (by Valiulis) and referring to the development of the active-service units, stated:

> The main feature of the guerrilla war – the use of mobile, full-time active-service units and attacking soft rather than hard army targets – were not invented by the chief of staff but were devised perforce by the field commanders such as Liam Lynch. All Mulcahy did was to order others to do likewise.[8]

This rather dismissive remark conceals a considerable degree of ignorance about the organisation and evolution of the Irish army. Many of the successful strategies which were adopted during the War of Independence were, of course, initiated by those who were involved in the fighting in the field and who were face to face with the realities of the conflict. But the extension of these tactics to achieve an orderly strategy, the burning of the three to four hundred police barracks, and the organisation and training of the flying columns and the active-service units could not have taken place without the guidance and control of the GHQ staff. And this is not to mention a great number of other more mundane responsibilities which were required to run a successful coordinated military campaign, such as the funding of the campaign, the divisionalisation of the army, the formation of companies, battalions and brigades, the appointment of officers, the development of policies relating to spies and informers, the supply of arms and equipment, the maintenance of communications, and the implementation of many other administrative, advisory and disciplinary procedures. This aspect of the war emerges clearly from the references quoted by Valiulis in her biography, and from a perusal of the extensive Mulcahy papers in the UCD Archives.

Mulcahy was by nature a 'backroom boy', happiest when completely committed to a specific task of organisation – a characteristic which became more pronounced as he became older. His commitment was to service, not only in his work as a soldier and a parliamentarian, but even in the smallest matters among his family and friends. He was not interested in power but, when power was thrust upon him, was well capable of responding to it. Although he was elected to Dáil Éireann in 1919, and participated in some formal parliamentary activities, during the period of the War of Independence he devoted his entire attentions and energies to the army and its organisation.

Like Collins, Mulcahy was 'on the run', a fugitive from the British authorities from January 1920 to the Truce in July 1921. He had several narrow escapes from capture while he was staying in his various hideouts, and he describes a few of these escapes in his annotation of Béaslaí's book.[9] The following refers to a raid on his office in Paul Farrell's flat in South Frederick Street, where Mulcahy had left several incriminating papers:

> Paul Farrell used to do some acting in the Abbey Theatre and he now and then wore kilts. I say that they sent for bloodhounds and they gave them a smell of Paul Farrell's kilt and they sent them out on the roof to look for me. Meantime I was quite all right in UCD and just visited the cordoned area from the outside. It was a particularly difficult time for us. It would have been about February 1921.

He gives a list of his hosts and the twenty-five places where he did his office work, or where he slept at night during his eighteen months on the run.[10] He received food, hospitality and shelter from many courageous people during this difficult time, some of whom had no connection with the national movement but all of whom showed intense loyalty to their fugitive guest. Sleeping accommodation was always uncertain; this October–November 1920 was a bad time, and another bad time was to arise around March 1921.

On another occasion, he eluded capture by escaping on to the roof of Michael Hayes's terrace house on the South Circular Road and clambering from there into the house of a Jewish couple, who provided him with an early breakfast and advised him when it was safe to leave. His mode of transport was the bicycle, but it is not clear whether he always carried a revolver. On the question of being armed, he had this to say:

> This question became really a problem in the latter part of the struggle. It wasn't a question easily settled.

He continues by describing the following rather embarrassing experience:

> I ran into an awkward situation on one occasion when, being without a revolver, I went into one of our places in Westland Row, middle way in the street near the church, and on the church side. In the front room on the first floor, one of the QMG's [Quarter Master General's] young assistants named Harding had some kind of an office and I went to him for a revolver; he gave me an automatic. I pointed it at the wall between two of the front windows and pulled the trigger; it went off. Harding just quietly said 'You should come here oftener.' However, with the noise of the traffic below, nobody came in from the next room to know what was up and I moved quickly away from the place – with lesson learned.[11]

It was the critical security situation in Dublin in March 1921 that inspired the chief of staff and the GHQ members to decide on the divisionalisation of the army throughout the country. This was in case the GHQ staff might be wiped out and the army in the periphery left rudderless, without coherent central control and coordination.

> The pressure in Dublin was such that it was clear that there was no great security for the hope that we might be spared any further serious loss in the strength of the GHQ staff or in the strong activists circle in Dublin; this led to thoughts for planning the divisionalisation of the country on the basis that there were very many areas in the country where the equivalent of a GHQ staff could be set up, to maintain the morale and the initiative of the Volunteers in the area.

Despite his formidable reputation as a highly principled and unyielding head of the army, he was in private life an affable and friendly companion and colleague. He had little of the exuberance and public charisma of Collins, nor did he have de Valera's aloofness and subtle detachment from his colleagues – attributes which are so frequently evident in successful political leaders. He did have the important ability as chief of staff to be completely committed to the task at hand, and at the same time to delegate responsibility freely to his colleagues, and to encourage them in every way. As Collins's reputation advanced, so did the number of his critics, but Mulcahy was not one of these critics. His admiration for Collins is clearly and frequently expressed in his papers and tape recordings; in fact, far from resenting Collins's increasing military and political reputation during the war, he did everything to encourage him in his multifarious activities, and to protect him from his critics.

THE WAR OF INDEPENDENCE: ARMY POLICY

Mulcahy formally directed the army during the entire period of the War of Independence. He was, as described by Maryann Valiulis, a forgotten hero in the sense that his reputation in later life lost much of the shine it had had during his military career. In the article 'The Lads who Freed Ireland' (April 1922) and an article in *Irish Indiscretions* (1922),[1] an American correspondent wrote of Mulcahy's dominant role in organising the military resistance to the British, and referred to his outstanding qualities as a strategist. He was responsible for army policy in the widest sense and for the activities and actions of the staff members and the commanders in the field. (That is not to say, of course, that his colleagues on the staff and the commanders in the field did not play a part in formulating policy and in initiating action.) His greatest and most seminal contributions, apart from his organisational role, was his insistence that the army should be organised on the ethical lines of a professional army, that unnecessary violence and killings should be avoided, and that the army must remain subservient to parliament and to the people.

His leadership was characterised by a policy of waiting and seeing rather than one of aggression, at least until the Dáil was suppressed in the autumn of 1919 and war became inevitable. The earlier period was an important phase in the evolution of the Volunteers in the context of organisation and consolidation, as well as in terms of defensive policy.

P. S. O'Hegarty, in his *The Victory of Sinn Féin*, writes:

> After 1916, there should not have been a shot fired in Ireland, nor a gun bought. They were totally unnecessary. We had the Sinn Féin policy, the men who made it, the enthusiasm and the support of the people. Without firing a shot, we could have forced from England anything that we have forced from her by the gun policy, and more. We would at the same time have maintained our solidarity, escaped Partition, and avoided the irreparable moral disaster [the Civil War] which has overtaken us.[2]

I discussed with my father the justification for the War of Independence and O'Hegarty's point that the war contributed nothing to the advancement of Ireland's freedom. Mulcahy stated that he thought that this view was important but that:

> We have very very little conception of the forces that were operating in Great Britain at the time against this country.

He mentioned the Ulster Volunteers and the powerful Tory influence supporting the Northern dissidents, which led to Britain changing the rules in relation to Home Rule in 1913, and the conscription issue and the fabricated German Plot in 1918. He stressed the harassment of the Irish political leaders as early as 1917, before the Volunteers were officially reorganised in October of that year. Here he referred to Ashe's repeated imprisonment for speaking in public about Ireland's right to freedom and his death in prison in September 1917 from forced feeding as an example of British intransigence. He held that the circumstances of British aggression and harassment of the people and the members of the Dáil were such that local and eventually national reaction in terms of military aggression was inevitable. It would be humanly impossible not to react to the cumulative effect of British aggression, which started as early as 1917 and continued for more than two years, before the Volunteers adopted an active policy of military resistance. Until the end of 1919, both the political head (Cathal Brugha) and the military head (Richard Mulcahy) of the army were committed to a defensive policy on the part of the Volunteers. The suppression of the Dáil in September 1919 was the final provocation. The suppression of the Gaelic League and the GAA at about the same time gives an indication of the degree of British harassment.

Mulcahy describes this harassment, which was noted particularly during the Sinn Féin loan campaign:

> Military and armed police breaking up meetings, suppressing newspapers, removing machinery, raiding individual people three or four times in one day, that is with persistency and very great pressure – it will be found that all this expresses itself in the daily papers of the time in spite of censorship, and in the pages of the official 'Irish Bulletin'.[3]

> There were rather strong reasons why after the establishment of the Dáil he [Brugha] would be strongly for controlling violence while keeping our powder dry; Cathal could very well, at that time, be laying down principles encouraging the Volunteers to a sense of responsibility by the power, the duty and the function that was on them, and in the light of that power, seeking control and discipline and subservience to the Parliament.

> In a local and spasmodic way, the violence of British agents in the country created individual occurrences in which there was bloodshed before September 1919. But it was when that tendency to violence by the British agents was crowned by the positive suppression of the Dáil by the British government that the positive element of violence was introduced as a policy, to provide clearance areas in the country where the writ for the Dáil could begin to run, and the smaller bodies of Volunteers, who were engaged in active hostilities, could have security and a certain freedom of movement.[4]

On the question of the war, he maintained that the Volunteers, as late as the autumn of 1919, were still committed to their traditional defensive role, and that this policy was supported by the political as well as the military leaders. Indeed, strictly speaking, the Volunteers were an apolitical force until the election of December 1918. A shift to a more aggressive policy was brought about by the increasing harassment of the Sinn Féin leaders and the Dáil by the police. And although the threat of conscription had passed by the summer of 1918, Mulcahy believed that a more aggressive policy was inevitable, and was justified on moral grounds by the approbation of the Catholic hierarchy when they supported the anti-conscription campaign:

> The bishops' manifest[o] declared that 'The Irish people have a right to resist by every means that are consonant with the law of God'. Doctor McDonnell of Cork, lecturing to the Central Branch [of Fine Gael], made the point that this declaration gave the Volunteers and their action the status and the justification of a national army under national control.[5]

Mulcahy deals with the defensive policy of the Volunteers and the change to a more aggressive approach at the end of 1919 in several tapes and in the annotation. He was not infrequently criticised by battalion and field commanders for his prudence and conservatism, and what they perceived to be his undue caution in developing an aggressive policy. He was certainly a foil to Michael Collins's more flamboyant and more aggressive approach. For example, his condemnation of the Soloheadbeg episode contrasts with Collins's failure to condemn the action.[6] Collins states:

> the fires of Easter Week . . . were blazing brightly again at Solohead, at Clonfin, at Macroom.

Mulcahy says of Collins and the men who took part in the action that 'Collins's attitude and manner would have been a comfort to them'. However, the trust and friendship he and Collins shared were not impaired by such differences, as is apparent from Valiulis's book and from many of Mulcahy's papers; nor was Collins less concerned than Mulcahy about the reputation of the army, despite his more tolerant acceptance towards sporadic actions on the part of the Volunteers. Nor did Mulcahy object to any other action apart from the Soloheadbeg and Inishannon episodes – and in these cases his objection, and that of Cathal Brugha, was to the apparent cowardly and unnecessary loss of life.

Mulcahy never expressed any reservations about allowing Collins to adopt such a prominent role in military affairs. I believe that, while he supported Collins in everything he did, his prudence and caution provided an important brake on the more impetuous people in the army. Without his control, and the limitations he placed on what he perceived to be ill-judged, aggressive behaviour, or behaviour involving unnecessary risk, it is unlikely that the army would have evolved along such professional and ethical lines as it did. It is also likely that, without his involvement, the people of Ireland might have been less receptive and less supportive of the army's activities, particularly during the bitter days of 1920 and 1921. The shocked reaction of the people of Ireland to the Soloheadbeg episode would underline the danger of the population being alienated by excessive army aggression and brutality. It was a different matter when, later, the reign of terror was instituted by the British in the form of the arrival of the Black and Tans and the Auxiliaries.

> The decision to proceed with an active, aggressive policy was taken in consultation between myself and the minister for defence, I imagine, but without any formal Cabinet discussion, and it was discussed with the Cork people, and no doubt with others in preparation for its extension in other parts of the country for several weeks before Carrigtwohill[i] on 4 January 1920.[7]
>
> The necessity for having a positive-use-of-force policy was only adopted under the compulsion of the suppression of the Dáil in September 1919. So engrained was the understanding of the disadvantages of violence in the work that we were doing, and the message that we wanted to get across, that the new policy only came into effective action and publicity with Carrigtwohill . . .[8]

In GHQ's contacts with the country, it was inevitable that some active and independent spirits would take affairs into their own hands. This trend was understandable in those areas where the British had been virtually cleared out by the widespread destruction of police barracks. There were many instances of peripheral impatience with the leaders in Dublin, and this was more evident in some areas than in others. Mulcahy refers, for example, to the South Tipperary Volunteers, who described GHQ in general and himself in particular:

---

[i] Carrigtwohill was first of the many police barracks to be attacked and destroyed.

[That] GHQ representatives, and particularly myself, were mealy-mouthed in our instructions, both with regard to sacrificing the lives of our own people, being careful not to keep identity marks and even being careful in not unnecessarily taking the lives of members of the enemy. In the whole of our policy, these things were matters of conscience with us. They were also matters of political expediency; they were also matters with common sense and in accordance with the spirit in which the Volunteers were first founded as a defence [force].[9]

Mulcahy's cautious attitude to unnecessary killings, even among the enemy, is reflected in his reference to 'the Compton-Smiths' in his speech during the Treaty debate, when he deplored the necessity of killing innocent men by both sides during the War of Independence. Major Compton-Smith was an Englishman who was taken hostage and executed by the IRA when the British authorities refused to reprieve the death sentence on a few Volunteers whom they had captured.[10] Another example of peripheral criticism of Mulcahy's approach is to be found in Desmond Ryan's biography of Sean Treacy,[11] where, in referring to excessive Volunteer quiescence before the war started, Treacy comments about the possibility that the Volunteer force, which had been laboriously built up, might disintegrate. He is quoted as saying: 'If this is the state of affairs, we'll have to kill someone, and make the bloody enemy organise us.'[12] (Treacy, with Dan Breen, was involved in the killing of the two policemen at Soloheadbeg in January 1919.)

When writing about the Volunteer policy of non-aggression, Mulcahy gives a list of episodes in Dublin, Meath, Clare and one or two in other counties which preceded the change to a more aggressive policy at the end of 1919.[13] He mentions the shooting of several detectives in 1919.[14] None of these events were arranged by headquarters but they were invariably initiated locally in response to local harassment. With one or two exceptions, they were subsequently approved by headquarters. Mulcahy had this to say on the matter:

Some of the 'fighting spirits' would look at this kind of thing, coming from me, as being office-chair-and-table kind of business. I was saved from being too thin-skinned about this by Diarmuid O'Hegarty's remark in certain circumstances that 'Mulcahy was the only one who came out of Easter week with a military reputation'.

On the matter of being prudent on the issue of conducting an aggressive policy, he remarks:

> Our general hesitancy both as a matter of humanity and as a matter of policy to taking life or risking our own people's lives has been used in various ways from time to time to discredit the policy of offensive resistance after circumstances had demanded that it be embarked on and to imply disagreements in policy in respect of it. Desmond Ryan implied in his lecture (No. 54) that Griffith was at variance with Collins and ourselves on the point; and Hayes-McCoy implies that there were similar disagreements on the part of members of Dáil Éireann and members of the Volunteer headquarters, stating something like, 'In fact these bodies still share the public dislike of activities which caused casualties to either side'.[15]

An example of his prudence is his response to a request to him to agree to a public funeral for Michael Savage, who was killed during the unsuccessful ambush on the Lord Lieutenant, Lord French. He refused, and defended this decision on the grounds of security, but he attempted to console Savage's colleagues by stating his resolve that the British would be pursued to the end. In the same tape, he states that the more ardent spirits were kept under control by GHQ, 'thus leading to much of the success of the Volunteers'. Apart altogether from the expressed opinion of Cathal Brugha and others to the effect that the Volunteers could never be anything but a threat to Britain, it would not have been reasonable or useful to encourage an attitude of aggression as long as the Dáil was there for propaganda-appeal purposes.[16]

What can we deduce from the general evidence about relations between headquarters and the country units? It is that, under the circumstances, and the severe constraints of the times, and bearing in mind the complete lack of traditional military and political discipline among the people of Ireland up to the early twentieth century, there was a remarkably cordial and harmonious relationship between country divisions and GHQ, which manifested itself progressively from 1918 to the signing of the Truce in December 1921. It is evident from the Mulcahy papers that country activities and pressures had to be restrained at times – and that headquarters held these powers of restraint.

It is also clear that no action was ever disapproved of by headquarters, apart from the Soloheadbeg and Innishannon episodes in early 1919. Indeed, the acceptance by headquarters of subsequent spontaneous country activities and innovations may have been an important factor in ensuring a stable and cohesive relationship between the Dublin military and political leaders on the one hand and the country brigades on the other.

The Soloheadbeg incident was initiated by the North Tipperary Brigade without the approval of GHQ. Two policemen were killed without provocation in the course of their routine duties when they were delivering explosives to a quarry. It was unfortunate that the action occurred on the day when the First Dáil met. The attack was widely condemned and, in particular, evoked the condemnation of both Cathal Brugha and the chief of staff.

Mulcahy discusses the event in detail, when he states that 'bloodshed should have been unnecessary in the light of the type of episode it was' and that 'it pushed rather turbulent spirits such as Breen and Treacy into the Dublin arena from time to time, where their services were not required and their presence was often awkward'. He described the effect the incident had on the Archbishop of Cashel:

> The effect on the archbishop, who many years after told me that he had regarded Soloheadbeg as part of official policy and that after it he withdrew his mind from such things and concentrated entirely on the religious and the moral aspect of his responsibilities and work, when, later, a monument was being erected at Soloheadbeg to mark the episode, he intimated to those concerned that he did not wish any priest in his diocese to be associated with it, and that as far as the parish priest was concerned, into whose parish the President, Seán T. O'Kelly, was going for the occasion of the unveiling, he was to receive the president with all due courtesy but not to be associated with the official proceedings. Sean T. had asked the executive council at the time [the second Inter-Party Government] what action he should take in reply to an invitation to be present. The executive council told him that they had no advice to offer him. He went there.[17]

Headquarters was apparently willing to compromise and to be tolerant of local intransigence, but there is no doubt, as David Fitzpatrick states in his *Politics and Irish Life 1913-1921*,[18] that central control by headquarters became more manifest as the war continued. On this subject, Fitzpatrick wrote:

> During 1918 and 1919, however, headquarters began to show greater adeptness at directing and supervising the Volunteers.[19]

And also,

> Headquarters provided advice, instruction, a little equipment and a welcome sense of national togetherness. In return, provincial units accepted the dismissal and appointment of commandants, provided [that] the families of local influence were not seriously inconvenienced; and to some extent they modified their military activities to accord with headquarters' preferences.[20]

The greatest source of conflict between GHQ and the provincial units during the war remained the shortage of arms. However, Mulcahy states that there was a general failure to appreciate the important part played by GHQ in imposing national policy on, and in achieving control of, the army as well as in creating a more formal military structure. The large amount of material in the University Archives testifies to the fact that, as the war progressed, GHQ gained increasing influence, without at the same time impairing the initiatives and energies of the local units.

Many actions were initiated locally without consultation with GHQ, usually in response to local pressures, but such actions usually received the approval of headquarters because they conformed to the military and ethical policies of the army and the Dáil. Despite these local, spontaneous actions, the documentary evidence available to us confirms that headquarters, through its policy of divisionalisation, its control and integration of the destruction of the police barracks and tax offices, its coordination of the activities of the flying columns, its control of the appointment of divisional, brigade and battalion officers, its effective imposition of discipline and ethical standards, its regular distribution of orders on a wide variety of military and organisational matters, and through its responsibility for supplies and training, gave us an army which evolved in an orderly and disciplined way.

The army's orderly evolution in the circumstances of the time is little short of remarkable. Not the least of these difficulties was the size of the British forces, which, during Lloyd George's intensified war in the spring of 1921, were made up of Black and Tans, the Auxiliaries, the remnants of the RIC, and 80,000 British regular soldiers.

The Mulcahy papers contain a large amount of material in the form of communications between the GHQ staff and the active-service units. The material testifies to the close and improving communication between the leadership and the army in the field up to and including the Truce. The material covered by the General Orders also testifies to the same situation. For example, a perusal of GHQ General Orders covers at random such subjects as recommendations about actions in military situations and in civil situations, advice about conducting correspondence within the organisation, the boycotting of the RIC, the medical treatment of the wounded, the seizure of arms by the enemy, the functions of the volunteer police force, emigration as a form of desertion, the organisation of the courts, the handling of women spies, the procedures as regards the death penalty, the treatment of deserters, rules regarding association with the enemy, the management of records, the recognition of bravery, reprisals, and so on.

The Valiulis biography underlines the important part played by GHQ staff in the evolution of the insurgent army and the subsequent army of the Irish Free State – an emphasis which is necessary in view of the general neglect by historians of the important and less obtrusive infrastructure which it provided and extended during the War of Independence. Without the stabilising influence and the prudent policies of the GHQ staff, which were sometimes resented by the fighters in the field, military initiative during the war could not have been maintained and expanded, nor would the subservience of the army to parliament and the people have been so certain, if and when independence was achieved. Mulcahy more than once underlined the control GHQ had over the country brigades, particularly in the later phase of the war, when different areas of country activity were formed into divisions, which were designed to be self-contained in the event of the elimination of GHQ by the British forces.

The organisation of the army along professional lines at and after the truce allowed Mulcahy, as minister for defence, and Eoin O'Duffy, chief of staff, after the ratification of the Treaty, to provide the forces on behalf of the Provisional Government which would deal effectively with the Irregulars during the Civil War. The military success against the anti-Treaty forces was largely achieved by the end of August 1922, within two months of the commencement of the Civil War, when all major cities and towns were under government control. The last eight months of the war was a war of attrition and a different challenge for the army, dealing as it was with local disturbances of guerrilla tactics and widespread but isolated outrages and vandalism. The Civil War was lost because of the lack of support by the great majority of people in Ireland (even among those who did not favour the Treaty), the support of the Treaty by the majority of GHQ staff and the Dublin Volunteers, and the availability of military equipment to the Dublin command from the departing British forces. The Civil War might have been avoided or made less damaging if Rory O'Connor and Liam Mellows, who occupied the Four Courts in April 1922, had agreed to a settlement with the Provisional Government and the Dublin command.

Dealing with the relations between the various members of the staff, Mulcahy refers to the excellent spirit which existed among them. There was never the slightest disagreement, and the work dovetailed in a satisfactory way: 'No suspicions, no withdrawings, no waste of time.' Speaking of attitudes which prevailed about the shortcomings and failures of soldiers and politicians during the War of Independence, he maintains that criticism was exceptional and recriminations rare and, as he put it, unworthy.

It was obvious that Brugha became more involved with the army and its policies after de Valera's return from America in December 1920, and that this was one source of Mulcahy's problems (an issue with which I deal elsewhere). The fact that the attack on the Custom House was organised shortly before the Truce in July 1921 was probably an initiative of Brugha and possibly of de Valera too. There is no mention of the proposed action in the minutes of the

Dáil, but at no stage in the entire period was there a mention of a military action in the minutes. Writing of the decision to attack the Custom House, my father said:

> Certainly, the initiative for such an action at this stage did not come from the GHQ staff. I was fully in on the discussions in connection with the proposal. Mrs Kilkelly, sister of Colonel Moore, had a house in Fitzwilliam Street near the corner of Baggot Street. For some time I had been using a room on the hall floor as an office. The discussions on this matter, as far as I recall, took place in the back drawing room upstairs. Cathal Brugha and de Valera were present at the discussions, and my recollection is that they were there with me on the day of the attack on the Custom House, while we were standing by waiting to see what the result of the operation was going to be. I think that it is Nowlan [Prof Kevin Nowlan, historian] who, in his lecture, points out that an action of this kind indicated a serious departure from previous policy on the part of the army. My feeling with regard to the destruction of the Custom House was the same as my feeling with regard to the sending of men to London with Cathal on an assassination policy – it was the feeling of being 'dragged'. There was no hesitancy on the part of the Volunteers in Dublin to undertake the job, nor was there any hesitancy at the level of the GHQ staff to pursue it or to argue against it in any way. Once the project had formulated itself in minds, whether inside, or spanning the threshold of, the Cabinet, as in the case of London, the men were provided and, unlike London, the job was done.

He adds:

> This article inevitably raises the question, whether the Custom House was not burned as a propaganda matter, however effective it might have been in dislocating the 'taxing departments', and the local government administration.[21]

On another occasion, I had the following conversation with my father:

RM: The burning of the Custom House was an action which you say was not initiated at GHQ staff, and, if it received approval from you, it was only because de Valera was keen about it. I take it then that it was de Valera [who] initiated the idea of the Custom House. You say you weren't keen but you cooperated in the matter. In fact, you and Collins and the people in the GHQ staff must have had very little to do with it. Did you do anything about the planning of it?

R: I had nothing to do with the planning of it. It was all in Traynor's[i] hands and the Second Battalion. I wouldn't say that Collins had anything to do with the planning of it. Collins would have been interested in it from the point of view that this was a kind of a blow that would affect the administration. I can't at all understand, if Collins was effectively interested in it, that the active-service unit and the Squad wouldn't be fully used in it.[22]

Seventy men were captured in the Custom House action, and several were killed. The loss of such a large number seriously depleted the forces in Dublin, and might have had catastrophic effects on the Dublin campaign, were it not for the early cessation of fighting that followed the Truce of July 1921.

RELATIONS BETWEEN THE ARMY AND SINN FÉIN

The Sinn Féin Cabinet papers, stretching as they do from March 1919 to December 1921, contain only a few references to the army, and then mainly to moneys provided to the Department of Defence. There are four mentions of sums of £1,000 and one reference to a grant of $1,000,000, but no other details to explain the latter act of generosity. Mulcahy was paid £350 annually but officially he was paid as assistant minister for defence and not as chief of staff.[23] The army was referred to only twice during the thirty-two months of Cabinet meetings, and then only in connection with the proposal about its reorganisation in November 1921.

Mulcahy provided the vital link during the War of Independence between the GHQ staff and the representative of the political section of the movement, Cathal Brugha. He also kept in touch with Arthur Griffith and Eoin MacNeill, both of whom were important figures on the political side and with whom

---

[i] Oscar Traynor, as commandant of the Dublin Brigade and successor to Dick McKee, was in charge of the operation. I have seen Traynor's detailed description of the planning of the action and its results in his private memoirs, *Oscar Traynor: A Record of His Experiences in the War of Independence*, which are unpublished but are in the possession of his family.

Mulcahy had built up considerable mutual trust and respect. His contact, and that of Collins, with Brugha and Griffith in particular was an important factor in maintaining an agreed policy and an understanding between the military and the civil authority, although it must be apparent that the main thrust of policy came from the military.

It is sometimes suggested that there was a lack of understanding between the army and the political wing of the independence movement, and that the army acted as an independent and unauthorised force. My father would strenuously deny that any such dichotomy existed in the situation, and he was highly sensitive to such assertions. There is a wide-ranging discussion about the relationship between the army and the Dáil in his papers. The following are only a few of the comments he makes on tape and in the annotation, where he underlines the close association between the army and the politicians:

> If there was any weakness in the situation, it could come from the fact that, so far from being too far apart and being autonomous of one another, the army chief, so-called, and the members of the government had relations more closely dovetailed into one another than would be normal between the heads of an army and the heads of a government.

He continues:

> There was no clash of any kind either of thought or feeling or action between any of the members of the government or members of the parliament, and those who were conducting the volunteer work, either at [the] top or throughout the country.[24]

If there was any other weakness in the situation, it was the depletion by imprisonment of the Sinn Féin leaders from 1918 to the end of 1920, when de Valera returned from America, and the ineffective role of the Sinn Féin standing committee and possibly the Dáil Cabinet. Cathal Brugha was the only formal political link with the GHQ staff, although he never appeared to attend the Sinn Féin standing committee, and his department and the army were seldom referred to in the Dáil Cabinet minutes. He played little part in formulating military policy, apart from approving of Mulcahy's conservative approach to aggression up to the end of 1919, and the more aggressive policy subsequently. The Dáil had no influence on the war – it rarely met and was also severely depleted in numbers – but Griffith and Eoin MacNeill, who were in close contact with Mulcahy during the hostilities, did not oppose the army in its policies. Mulcahy attended the standing committee of Sinn Féin from October 1918 to March 1919, so clearly he had some contact with the residue of the Sinn Féin membership, and during this short period he was elected a member of the subcommittee to prepare a submission on Ireland's demand for independence for the forthcoming Peace Conference.[25] There was much misunderstanding about the pivotal role of GHQ during the War of Independence as a consequence of the long delay in the issuing of the Mulcahy papers. By the time these became available, many views about the war and its leaders had become distorted and fixed in our historical literature.

Nothing written by Mulcahy of the revolutionary army could be construed in any way as suggesting disloyalty or an independent attitude on the part of the soldiers. In his later notes on Cathal Brugha, Mulcahy emphasises the close contact which existed between himself, as chief of staff, and Cathal Brugha, as the minister for defence. Perhaps Mulcahy's attitude to the question of the army's relationship with the civil authority is best summed up in the following letter he wrote to Bishop Fogarty of Killaloe after the publication of P. S. O'Hegarty's book *The Victory of Sinn Féin*:[26]

> When you said on Friday that you were sending a copy of P.S.'s book to a few influential friends in America, I said that there was a comment I would like to make on it for their information, so that at least one very serious misrepresentation contained in the book would be offset to some extent. And the comment is this: one of the main things that it does is it paints a picture that suggests that 'the greatest achievements of any Irish generation was brought about by a military terrorism in which a civilian government existed merely as a machine for registering military decrees and under which every argument, save the gun, was eliminated'[27] in a situation in which the 'political machine became a tool in the hands of the military side of the movement so that in the end

the whole thing was moulded by men who were incapable of regarding democratic government seriously only in so far as it could be manipulated or forced to do what the military mind wanted'.

We can only imagine that ordinary people reading the book will read that the 'military mind' is the General Headquarters Staff of the time, and that the 'political and democratic machinery of government' is the Cabinet and the Dáil. If P.S.'s painting of the position is accepted as he has put it, it contains to my mind a very great danger to the State on some possible future occasion. The fact is that his painting of the situation is entirely wrong, and the inferences that ordinary people would draw from his painting, if anything, more wrong. I feel that it is of very great national importance that the names of the old members of the GHQ staff should not be invoked by some future decade or generation to show that national progress can only be made in any doubtful national situation by taking the 'Civilian Government' by the throat. It is my personal opinion that no group, pre-Truce, realised the necessity for building up and making as effective and as prominent as possible our Civil Departments than did the individual members of the General Headquarters Staff. And no people suffered more by the more or less ineffective work of some of those departments than did the General Headquarters Staff and the Volunteers generally.

I have told P. S. O'Hegarty, with whom I discussed the matter, that the time has not yet come when it is either desirable for some of us to 'look back', but that I personally have a considerable lot of material that would support this latter statement of mine, and would give the lie to the very serious suggestion of his that I refer to. For instance, I attach for your Lordship's information a copy of a letter sent by me on 4 June 1921 to Cathal Brugha, the minister for defence, which is typical of our attitude on this matter. I have papers to show that the Military Authorities felt it was not right that civilians should be tried by court-martial, that the work should be done by the Home Affairs Department, that the Military Authorities saw danger in 'allowing people to feel that the Defence Department was, perhaps, trying to run the Government' in connection with matters that should have been done by the Local Government Department, and where we considered that the prestige of the Local Government Department itself demanded that they should do particular work. The papers dealing with the organisation and development of the police, and police work, show a very serious attitude towards civil administration on the part of the military authorities, and a very irresponsible one on the part of the civil departments.

In May 1921, the military authorities made complaint of the fact that there was no conception of any organisation extra-military, and that military work was suffering as a result of that fact. And in the autumn of 1921 the position was such that I asked of one of our senior officers that he crystallise into a memorandum, for the information of the Dáil Cabinet, the disabilities and the weaknesses that the military organisation suffered under through the absence of effective civil administration for a large number of matters that were proper to be dealt with by the civil authorities.[i]

It is absolutely untrue that the guerrilla warfare was not fully approved of by the Volunteer Executive and by the Dáil Cabinet. It must be perfectly obvious that there was good reason why it should not be publicly made clear that the Dáil Cabinet was responsible for the guerrilla warfare. Members of the Dáil Cabinet had to take public action, and be in public, in circumstances that very often involved arrest, and we could not send the members of the Cabinet into their captor's hands with a rope tied round their necks, as would have been the position if it had been in any way publicly made clear that they held themselves responsible for the conduct of the War. The published report of the Dáil Proceedings for 1919 and 1921 showed that the Dáil supported the Volunteers by monies, and imply entire support of their action. At the very first private meeting of the Dáil, after the public meetings in January 1919, I personally supplied a report on the condition of the Volunteers at the time as minister for defence. There was no explicit authority from the executive of the Volunteers to do so, but the implication must be accepted as the Volunteers put themselves

---

[i] This was one of the factors which led to the disagreements between Mulcahy and Collins and the Dáil minister in charge of home affairs, Austin Stack.

at the disposal of the Dáil once the Dáil was elected. The proceedings, however, do not report that such a report was made. O'Hegarty's statement with regard to Griffith's attitude to the military mind is utterly misleading. I was, personally, in the most close contact with Griffith and there was a very great sympathy and understanding between the two of us – and O'Hegarty's whole representation of Griffith's last days are utterly absurd and untrue. It is worth mentioning too that O'Hegarty, who considers that a shot should not have been fired after 1916, was of the opinion in February or March 1919, when we called off the reception for de Valera at Mount Street Bridge after his escape from Lincoln, and the release of the other prisoners there, because of a Proclamation issued and action intended by the British Military Forces in Dublin – O'Hegarty considered that our calling off of the reception was 'the biggest blow that Ireland had ever received since O'Connell called off his Clontarf Meeting and was, in fact, a much bigger blow than that'. To deal adequately with the points I touch on would take a very deep going into certain matters, but what I have said will, perhaps, serve some kind of offset to some of his statements.

THE IRB

The role of the IRB during the War of Independence is a subject of controversy. The IRB, with Brugha, spearheaded the revival of the Volunteers as early as November 1916 after the Rising and was an important influence during the war. Its members were active in the Volunteers and in particular they were associated with Collins in his military and intelligence work. However, it is emphasised in the Mulcahy papers that the council of the IRB, and the leaders of the IRB as such, had no part to play in formulating military policy during the war. Military policy, whether it was arrived at electively or in response to circumstances, was formulated by the leaders of the Volunteers and approved by Brugha, representing Sinn Féin and parliament, and not by any other group.

Mulcahy was conscious and appreciative of the part the IRB members played in Collins's intelligence work before and during the War of Independence, and in establishing communication channels with the country forces and with contacts in Great Britain. As far as I can ascertain from his papers and recordings, he had no formal contact whatever with the IRB during the entire period from 1913 to 1924, although he was always thought of as an IRB man, even as late as 1924. His remoteness from the Brotherhood is apparent from the conversation he had with Sean MacEoin about the IRB on the telephone, which is recorded on tape. Unfortunately, it is difficult to understand MacEoin's contribution to the conversation because his voice is poorly transmitted on the phone.

However, it is clear from Mulcahy's responses to MacEoin's comments that the IRB was alive and well up to the time of the mutiny in 1924, and that Mulcahy was unaware that both Sean McMahon[i] and Sean O'Muirthile, who were on the Army Council during the Civil War and until they were sacked at the time of the mutiny, were also leaders of the IRB. They were attempting to resuscitate the Brotherhood 'to further the national and cultural aspirations of the country', whatever that may mean. Mulcahy at all times in his papers denies that the IRB had any significant presence during the war and immediate post-war years. It is likely that, because of his unique position as political and military head of the army during and after the Civil War, those members of the IRB who were closest to him were reluctant to inform him about their connection with the secret organisation, nor was such a revival by the senior officers of the Free State army in any way a sinister development in relation to the new state or the role of the army in defending the state.

The following is a note he makes about the role of the IRB. It is a good example of my father's propensity as he got older to indulge in long sentences and complex metaphors. Of course, because much of his writings was dictated rather than written, his style tends to be conversational and is sometimes influenced by Irish idiom.

> The secret organisation remained as a kind of humus in the political ground on the one hand, and on the other it was the core of the kernel of the intelligence organisation effectively built up by Collins and controlled by him, that disrupted and outwitted the secret service, destroyed its murder arm, and on the other hand, manipulated the

---

[i] Sean McMahon was active in the IRB and IRA during the War of Independence, and chief of staff during the Civil War after Collins's death.

machinery that so controlled the 'water ways' that de Valera could be brought from Lincoln to Ireland and then to the United States and then back home again, and was the basis of the security which prevented the country ever having to feel that either its parliament or its executive government had been destroyed by enemy action.[28]

THE FIRST DÁIL

Mulcahy had little to do with politics up to the time of the ratification of the Treaty, although he had been a member of the Dáil since its inception, and minister for defence in the Dáil Cabinet from January to April 1919. He was appointed assistant minister for defence on de Valera's return to the Cabinet in April 1919 and remained so to January 1922, although at no time did he attend Cabinet meetings. He was one of those chosen as a candidate for the First Dáil in December 1918 but his choice was made only at the last moment, when the chosen candidate for Drumcondra/Clontarf constituency, Harry Boland, was transferred to his home constituency, Roscommon.[1] He was at the time a second-year student of medicine at University College Dublin, as well as being chief of staff, but as his staff duties increased during 1918 he was obliged to abandon a medical career. His success against the Parliamentary Party candidate could be partly attributed to his fellow students, who came out in force to canvas and speak on his behalf. His contact with University College was important subsequently because one of his offices, and an important retreat for him when he was on run between January 1920 and July 1921, was the Department of Physiology at Earlsfort Terrace. Mulcahy was the last of ten speakers at a Sinn Féin election meeting in the Mansion House. In a report afterwards, P. S. O'Hegarty, writing of him, said: 'the last speaker would have been interesting but he spoke in a monotone'.

My father made some comments on the occasion of the fiftieth anniversary of the First Dáil meeting. The text is fairly characteristic of his last few years in that he is wordy and tortuous in his allusions and metaphors. Nevertheless, he deals in considerable detail with the significance of this first meeting of a native and democratic parliament, particularly in terms of the wishes of the population, the rejection of British control of Irish affairs by the people, and their willingness to face up realistically to British aggression. He goes on to say how the meeting marked the beginning of a process which had its successful conclusion in the Truce agreement in July 1921. At all times he emphasises the crucial role of the people. He obviously, and perhaps a little naively, attributes to 'the People' sentiments which reflect his own strong democratic idealism. He talks about the achievements and triumphs of the First Dáil. He describes in detail the transferring of power from the standing committee of Sinn Féin to the Dáil in January 1919 and the procedures and meetings whereby this process was brought about. Committees were formed for specific tasks, such as the preparation of a declaration of independence, and a group to visit London to influence the representatives of other countries to support the Irish cause in the peace negotiations. He provides the names of the members. A liaison group (Mulcahy and Harry Boland) was, at his suggestion to the standing committee, organised to protect political meetings from British police and army aggression, and to press for the release of prisoners after the overwhelming success of Sinn Féin in the 1918 general election.

He talks about the democratic programme which he formally proposed in Irish in the Dáil, and Griffith's very positive response to the policy it contained. This programme was drawn up by members of the Labour Party (Thomas Johnson and William O'Brien) at the behest of Sinn Féin. Griffith saw in this programme support for his own belief in the innate qualities of energy and talent of the Irish people, whatever their religion, politics, or gender.

Much of what Mulcahy records is redolent of his own idealism and political philosophy when he talks about the Irish people and their struggle for independence. He refers to Pearse and to his support of Home Rule in 1912, and to his change of outlook by 1916 – a change Mulcahy attributed to the fact that the Irish Parliamentary Party followed the British rules during the years of the Home Rule movement but that, when the Irish were about to achieve their political objectives, the British changed the rules. He likens the thrust towards independence to a river which becomes turbulent when it meets the turning tide at the estuary. This is one of his most sustained metaphors and he continues to rely on it for several sentences. He finishes this subject by referring to the meeting of the full Dáil in April 1919, made possible by the release of all the prisoners in early March, after the escapes of de Valera, McGarry, Milroy and Barton from jail. The full Dáil met on 1, 2, 4 and 10 April 1919 and was followed by a Sinn Féin Ard-Fheis on 11 April.

Apart from his attendance at the infrequent Dáil meetings and his participation in certain formal political activities, such as attending the American delegates to the Peace Conference while they were in Ireland,[2] his address on the democratic programme in the First Dáil in 1919, and proposing, with Sean MacEoin,[i] de Valera as President of the Dáil in August 1921, he was completely absorbed in his military responsibilities. He claims that he had little knowledge of the intricacies of the political situation from the time de Valera came back from America in December 1920 to the time of the Truce in July 1921, because he was so heavily committed to the organisation of the army. He was also sufficiently removed from the political scene during the Truce in the autumn of 1921 to be able to say that he failed to appreciate the long-term implications of the rift which was occurring between the leaders at this time. However, he was obviously a close observer of the political as well as the military scene, if one is to judge from his writings and his papers. Because of his intimate contact with the revolutionary movement and its principal architects, and his unique collection of papers, he may well have been the most authoritative commentator to have survived the period. Many of his associates thought that he was the survivor of the War of Independence and Civil War best qualified to write about these turbulent times.

SINN FÉIN

The original Sinn Féin organisation was established in 1905 by Arthur Griffith, with the dual monarchy as his constitutional solution to Ireland's aspirations for self-determination. Its precursor was the Irish National Society of London. Sinn Féin's early history is dealt with by my mother and father in discussion. The post-1916 party was established in October 1917 with the coming together of a number of individuals and organisations with nationalist aspirations. It had a constitution which included an extremely complex system of committees and councils which need not be described here, except to say that its standing committee was the only body which met regularly before,

---

[i]'The Blacksmith of Ballinalee', famed for his military exploits as commandant of the Longford Brigade during the war.

during and after the War of Independence and which was responsible for conducting the regular business of the party. Its annual convention, or Ard-Fheis, met each year except for 1920 and was the party's legislative body. Students interested in the history of Sinn Féin and its evolution will find a detailed description of its post-Rising structure in Michael Laffan's *The Resurrection of Ireland: The Sinn Féin Party 1916-1923*.[3]

It might be appropriate to record some of Mulcahy's views of the part Sinn Féin played, through its standing committee, in the struggle for independence between 1917 and the Treaty. He refers to Sinn Féin frequently in his tape recordings and the annotation, confirming the apparent indolence of the political wing of the movement during the period of the war. He refers to the constitution of Sinn Féin, its influence on the Treaty issue, and the ineptitude of its members in dealing with the divisions which occurred following the ratification of the Treaty. According to Mulcahy, Sinn Féin and the Dáil had little effect on the struggle against the British, apart from some of its individual leaders. The Volunteers were the only organised body which was effective, and without them the courts and other services organised by the Dáil could not have functioned. Wherever the political strength of the people came from, it apparently did not come from any drive from the top of the purely political organisation.[4]

Páidín O'Keeffe recorded many conversations with my father during their retirements. O'Keeffe was the paid secretary of Sinn Féin and continued in that capacity during the war, except for his year in prison from March 1918 to March 1919. The first of the two Sinn Féin minute books in the UCD Archives records the seven-page proceedings of the eighth annual congress at 6 Harcourt Street on 4 October 1912, with Arthur Griffith in the chair. There were twenty-three further meetings of the National Council up to and including 10 July 1913. The minutes of the first meeting were unsigned but the subsequent meetings were signed by Arthur Griffith, Constance Markieviez or Jenny Wyse-Power.

The second book includes the minutes of the standing committee from 5 June 1919 to 24 March 1922. The committee had seventy-eight weekly meetings during this latter period but, according to my father and Páidín

O'Keeffe, its main characteristic was its concern with minor matters of detail rather than matters of policy or organisation. At times, Parkinson's Law prevailed. The committee had no semblance of the functions or powers of an executive body of a dominant political party. It was unwieldy because of lack of clear leadership. The meetings during the war up to the Truce were mostly brief and poorly attended, and were suspended entirely from November 1920 until February 1921, after de Valera's return from America.

The attendances after de Valera's return improved greatly and the proceedings lasted longer. However, these meetings were not concerned with any political matters of great import, apart form approving the nominations for the 1918 election (which were submitted by Michael Collins and his IRB colleagues Harry Boland and Diarmuid O'Hegarty, and which were accepted) and making the necessary arrangements to transfer some of its functions to the First Dáil, which met in January 1919. Certainly de Valera kept all political matters close to his chest. The army and the military were not mentioned once during the entire seventy-eight meetings, nor did Cathal Brugha as minister for defence and in his other capacities (he had been a member of the standing committee) attend any meeting from March 1919 until 22 March 1922. At the meeting on 22 March 1922, he acted as proxy for the joint honorary secretary, Austin Stack, but, significantly, this was after the Treaty split. Brugha may have resigned from the committee and simply confined his business to the Cabinet, which at the time was less onerous. Brugha had attended eight meetings up to March 1919. (The minutes of the standing committee before 5 June 1919 are available in the National Library.) Apropos of his earlier attendances, O'Keeffe said '[I] never saw Brugha doing anything except attending meetings of the standing committee and saying nothing' and 'but Cathal had no work to do, he never did anything'.

From April 1919, the Cabinet of Dáil Éireann assumed many of the political functions of the standing committee of Sinn Féin. It is not surprising therefore that few matters of a political nature were on the agenda of the standing committee, nor is it surprising that Cathal Brugha, who was a member of the Cabinet from January 1919, failed to attend. His department's affairs were clearly a responsibility of the Cabinet. Throughout the twenty-one months up to December 1921, when 115 meeting of the Cabinet had taken place, the army was discussed only twice – in relation to its proposed reorganisation in November 1921[5] – nor was the Department of Defence mentioned, except to confirm its financial support on a few occasions. Brugha continued his business activities and refused his salary of £500 as minister for defence.[6] He suggested that the money should be provided to support the chief of staff, which it was.

A few conclusions may be reached from a perusal of the standing committee and Cabinet papers. Firstly, it seems that Mulcahy had little conception of the activities of the Cabinet while he was beavering away organising the army. Despite his appointment as assistant minister for defence, he never attended Cabinet meetings, nor do I think he was ever informed of the meetings or of its proceedings. During the three months from January to April 1919, when he was minister for defence, there was only one Cabinet meeting, and that came just before the reshuffle in early April, when he was replaced by Cathal Brugha as minister. Mulcahy provided a report of the army's activities at this meeting.

Secondly, I believe that Brugha was not greatly involved in political or military activities, at least until de Valera's return from America in December 1920, but following this time his presence as minister gradually became more intrusive and on some occasions his actions as minister were inappropriate. Thirdly, it seems that Mulcahy was not the only one to be remote from Cabinet activities. The entire military campaign up to the Truce seems to have been little influenced by the Cabinet or the Sinn Féin Party. One can understand the contention by Mulcahy and Béaslaí that the army provided the major, and probably the only effective, role in the fight against the British and that the absence of the available Cabinet leaders from the standing committee, with the exception of Griffith and Stack, reduced the influence of Sinn Féin. Of Austin Stack, O'Keeffe said: 'Of course Stack was not capable of doing anything.' He implied that Stack had the 'Casement cloud' on his mind since the Kerry debacle at the time of the Rising. Of course, the absence of de Valera and his notorious reputation of sharing little with his colleagues had a stultifying effect on any possible political activities.

The small attendances and the rather trivial matters dealt with at earlier meetings of the standing committee were not surprising in view of the president's absence in America. However, despite de Valera's presence at most of the later meetings, no matters relating to the Truce, the Treaty or the Treaty disagreement were raised. This confirms that de Valera kept things close to his chest – at least from the organised Sinn Féin Party. It is not surprising that during one conversation, Mulcahy complained about de Valera's failure to keep him and his staff informed of political progress during the Truce. Elsewhere, Mulcahy implies that de Valera's only confidant and advisor was Erskine Childers. One would expect that Collins would have kept Mulcahy up to date on political matters during the Truce and in the immediate post-Treaty period. Whether he did is not clear, nor is it clear that he met Mulcahy during his many visits to Dublin during the Treaty negotiations. I suspect that Mulcahy was too absorbed in army matters to concern himself with political developments at the time, nor do I think that Collins was particularly communicative with him, as Collins drifted out of army activities coming up to the Truce of July 1921. I do not think that Mulcahy met Collins more than once or twice during the Treaty negotiations.

Mulcahy was in full agreement with O'Keeffe that the standing committee had little influence on matters of political, social or economic importance. One of the subjects on its agenda was the Belfast boycott, which was originally imposed in response to the vicious attacks on Catholics in Belfast in July and August 1920. According to O'Keeffe, he, as secretary of Sinn Féin, had the unwelcome task of being involved in organising the boycott. The boycott was supported by the Dáil Cabinet and apparently by Griffith and Collins. Griffith's support is surprising and seemed to be a lapse of political judgement, but according to P. S. O'Hegarty's view,[7] Griffith supported the measure and was influential in opposing some of his Dáil colleagues who were not in favour of the boycott. It is perhaps less surprising that Countess Markievicz, the minister for labour, declared in the Dáil on 17 August 1921 that she had taken charge of the boycott earlier in the year and that, since then, the work had been going forward well. She refers to the twelve organisers and the four hundred committees under her control, and says:

... it was almost impossible for a Belfast merchant to sell a pennyworth of goods in any part of Ireland.

The Dáil Cabinet first discussed the subject on 13 November 1920, when it proposed the setting up of a Belfast committee, under the control of Michael Staines, to direct the boycott. There is no evidence that any member of the Cabinet, including Arthur Griffith and Michael Collins, were opposed to the boycott, but the Cabinet records are scanty and do not mention the names of those who attended, nor do they include the discussion which ensued. Nevertheless, it is likely that O'Hegarty was correct in his view. It is difficult to believe that they would have proceeded with the campaign against the wishes of Griffith, who was acting president in November 1920. The boycott was mentioned again in the Cabinet on 21 October 1921, and there appears to have been no objection to its continuing. It was finally suspended by agreement between Collins and Craig. The boycott had a hugely divisive effect on relations between North and South, and was apparently a factor in influencing many loyalists who were initially uneasy about partition. It was a 'British solution to an Irish problem'.[8]

I have no idea if Mulcahy supported the policy or had any thoughts about it at the time, but he had this to say about it in 1961:

> The opportunity for disorderly interference with the goods of others and for pillage afforded by the boycott was an important element for detonating irregularism, which probably brought all the robbers over on the side of the anti-Treaty forces. A book was published, [Patrick Kavanagh's 1938] *The Green Fool* (I think), which gave a rather lurid account of Civil War robberies in story form; and there was a whole area around Ferbane and the Shannon which earned a notorious name. The Belfast boycott was a very disturbing influence of this kind, particularly in the Civil War days. Even in pre-Truce days it may be found to have encouraged 'commandeering' by reasonably disciplined Volunteeer units.[9]

The failure of the standing committee to have a meeting between October 1920 and February 1921, during and after the Clune truce initiative,[i]

---

[i] Archbishop Clune from Australia was sent to Dublin by Lloyd George in November 1920 in an attempt to arrange a Truce.

confirmed that it had little part to play in political matters. The February meeting was only convened because of de Valera's return from America. It may be that political initiatives were confined to the members of the Dáil Cabinet who were still in Dublin, or perhaps solely to Griffith as acting president, and to Collins after Griffith's imprisonment in November 1920. The Cabinet papers of 30 November and 18 December 1920 refer to peace negotiations, and on the second date the matter was left in the hands of Griffith. The Clune negotiations failed in December 1920 but from that date, up to the Truce of July 1921, there were recurring background activities, through various unofficial channels, aimed at a truce. During this time, de Valera was granted immunity from arrest by the British in the hope of providing an effective link on the Irish side, and it is also believed that this immunity was granted to Collins in the later months of the war. A reference to the Sturgis diaries will confirm that the greatest obstacle to finding a truce during the first six months of 1921 was the difficulty of contacting de Valera.

THE TRUCE

The Mulcahy biography makes a valuable contribution to our knowledge of the six-month period of the Truce. It underlines the difficulties which were created for the army in general and for the chief of staff in particular during this time. The frustrations, antagonisms and personality clashes during this uncertain time contributed, in Valiulis's analysis, to many of the divisions which were to occur after the Treaty was ratified.

The arrival of a large influx of new Volunteers during the Truce added to the stresses of army organisation and the maintenance of discipline. Mulcahy, as head of the army at this time, became the object of every sort of complaint from fellow officers, politicians and civilians. In the absence of a police force to maintain civil order and to deal with civil matters, the army bore the brunt of all the problems which arose in the country during this time of uncertainty. During the war, Volunteers showed a strong sense of responsibility and discipline, but the Truce led to some acts of behaviour which prompted civilian protests. Drink for the first time became a problem, and often led to bad public behaviour and to the intimidation of civilians. All complaints had to be investigated and required a response from Mulcahy and his staff. In the words of his biographer, Mulcahy always emphasised to his men the honour of the army and, because of 'the army of complainers' among the public (in his words), it was a particularly frustrating time for him. In the absence of police, or an effective government Department of Home Affairs, and with the arrival of the 'Trucileers' (a pejorative term applied in particular to those who joined the army in parts of the country, such as Kerry and Wexford, where there had been little activity during the War of Independence), he was caught between the demands of his political colleagues, his officers and men, and the civilian population.

It would be hard not to agree with Valiulis's views about the adverse influence of the circumstances created by the Truce on the genesis of the Civil War. However, Mulcahy qualified this opinion when he claimed that the Truce period would have had little adverse influence on subsequent events if de Valera had not so promptly and savagely attacked Griffith and Collins after the Treaty agreement had been signed in London.

Brugha's antipathy towards Collins commenced towards the end of 1920 and worsened during the following year. It was sustained during the Truce, although what was equally important from the point of view of the relationship between some members of the Cabinet and the GHQ staff was the less obvious antagonism between Brugha and Mulcahy. This subject is dealt with in some detail by Valiulis and it is almost certain that Brugha's antagonism towards Mulcahy was related not only to Mulcahy's determination to protect Collins from criticism from Brugha and Stack but also to his resentment that the army's unique role in bringing about a Truce was so clearly in the minds of the people, and to the obvious public perception that the army leaders were the outstanding figures in achieving British recognition of the Irish demands.

Mulcahy deals in considerable detail with the conflict which developed between Brugha and Stack on the one hand and Collins on the other. This conflict inevitably led to the wider division which developed between some members of the Cabinet and the army leaders, and which became more manifest on 25 November 1921 when de Valera, at a Cabinet meeting, attempted, without success, to found a 'new army'. All members of the GHQ staff attended the Cabinet meeting by invitation. The main purpose of the exercise appeared to be the attempt by Brugha and de Valera to have Stack appointed to the staff. In the words of de Valera, Stack would hold a watching brief for Minister for Defence Cathal Brugha. Such a reason was unlikely to appeal to the chief of staff and his colleagues.

The members of the staff resented de Valera's intrusion, having little confidence in Stack as a suitable addition to the army leadership. Each member of the staff expressed his opposition to the proposal, and they left behind them an irate president who shouted after them: 'Ireland will give me a new army'. The resentment of some of the staff was such that both Eoin O'Duffy,[i] the assistant chief of staff, and Liam Lynch, the senior commanding officer in the South, sent letters of resignation to Mulcahy in protest at de Valera's intrusion. Needless to say, their resignations were ignored by Mulcahy and the Cabinet.[1] Sean Russell, who was soon to become passionately anti-Treaty and to continue his military struggle for a republic long after de Valera's new constitution was adopted in 1937, said to Mulcahy after the meeting:

> I didn't think that there was a man in the country who would speak to my chief like that.

Russell had been appointed director of munitions on the GHQ staff late in the War of Independence. His later IRA activities brought him to Germany during the Second World War. He died in a German submarine when he was returning to Ireland.

The 'new army' had already been discussed at Cabinet on two occasions before the 25 November meeting. On 15 September 1921, it was decided to put the army on 'a regular basis', with Austin Stack to attend staff meetings and Cathal Brugha to chair the meetings on special occasions. On 4 November, it was confirmed that the arrangements to 'recommission' the army were to go ahead, and all GHQ and other heads were to be reappointed. On this occasion, there was no mention in the minutes of Austin Stack. The staff's unanimous opposition to Stack was almost certainly related to his reputation as an inefficient minister for home affairs and to the army's resentment that so many of the responsibilities proper to his department had to be adopted by the

---

[i] IRA leader in Monaghan and subsequently member of GHQ and the 1919 Dáil. He was noted for his success in organising the civic guard after the Treaty. He headed the Blue Shirts and Fine Gael for a brief period in the 1930s.

Volunteers. It is somewhat surprising that Griffith, and particularly Collins, would, as Cabinet members, agree to such interference with the army; but I expect that their heavy responsibility as plenipotentiaries left them no time to attend to other Cabinet matters, apart from their travel over to report on their negotiations with the British, and that they may not have been present at the two meetings. The basis of the conflict about the appointment of Stack was certainly symptomatic of the widening divisions which were developing between the army heads and certain members of the Cabinet.

Despite the failure to get agreement with GHQ at the Cabinet meeting on 25 November, the minutes of the meeting gives an uncharacteristically long account of the proceedings and fails to mention GHQ's attitude.[2] It provides a list of the newly appointed GHQ staff, with no changes apart from the addition of Stack as joint deputy chief of staff with Eoin O'Duffy, the latter to be chief of staff in Mulcahy's absence. It states: 'The supreme body directing the army is the Cabinet' and that all commissions derive from the government and must be sanctioned by the minister for defence. The minister can nominate or veto members of the army but

> He must produce a working army. The chief of staff is the professional or technical head of the army, and when in command is supreme on the field of battle as regards the disposition of his forces.

I need hardly say that Griffith and Collins were not present at the time of these proceedings. They were on the boat back to London, having attended the earlier part of the meeting.

Of course, it was reasonable of the Cabinet to adopt this policy towards the army, and I know that Mulcahy was in full agreement with the principle of civilian control. However, the circumstances were hardly likely to be accepted by the army leaders, where a successful and efficient staff was being asked, without prior consultation, to accept an unpopular addition who was deemed inefficient and who was already on poor terms with some of the army leadership. And the rationale of the appointment was, to say the least, undiplomatic, where Stack was 'to act as Brugha's watchdog'. In a proper army/Cabinet relationship, I would have thought that the link with the minister for defence was one of the chief of staff's functions.

Intervention in military affairs without consultation with GHQ by Brugha and Mellows was particularly evident during the Truce. The chief of staff resented this, believing that certain of these interventions were matters which concerned the military heads of the army and were not of concern to the civil authority. Valiulis, writing about the Truce, noted that the chief of staff was not invited to meet the head of the British army in Ireland, General Macready, to arrange the Truce terms, which would have been normal protocol. She implies from Mulcahy's comments that the failure to invite him may have been related to 'the British refusal to recognise the IRA' and/or the fact that 'It was not yet time for the members of the army to come out in the open'. Neither reason seems plausible to me. My father's note on the subject tends to hedge on the matter:

> There was no necessity, from my particular point of view, to stand on any ceremony in the matter; it was sufficient for me that a truce was being arranged, and that full responsibility was being taken and an effective truce was being arranged at the political level of responsibility.[3]

It would seem to me that the politicians who attended the Truce talks, de Valera and Brugha, should have been anxious to emphasise the status and equality of the two military forces by insisting that Macready was met by his counterpart from the Irish side. I suspect that the chief of staff was excluded by Brugha for personal reasons and because Brugha by this time was determined to play a more active role in controlling the army – a trend which started with de Valera's return from America and continued right up to the signing of the Treaty. This suspicion is strengthened by Brugha's action in appointing Eamonn Duggan[i] and Robert Barton[ii]: two relatively junior officers of the IRA, as officers without consulting with the chief of staff. These two junior officers apparently attended the Truce negotiations. This could only be interpreted as a casual dereliction of protocol at best, or as a deliberate discourtesy at worst. Later, other liaison officers were appointed without consultation with the chief of staff.

Mulcahy refers to the appointment of Barton and Duggan as liaison officers

[i]Solicitor, TD for Louth/Meath in first Dáil, signatory to Treaty.
[ii]Wicklow-born, ex-British army officer; TD for Wicklow and minister for agriculture in First Dáil. Later signatory of Treaty but eventually opposed it and retired from politics.

in his papers. He stresses in these notes that they both continued as liaison officers with the British military authorities during the Truce without his acquiescence and without consulting him. Barton had been in jail until a few days before the Truce and, on his release, was immediately appointed a commandant in the army. Although he was only a few days back in the army, he was appointed one of the two to represent the Irish military authorities. Mulcahy thought that his subsequent appointment as one of the plenipotentiaries on the Treaty delegation was 'bizarre'. At no time does he speculate about the influences which accounted for Barton's unexpected appointments, but Barton's cousin, Erskine Childers, may have been involved, or Collins may have recommended him. He had always been a close friend and admirer of Collins. The only Cabinet reference to the liaison officers was to discuss how much they should be paid.[4]

A further action of Brugha's was to set up a Commission of Defence during the Truce without discussing the proposal with the chief of staff. When Mulcahy wrote to Brugha to enquire about the proposal, he received a rather dismissive letter of explanation from his minister.[5] Nothing appears to have come out of the commission.

It was rather typical of my father that he would not allow such breaches of protocol to become a contentious issue. He was certainly justified in resenting Brugha's increasing activities during the Truce in contacting individual members and groups of the army, and in conducting business with them, without the knowledge and agreement of the chief of staff or other senior officers. That Brugha's involvement in army affairs was not on major questions of policy but on more mundane matters is suggested by the following comment by Mulcahy on the Robbie affair, which was an administrative issue:

> The Robbie papers and the developments in relation to myself that flowed from them indicate that the things about which Cathal was at variance either with Collins or ultimately with myself were not matters of policy or of principle, nor were they matters of the kind that normally come for discussion at a higher level of political or executive level. Cathal's correspondence with me about the Robbie case begins about 10

July. It continues until 13 September, when I am told 'you will hand over to the deputy chief of staff all monies, papers, books and other property of the department in your possession'. And two items of monies are specifically referred to: a suspense account of £996 odd, and another £500 'transferred from your account to that of the Director of Purchases, but which amount the latter yesterday reported he had no record of having received from you' – the deputy chief of staff intended to be Austin Stack and the director of purchases being Mellows – and on the above instructions being carried out, I shall have your salary up to date paid to you.[6]

Mulcahy may have been too tolerant of Brugha and others who failed to deal with him according to normal protocol. He was deeply committed to maintaining the army as the servant of parliament and the people, and on all occasions he maintained a formal and proper approach to those whom he recognised as the representatives of the electorate. I feel that, in dealing with people who had no greater claim to prominence in the national movement than himself, he was perhaps too deferential to his senior political colleagues, and that he may have diminished his own influence in this way. He was at fault in not protesting about some actions taken by Brugha (and later by O'Higgins) in matters which were clearly the remit of the head of the army, and not of the civil authority. To appoint military liaison officers without consultation with the head of the army, to arrange a military truce with the head of the British military without consulting the head of the army, to maintain contact with army officers on military matters without the knowledge of the chief of staff – such breaches of protocol by political leaders should have evoked a more vocal and indignant response from Mulcahy. Indeed, if he had been more protective of the privileges of his office, he might have avoided some future misunderstandings. While his failure to protest may have been best from the national point of view, I am certain that his refusal to protect the authority, rights and dignity of his office harmed his standing with the political leaders. His characteristic of accepting the actions of his superiors, however he may have disagreed with them, was to contribute to the overshadowing of him during his later political career.

Other problems were to occupy him during the Truce. There was a massive increase in the number of young men who wished to join during these six months: the 'Trucileers'. According to Mulcahy, problems were also caused by Brugha and others during the Truce, which may have damaged the attitude of the rank and file to Mulcahy and Collins. Mulcahy had this to say on the subject:

> The influence of the Truce should not be exaggerated. It was a difficult time, lasting more than five months, and full of uncertainties about the future role of the army and the likely outcome of the negotiations with the British. But in general, discipline and adherence to the conditions of the Truce were maintained.

Local and foreign newspaper correspondents, who were invited to one of the training camps in the Dublin Mountains during the Truce, were loud in their praise of the organisation of the camp and the disciplined behaviour and training of the eight hundred volunteers who were there to receive the chief of staff and his visitors. They were impressed by the chief of staff's address to the troops and the Volunteers' response, which confirmed their clear commitment to the army and the nation. Despite the difficulties experienced by the chief of staff and GHQ during the Truce, both in their relations with the political leaders and with the soldiers in the field, Mulcahy states that, without de Valera's intervention immediately after the signing of the Treaty, the effects of the Truce would not have led to a split in the army. The question of de Valera's culpability in provoking the Civil War is dealt with in a later chapter.

THE LEADERS

MICHAEL COLLINS

Collins was in the GPO as a junior officer during the 1916 Rising and was appointed secretary of the National Aid Association after his return from Frongoch. He became director of organisation on the Volunteer executive in October 1917. He was director of training and adjutant general on the GHQ staff from March 1918 and was subsequently director of intelligence until the ratification of the Treaty. As chairman of the Provisional Government and therefore de facto head of state, he returned to the army as commander-in-chief from 13 July until his death on 22 August 1922.

Mulcahy first became closely associated with Collins when they were appointed to the Volunteer executive in October 1917. He has recorded extensive memoirs of this association. Among these memoirs I have included a number of comments of my own which may throw further light on the relationship between the two leaders. My father's relationship with Collins has always intrigued me. As chief of staff, and therefore Collins's military superior, Mulcahy had an intimate association with Collins during the entire War of Independence. This is clear from the following paragraphs. That he admired Collins for his many attributes is evident, just as he never showed any resentment as Collins's military reputation soared during and after the war – and as did his political reputation before and after the Truce. At all times, Mulcahy showed an extraordinary sensitivity to criticism of Collins (as he also did to criticism of Griffith), particularly on the Treaty issue and its aftermath.[1] For instance, during the Truce he was outraged when he received a letter from Sean O'Hegarty, the IRA leader in Cork, reporting that Collins was drinking and carousing during the Treaty negotiations in London. Despite the chief of staff's vigorous demand for evidence on this issue, it was not forthcoming. It is clear from the tape recordings that he believed that Collins could do no wrong. The deaths of Griffith and Collins in August 1922 at the height of the Civil War were, in his view, the ultimate tragedy for the new Irish State.

It was typical of my father that when Constantine Fitzgibbon described Collins getting out of a prostitute's bed in the first page of a novel he had written, Mulcahy became so irate that he pressed the then minister for justice, John Kelly, to refuse Fitzgibbon his naturalisation papers. Despite several approaches by Mulcahy to the minister, he failed to stop Fitzgibbon becoming an Irish citizen. He even described Fitzgibbon's writing as 'foul penmanship'. While Collins was widely admired for his extraordinary achievements, not many people would share Mulcahy's extreme sensitivity about him. Collins's robust personality would hardly evoke such sentiments.

Mulcahy remained chief of staff until the ratification of the Treaty in January 1922. As such, he was the head of the army during the entire War of Independence. He describes elsewhere that while the members of the staff had clearly defined roles and duties, at least during the later stages of the war, there was of necessity much duplication of activities and responsibilities. Nowhere was this more evident than in the case of Collins, who was given a free hand. He took this opportunity with alacrity and great energy, undertaking a multitude of commitments, including many which might appear to be the responsibility of the chief of staff or his assistants. Indeed, apart from his intelligence work, Collins was involved in other areas, including contact with the commanders in the field. However, he was obviously assured that his initiatives would have received the chief of staff's support and would have conformed to general-staff policy. Collins's intelligence work was organised through a network of colleagues, most of whom were members of the IRB. His extensive links with the country brigades were also probably maintained by IRB contacts.

Collins's wide-ranging activities and his soaring reputation were never a source of resentment or irritation to my father. On the contrary, his energy, his organisational ability, his great capacity for work, and his powerful influence on his colleagues was a great source of satisfaction and admiration for his chief, who shared with Collins the same dedication to work and to meticulous organisation. A lesser man in his senior position might have felt resentment towards his colleague in such circumstances, but the following quotations from his annotation clearly confirm Mulcahy's appreciation of Collins and of his great contribution towards the foundation of the State.

I have a strong impression from discussions with my mother and her sister, Phyllis O'Kelly, second wife of Sean T. O'Kelly, that the Ryan sisters had certain reservations about Collins in relation to Mulcahy: that his boisterous, flamboyant and charismatic nature tended to eclipse my father's more muted role during the war and that he did not sufficiently show his appreciation of his chief's contribution to the struggle. To the best of my knowledge, such sentiments were certainly not expressed to Mulcahy, who would have reacted angrily to such a criticism. Phyllis, who met Collins frequently when he visited the chief of staff at his home at 19 Ranelagh Road during and after the war, told me that 'He was a rough type and more or less ignored the women' – not surprising in view of his preoccupation with his multifarious military and political commitments. There is little doubt that Collins was by nature a rugged individualist and may have been driven by the vanity which is so often at the basis of such a person. Mother may have been right in believing that he was less conscious of the standing of his chief of staff colleague than he should have been, that he was prone to act too independently of his chief and that, in the later phase of the struggle, he did not keep him fully acquainted with political developments. Despite Collins's many surviving letters, I have no knowledge of any tribute or comment made by Collins about his chief.

Mulcahy's appointment as chief of staff allowed Collins the freedom of action which was fundamental to the success of his intelligence work and to the survival of the army. He not only encouraged Collins in every way but also provided him with vital protection from his critics on the political side, who responded adversely to Collins's military and political successes, and to his rather flamboyant and sometimes abrasive behaviour and personality. It was an extraordinary and fortuitous partnership, not least because his chief never showed a trace of resentment as Collins became more prominent both nationally and internationally. Mulcahy's admiration of Collins's role was the result of his commitment to the success of the revolutionary movement. He was completely committed to army organisation and its good reputation and had little interest in his own public image.

Although in the early years he was apparently as well known as Collins as a leader in the War of Independence, he had a largely administrative role in co-ordinating the headquarters staff, as indeed did Collins. His profile has obviously diminished over the years. Unlike Mulcahy's, Collins's reputation has advanced with the years and with the increasing media and literary attention to him, so much so that nowadays we hear little of any other military figure in the war. I have a list of forty books published about Collins, and they continue to appear; there is a strong commercial factor driving the current cult of Collins.

Mulcahy writes of their association during the war, but there is little direct correspondence between them available and there is no evidence that there was much of it to begin with. They apparently met regularly and committed little or nothing of their decisions and conversations to paper. They met at Mulcahy's apartment in Oakley Road at the beginning of the war and later at 19 Ranelagh Road, where my father went to live in 1920. The nature of their relationship is probably best described in Mulcahy's characteristically conversational, almost poetic, style in the following quotation:

> I opened and kept open for him all the doors and pathways that he wanted to travel – our relations were always harmonious and frank and we didn't exchange unnecessary information. We each knew what the other was at and particularly in his domain of intelligence, I had no occasion to be questioning him. Over many matters we exercised a constructive and practical Cistercian silence.[2]

Collins needed the protection of his military colleague, particularly after de Valera's return from America. Historians have paid too little attention to the antagonisms which Collins evoked and which developed after this time, particularly among the politicians. Nor have the reasons for these antagonisms been properly evaluated. Collins did not suffer fools gladly and was inclined to be abrasive with the incompetent. Whatever about this tendency of Collins, Mulcahy had this to say about him:

> It can be seen that there was never on Collins's part any note of mere domineering or anything but the offer of the most effective service in a most reasonable manner and terms. Without in any way overpowering or wanting to overpower their judgement in any matter, where their judgement might differ, he would in fact in matters of practice have earned in practical affairs a certain ascendancy over them.[3]

Mulcahy refers on several occasions to the antagonism shown towards Collins by Brugha and Stack, and speculates about the cause or causes of their antipathy, an antipathy which appeared to surface in early 1921 when de Valera returned from America:

> In my joint dealings with Collins and Brugha together I could not say that there was any friction between them until it developed over the question of the Scotch accounts in the end of 1920.[4]

Various factors may have been responsible for the antagonism, including Brugha's criticism of Collins's handling of certain financial transactions in relation to the supply of arms from Glasgow: the Scotch account. There were many who thought that jealousy of Collins on the part of Brugha and Stack may have been a factor, and such an opinion was expressed by de Valera early in 1921 when my father complained that Brugha's quarrel with Collins was endangering the security of the members of the GHQ staff. On that occasion, de Valera said to him: 'You know I think Cathal is jealous of Mick. Isn't it a terrible thing to think that a man with the qualities that Cathal undoubtedly has would fall a victim to a dirty little vice like jealousy.'[5]

Stack was a close associate of Brugha, and his antipathy to Collins may have influenced Brugha. Stack had disliked Collins and his dislike was attributed to Collins's dismissive remarks to Stack when, at the time of the Easter Rising, Stack and other local Kerry people failed to land the arms from

Germany, and when Roger Casement was captured. Fionan Lynch, in a conversation with me, referred to Collins's lack of diplomacy with Stack as a likely cause of the rift between the two men. Páidín O'Keeffe, in his conversations with my father, also refers to Collins's propensity to offend. On this matter, Mulcahy said:

> I find it difficult to think that the resentment spoken of is related to the 'fame and power' side of Collins. It could easily have been originally generated from Stack, that is, there was the same element of reaction in Cathal Brugha as in Stack but only to a smaller extent. It would arise from Collins's manner, from Cathal's feeling that the IRB membership had not come out in the Rising, from Stack's apparent failure in Kerry in the Rising, and from whatever feeling might have been generated by the way in which any IRB inquiry into the 1916 Kerry episode might have rubbed Kerry the wrong way. When Cathal [Brugha] became the public exponent of this hostility to Collins, he spoke with the joint figure of himself and Stack. I'm not clear what kind of public attack on Collins Stack ever made – look up the Dáil discussions on the Treaty.[6]

On the question of the Scotch accounts, my father said:

> [Brugha] did definitely imply that monies that Collins had control of, at any rate in his position as a member of the GHQ staff, and which were supposed to be used for the purchase of arms, were being wasted or mis-spent or unlawfully made use of by Collins or by persons to whom Collins distributed these funds.

When Mulcahy had discussed the situation with Brugha in attempting to defuse the disagreement, Brugha replied: 'As long as the ordinary laws of accounting are attended to, that is all I require.' Mulcahy goes on to say:

> He wanted for some particular reason to have Collins removed [from] his position on the GHQ staff. Apparently he gave no consideration at all to what Collins's work meant, not only to the staff, but to the Government.[7]

And he adds:

> A glance at some of this correspondence revealing the accidents, disappointments, dangers and achievements in this line of purchasing and transporting arms would reveal also the pettiness and the mean lack of imagination on the part of men like Stack and Brugha and perhaps Mellows. The mentality is not understandable.

In a further comment about Stack, he says:

> . . . it is impossible to envisage what kind of a spirit, a heart or a mentality Stack could have had or have developed that would bring him so bitterly and so disastrously against Collins and drive the country into civil war.[8]

It is difficult to quantify the effect of these various factors, but the attitude towards Collins was sufficiently strong for Brugha to ask for Collins's resignation from the army. It is surely likely that the divisions which existed in 1921 between Brugha and Stack on the one hand and Collins and Griffith on the other (and later Mulcahy) had some influence in leading to the Treaty divisions and the Civil War, even if this view is largely discounted by my father, who said that such differences as the Cabinet divisions and army problems during the Truce would not have led to a serious political or military split on the Treaty if de Valera had not so aggressively, disastrously and promptly rejected the settlement in public. Throughout the annotation, one finds an impression of a deep sense of mutual trust, harmony and respect between Mulcahy and Collins. They shared a number of attributes. Mulcahy was trained in the British civil service, and Collins had had the same type of training in London. Despite the contrast in their personalities, they shared the same boundless energy and flair for organisation. In one of his personal remarks about Collins, Mulcahy states:

> He was the person who, by his approach and by the contacts he made, prised open the whole system of the British intelligence system and enabled it to be destroyed; in that, his character has its place; a vast amount of stuff could be assembled associating his smiling buoyancy, his

capacity for bearing tension, clearness of mind, perfectly controlled calm and a devil-may-carishness completely concealed. His clarity of mind and his whole manner and demeanour, together with his power of concentration on the immediate matter in hand, gave him a very great power over men. There was little doubt that his position in the IRB and what he apparently wished to make of the IRB and its tradition gave him, in relation to those people that he was most responsibly and closely dealing with in matters of high secrecy, some kind of mystique which was a kind of cement in matters of loyalty and service; it probably helped particularly to penetrate, and to make as effective as it was, the group of his associates inside the detective force and the police.[9]

His character, his ability and his impulses and tendencies spurred him to make use of his associations. His IRB associations stemming from Frongoch, the further extension of his contacts through the work of the National Aid Association, of which he was secretary, his position of director of organisation (on the resident executive), his contact with the Sinn Féin organisation, which became more powerful and important after the German Plot arrests, all widened the base over which he could use his great energy and stimulate activity in other individual persons and in groups. He was effective with pen and tongue. When, in correspondence and instructions, he was dealing with sluggish material, he has been known to make five copies of a letter, sending out if necessary periodically the third, fourth, fifth copy, as an effective reminder, with considerable labour-saving elements.[10]

Speaking of Collins's administrative approach:

This sample of Collins's correspondence is important and interesting and what has to be understood is the type of control that such correspondence exerted over the people in the country who received it, and who, in relation to individual letters, had to answer details arising out of the questions asked and who, in relation to the somewhat very elaborate forms that had to be returned monthly or so, were forced to keep in touch with the actual details of their whole area over a rather wide field of observation.

A number of these forms, for the greater part of the country, are available over a substantial period of time.

The scheme of things provided a very important link between the person at the receiving end of Collins's correspondence and various other people all through his area, with whom he was required to keep in authoritative contact, directing their efforts in assembling information on the one hand and in carrying out activities on the other. This technique can be reviewed in relation to wider aspects of the situation in my own correspondence and papers. There were similar lines of contact and direction coming from the adjutant general, the QMG, the director of organisation, the director of training. Some of the 'fighting spirits' would look at this kind of thing, coming from me, as being office, chair and table kind of business. But when Collins wrote 'for God's sake, buy a pen and a bottle of ink', they knew what he meant, and they knew that he was telling them very plainly that they weren't being asked to do anything that wasn't fully within their power.[11]

From the point of view of public recognition and appreciation, the Collins that stood by the grave of Ashe in September 1917 and the Collins of January to March 1920 were two figures of very different dimensions. If, internally, he had grown in power, strength of will and flexibility, as he had, he had done it by tireless, vigorous, almost turbulent hard work, applied to his office work as much as to his widespread and general personal contacts. The impulse to make the necessary movement from place to place, and to meet an increasing number of different people to deal with various facets of work, added to his daring, gave him enormous momentum.[12]

A few pages later, in an account of Collins's recreational activities and of his character, Mulcahy talks about Collins's propensity to indulge in horseplay:

There were very many reasons why Collins indulged in a certain amount of rough and tumble, and, of course, a little of that, particularly encountered by people 'on the fringe', can be very much exaggerated. He was capable of an intense amount of concentration over what might be called documentary or office work; his own natural capacity, his early office schooling contributed to this; he was intensely interested in contact with persons – for a purpose – his purpose carried his concentration into these contacts as zealously as his concentration was carried into office work, or what might be called his personal planning and contemplation-related thoughts; he couldn't slow down, he was entirely geared for action. It would be an exaggeration to say, however, that 'horseplay' was his recreation, but in part it provided perhaps a substitute for that and was a kind of escapism; it was also a definite part of his diplomatic technique. It is unnecessary to say that in those times Collins necessarily had a lot of contact with people of all kinds who as a matter of inquisitiveness or self-importance would like to know some of the things in his inner mind; some with Volunteer or political responsibilities might like to know something which Collins might have reason for considering that they should not know; others might want to know something from the point of view of being able to gossip and boast in a human way about what they knew; a list of his 'joints' would indicate the type of places in which he had occasion to meet people, very often of a mixed kind, where light banter, indulged in to protect himself against serious conversation, could easily develop into a little rough and tumble. The basis of this is a natural kind of desire not to slow down, continually exercised energy of some kind, mental protection against awkward or inquisitive persons, escapism.[13]

Collins dealt particularly with the aggressive activities of urgent and spot intelligence in relation to enemy activity. And there was a kind of a 'quick-silver' instinct about his mind and action in moving about.[14]

In the light of this it is worth recording that at this moment, i.e. October 1920, Collins was on the eve of (1) 21 November 1920, which marked the climax of his great intelligence work which on that date enabled a great spy offensive on the part of the British to be exterminated by the Dublin volunteers, (2) and on the arrest of Griffith immediately after that, to assume in addition to his volunteer work, his work as minister for finance [and] the responsibility of acting president.

The appreciation of Collins and his work and their mutual association expressed by Griffith in the Treaty debates wasn't germinated in London; it had grown progressively since Griffith and Collins became associated in the work of Dáil Éireann after its establishment. The only time probably that Griffith had any anxiety with regard to Collins was when he thought it possible that he was endangering the safety of the Treaty by the length to which he appeared to be prepared to go to placate the anti-Treatyites and to shepherd them away from preventing a general election in 1922 or avoiding anything like civil war.[15]

As regards their specific roles on the GHQ staff, he writes that Collins was in full control of intelligence work, which started before the setting up of the staff when Ned Broy first contacted him indirectly in the summer of 1917. Broy was on the British administrative staff in Dublin Castle and was Collins's vital source of intelligence information.

More than once, Mulcahy refers to Collins's enormous capacity for work, his genius for organisation and his ability to stimulate others. He states that, as regards work outside Dublin or large-scale work of any sort, there was the closest possible consultation between himself and Collins. Whilst Mulcahy's reticence and less overtly sociable persona was in striking contrast to Collins's gregarious and convivial character, the two men shared the same commitment to organisation, to providing meticulous directions, and to demanding appropriate responses from their subordinates.

Through Collins's system of keeping contact with companionable groups, and his system of joints [clandestine meeting places] for meetings with such as these, he could exercise a very considerable amount of executive power, and he would never be out of reach when wanted, if [Harry] Boland or anybody else thought there was a matter that he should come in personally on.[16] It is quite true that Collins always moved with the most easy freedom wherever his many activities required him to move. For him, as for the rest of us, the bicycle provided mobility; this was our main protection. He wore no disguise, moved with an assurance that disarmed everybody, and bluffed his way through almost impossible situations.[17]

Béaslaí is perfectly correct in saying that Collins 'remained unshaken in his loyalty to his chief', that is to de Valera, [after the ratification of the Treaty]. Following one of the occasions upon which he was home [from London] and had some talk at the Cabinet and with de Valera, he remarked to me that one of the things that de Valera had said to him was something like 'when a settlement does come, it is only the people who are no good will be against it'.[18]

I have never known anything but the greatest cooperation and cordiality between Collins and Griffith during the whole period. It must have been with the greatest possible confidence that Griffith accepted him as a colleague to go to London with him. I am certain that there is no one whom he would most wish to have with him in such circumstances than Collins. That he would be justified in such a feeling is shown by the result of the negotiations, and Collins's attitude after the Treaty was signed. Not until the question of an election pact with de Valera, into the discussion of which, and the planning of which, Collins was forced by circumstances, did I see Griffith disturbed – and seriously disturbed. Griffith was concerned with giving the people a chance of declaring unequivocally whether they accepted the Treaty or not; he knew very well that they wanted to accept, but he also knew that what was possible to achieve through the Treaty could be very prejudicially affected by the firmness or otherwise with which the people's acceptance was expressed. At that particular time, Collins, suffering under his stresses, could speak rather testily about Griffith, and Griffith, under his strains, was alarmed and disappointed in Collins.[19]

Having referred to the sacrifice made by the leaders of the 1916 Rising, Mulcahy noted:

Collins was making an analogous sacrifice in his capacity as chairman of the Supreme Council of the IRB, when he went to London as a negotiator. But as MacDermott and Pearse didn't sacrifice their lives without some hope and some faith of definite achievement and progress towards Irish freedom and the road to an Irish Republic, so Collins didn't go to London without hope and faith and with a lot more assurance perhaps than the 1916 men had of progress towards Irish freedom – and on the road to an Irish Republic, though no one even at the Supreme Council of the IRB level would have assured him that he could get a republic agreed to by the British, or that, even if they demanded that he should, would have persisted in that demand on the light of Collins telling them, prior to his going to London, that he couldn't get it for them.[20]

Referring to Collins's visit under an assumed name to Stack in Manchester Jail, while Collins was on the run, Mulcahy said it was 'typical of his audacity':[21]

When Béaslaí suggests that Collins did not think that he was the right man for the task, it is that Collins's difficulty was that de Valera should have led the delegation. With de Valera and Griffith members of the plenipotentiaries group, Collins would not necessarily have thought that his presence on the group would not be an additional strength. He would feel, however, if he were not one of the plenipotentiaries, that he had complete confidence in such a pair and that he would be in a stronger position to help them in their consultations and outside discussions, but more particularly, that he would be in a stronger position to support them ultimately in the work of getting accepted whatever decisions they might come to. He would then have been pleading for the acceptance of work done by the leaders who had done their best.[22]

Collins went as a soldier 'at the orders of a superior officer', although against his own judgement. He objected strenuously against de Valera's decision not to go to London. He considered that his military position and military record debarred him from being a suitable member of the negotiating body. The fact is that after de Valera and Griffith, Collins was the outstanding personality who should be with them; and the question cries out for understanding why these three names were not the first selected, and the persons most willing to serve and most able to guarantee complete confidence and support.[23]

In relation to the antagonism shown by Brugha and Stack to Collins during the Truce and the negotiations:

> There is the temptation to ask, what on earth did either Stack or Brugha think they were [doing] sending Collins with his uncurbable desire to work and serve into the middle of the London negotiations, while bedaubing him in this particular way, either in relation to the efficiency of the organisation in Britain that he was depending on for this work, or in relation to dishonesty on the part of either himself or persons in Britain in relation to money matters. [This refers to the Scotch account controversy.] The question arises as to what Collins thought of it all; he pushed it all from him as something that would be smothered out of existence in coming achievements; the true answer would be that he did not think of it at all; all his energies and all his thoughts were absorbed with the many works in hand and now particularly with work bearing on the negotiations in London. All the circumstances of the time were vigorously dynamic. He was now associated with Griffith in very definite pinpointed responsibility and power to take the possibilities shown by Lloyd George's approach in his letter of 20 of July, explore them, expose their realities and help to formulate the proposals in a way for presentation to acceptance by the Dáil. I doubt if he bothered to consider what kind of a group he was leaving behind as the remnants of the Cabinet. I feel that he still trusted de Valera, felt that he was out for making peace and that he understood the necessity for it, and that he left out of his mind any unnecessary doubts that would interfere with the freedom of his thought or his consultations and work at the Irish plenipotentiary level.[24]

He speaks of Collins and the immediate impact of the Treaty crisis:

> It is somewhat humiliating to find ourselves considering these things in the light of the terrible moments that had to be faced by so many people at the end of the year 1921. The crisis breaks particularly around Griffith

and Collins, and the decision that was taken on the night of the 5/6 December. Collins, in the light of all he meant in terms of work, development and achievement in so many areas previously, and his astounding exertions and activities from the beginning of January 1922 to the date of his death, appears a particular figure in the light of his character and doings and sacrifices . . . But in the light of what Griffith meant back to 1899 and in relation to the beginning of everything, a special poignancy attaches to him.[25]

De Valera's suggestion, soon after his return to Ireland from America, that Collins should go to America to complete de Valera's unfinished work and to patch up the divisions Dev had left behind, may partly have been motivated by a conscious or subconscious resentment of Collins's public notoriety and his dominance of the political scene. At least Dev must have felt that he could do without Collins, even at this crucial stage of the War of Independence. It seemed an extraordinary suggestion, and Mulcahy had this to say about it (with his latter-day long sentences and verbal tortuosity!):

It was possible for us to hear of the proposal by de Valera that Collins was to be sent to America with a long list of things to be done and to smile at the pungent if laughing word of Collins to his pals that 'the long **** won't get rid of me as easy as that'. But it is fantastic now to look back over notes and to think that in the many-sided crisis that existed for the people generally and such institutions of the government, including the Dáil and the army, as were at work, the president, returning after an absence of more than a year and a half in America and practically another year absent before that in English jails following the arrests in May 1918 in connection with the German Plot, would, in relation to Collins, have nothing else to suggest but that he should go away on the kind of work set out in pages 1-5 [of Vol. 2 of Béaslaí's biography]. It was only a person living in fairyland and having no sense of action or what, in the carrying out of action, mutual and seasoned trust among men means, who could think that even in the military arena alone, Collins could be spared at such a moment. The minister for defence was concerned more with an examination of what were called the 'Scotch accounts' with, I fear, a certain amount of cooperation from Mellows – also returned from America – in the development of an antagonism against Collins and with a view to damaging him by surrounding him with mean insinuations; pursuing the matter in such a way as to endanger the safety of the members of the GHQ staff by requiring them to attend meetings to discuss these things at a time when, normally, I wouldn't allow more than three or four of them to meet at one time.[26]

De Valera's letter to Collins about going to America is dated 18 January 1921. That, in a fortnight after his return, he should have contemplated the idea of sending Collins to America, and drafted the actual details of the letter of the 18, is a thing that nobody immersed in the home circumstances of the time could possibly understand. And if Mick's [Collins] reported comment on the suggestion cannot be regarded as just a word of one syllable, it must certainly be regarded as just a compound word, because he couldn't express anything but just 'surprise' – surprise at something beyond understanding, and at a time too busy and too full of pressure to feel that it was necessary to understand it. Any understanding could afford to wait in the development of his contacts with the man whom he had been out of personal contact with for nineteen months, although he remained in close communication by letter with him. Collins's cooperation with Dev and his confidence in his person as leader never developed any weakness or questioning.[27]

The coming of Craig[i] and [Lord] Derby, and the movements and talks of other persons with peace feelers had stirred the atmosphere a good bit by June 1921. The submission by 'the Hearst' man of a number of questions to Collins emphasises the fact that, apart altogether from Collins's general work and activity, the arrest of Griffith in November 1920 had put the final touch to bringing Collins into the forefront of the political sphere of importance and contact. Even if de Valera had not gone to America, Collins's position as minister for finance, balanced by his equally important position in army matters, would always have held

[i] Sir James Craig, prime minister for Northern Ireland from 1921-1940.

95

him on the level with both de Valera and Griffith.

Collins was fortunate (in the historical sense) to have died at the height of his fame, and to have his reputation enhanced by subsequent historians and writers, so that he has become a legend. He is perceived by many as a lost saviour to his country, but he, like other heroes who had the good fortune to survive the revolution, would have found himself facing the realities of a political and social situation where the gilt of his fame might easily have worn thin with the passage of time and the interpersonal problems and conflicts which are inseparable from the rough and tumble of political life, particularly at a time of profound change. Collins raised many antagonisms during his time, which are referred to by Páidín O'Keeffe in his conversations with Mulcahy. It is likely that, if he had been faced with the many difficulties of the fledging new state, he would have experienced the same problems encountered by his surviving colleagues.

It was Mulcahy's belief, consistent with his admiration for the man, that Collins would have been the saviour of the country if he had survived. Mother and I, in commenting on my father's view, took a somewhat more pragmatic view of the hazards to one's reputation of survival in politics, particularly in the bitter post-Civil War milieu, with its severe recession, and with massive unemployment, aggravated by the post-war demobilisation. However, Mulcahy may have had a point in that Collins's influence in the Cabinet might have eased the demobilisation problems and might have prevented O'Higgins's intrusion into army affairs, with the consequent Army Mutiny and its adverse influence on the government and its supporters. How Collins would have coped with the rough and tumble of political life in the Ireland of the 1920s is anybody's guess.

Mulcahy was still alive, and living in the mundane political world of post-Treaty Ireland, with its chronic problems of recession and reconstruction, made worse by the bitter political divisions. His reputation, which during the War of Independence was closely linked with that of Collins, slowly atrophied as he faced the problems of the Truce and the Civil War, and its aftermath of bitterness and disillusionment, and as his admirers and those contemporaries who thought so highly of him gradually departed the scene. Collins died at the right time for himself and for his reputation – although not at the right time for Ireland. Apart from his outstanding military role, he deserves to be remembered for his seminal contribution to the political evolution of the Irish State. However, his reputation might have suffered too if he had survived to face the rigours of post-Treaty Ireland. After 1924, Mulcahy's reputation began to yield to the influence of the commonplace. He himself, because of his tendency to self-effacement, his lack of political mystique and personal ambition, and his inability to have recourse to the devices that make a politician popular with the crowd, was at least partly responsible for his own declining reputation. Collins is a folk hero, at least in the minds of the media and among some of his biographers, mainly because of his military exploits rather than because of his great administrative skills during the War of Independence. John Regan, in his article on Collins,[28] underlines this point when he writes:

> But like the seldom-published photograph of Collins at his department desk, the Michael Collins of the Department of Finance does not have the same appeal as Collins the gunman.

I am reminded again of the constant theme in my father's writings and conversations, which is his sensitivity to criticism of Collins and Griffith. In his opinion, they were the two great architects of the independence movement, and their deaths in August 1922, at the height of the Civil War, was the ultimate tragedy for the new Irish Free State. During a recorded conversation, Mulcahy reacts strongly to implied criticism of the two leaders, and during the same conversation he expresses his dislike of Prof. Desmond Williams, who was Professor of Modern History at University College Dublin and who, during a Thomas Davis lecture, said that both de Valera and Collins shared the blame for the Civil War, Mulcahy disagreed profoundly with Williams's conclusions on the genesis of the Civil War, but perhaps Williams may have had a point when we recall Páidín O'Keeffe's comments about the alienation of some deputies by Collins.

Several references are contained in the tape recordings to the influence

Michael Collins may have had in provoking resistance to the acceptance of the Treaty and thus to the subsequent split in the army. These references are quoted from conversations Mulcahy had with Páidín O'Keeffe, who came into intimate contact with all the political and military leaders during this time. He talks about the various personal problems and stresses which arose among leaders. He was pursued relentlessly by my father in the early 1960s to record his experiences during his tenure of office with Sinn Féin. He was equally well informed about Sinn Féin, the IRB, and the background to the formation of the Sinn Féin and Volunteer executives in 1917. He refers to these in several of the tapes.

O'Keeffe had a prodigious memory and was an observant and uninhibited critic of those whom he served. On several occasions he spoke about Collins, particularly in relation to his frenetic activities and the effect his dominance had on his colleagues. He maintained that part of the vote against the Treaty was an anti-Collins vote, and that Collins first caused a degree of antagonism because he, with Harry Boland and Diarmuid O'Hegarty, three Volunteers and prominent IRB men, had the choice of candidates for the 1918 election – a fact which was resented particularly by those who had aspirations to be invited to enter the Dáil but who failed to be nominated.

Michael Collins died towards the end of the engagement at Béal na mBláth. Because of testimony at the time, it was believed that he was killed by one of the last bullets fired by the Irregulars, which ricocheted off the armoured car or off the road before it entered his head. Although occasional suggestions have been made that he was shot by one of his own men, the circumstances of his death makes such a possibility highly unlikely. The late Terry de Valera tried to convince me that this was so, but he obviously had a motive to accept this view. Collins was laid out in 58 St Stephen's Green, a private wing of St Vincent's Hospital. According to Mr Fletcher, of the Department of Anatomy at UCD, who was a young attendant in the department at the time, a post-mortem examination was carried out by Jimmy Redditch, the head porter at the Anatomy Department of the Royal College of Surgeons, with Oliver St John Gogarty in attendance. It is likely that the procedure was confined to a superficial examination of the head wound and to preparing the remains for embalming and the lying in state at City Hall from 25 to 27 September 1922. Fletcher told me that the embalming fluid used was formalin, and that eosin was added to retain a pink colour in the face. This would be confirmed by Lavery's painting of the dead Collins, which shows him with normal or even a slightly exaggerated lifelike coloration.[29] Perhaps Calton Younger, in his *Ireland's Civil War*,[30] is correct when he states that no post-mortem was carried out. Unfortunately, despite enquiries with the college more than forty years ago, I was unable to obtain any record of the examination, nor was such information available from the hospital.

Béaslaí quotes[31] Emmet Dalton, who was with Collins when he was killed: 'There was a fearful gaping wound at the base of the skull behind the right ear.' And Calton Younger writes that the body was examined by a Dr Leo Aherne in Cork, who, 'like Dr Gogarty later, was sure that the wound was caused either by a ricochet or a spent bullet'. Ulick O'Connor, in his life of Oliver St John Gogarty,[32] writes of Gogarty: 'With fine skill, he was able to hide the gaping wound in the back of the head.' The photograph in Younger's book of Collins's body lying on a bed in Cork with a wide white bandage around his head was consistent with his having an extensive head wound.

However, in a conversation recorded by my father with Gerry Ryan of Tipperary, it is stated by the latter that the body was inspected by a British army officer. According to Ryan, the officer described a small entry wound and a large exit wound. The absence of a large entry wound would strongly support the view that he was killed by a ricochet bullet and not by one of his own men.

Kathleen Galvin, who was acting night matron on the morning of 24 August, gave me a most poignant account when I was a young consultant there in 1951 of the arrival of Collins's horse-drawn gun carriage. The remains arrived at the North Wall very early on that morning. She described the moment, about four in the morning, with the sun just rising, and shortly after rain had fallen, and with the cobblestones glistening in the early light, when the gun carriage appeared and moved slowly from the Shelbourne Hotel to the hospital steps, preceded by a makeshift army band playing the moving and evocative Scottish dirge 'The Flowers of the Forest'. She talked about the emotional turmoil of that moment, and of the intense sadness which prevailed.

Mulcahy spoke with two colleagues who were in the Free State army at the time of Collins's death. One was Frank Holland, who was leader of the pipers' band before the advent of Fritz Brasé as head of the army school of music. Frank was with the pipers at the North Wall when Collins's remains arrived in the early morning. It was he who said that the dirges played were 'The Flowers of the Forest' and 'Lord Lovett's Lament'. At the end of Mulcahy's interview with the two ex-soldiers, they all three attempted to sing 'Lord Lovett's Lament'. I remark in my abstract of the tape:

> Holland's description was followed by an atrocious rendering of the latter dirge by the three, confirming that the larynx undergoes the same functional deterioration with age as the other organs of the body!

I also had a description from Kathleen Galvin of Kitty Kiernan's arrival at St Vincent's Hospital later in the day. She was dressed in a dark grey suit and a white hat. She 'was swooning and behaving in a most dramatic way' before she laid a lily on the coffin, and then sat beside it for a prolonged period in a trance.

My father talks about Collins's death on tape. His death evoked my father's well-known message to the army, which was aimed at preventing reprisals, and which was published immediately after the news of Collins's death had reached Dublin:

> To the men of the Army
> Stand calmly by your posts.
> Bend bravely and undaunted to your work.
> Let no cruel act of reprisal blemish your bright honour.
> Every dark hour that Michael Collins met since 1916 seemed but to
> Still that bright strength of his and temper his gay bravery.
> You are left each inheritors of that strength, and of that bravery.
> To each of you falls his unfinished work.
> No darkness in this hour – No loss of comrades will daunt you at it.
> Ireland! the Army serves – strengthened by its sorrow.

This message was followed one week later by Mulcahy's homily delivered over Collins's grave (see Appendix 1). Mulcahy's deep commitment to his religion, his spirituality, his interest in Irish history and Ireland's culture and language, is clearly evident from this homily. A later panegyric over the graves of Thomas Ashe, Peadar Kearney and Piaras Béaslaí is equally full of references to God's Providence and the Christian path to perfection, to the Kingdom of Peace on earth, to recent Irish heroes and to the spirit of Fenianism. He speaks with confidence about the nation's hopes and resurrection, and his quotes in the Irish language bear witness to his idealism.[33] The Béaslaí homily is in its own way a tour de force but, although it was delivered fifty-one years after 1916, it is hard to reconcile its contents with my father's military performance at Ashbourne. Perhaps it is not surprising that Kevin O'Higgins called Mulcahy a 'soldier saint'.

Writing of the Dáil debate on the Treaty, Nichevo of the *Irish Times* gave a pen picture of several of the leaders, including Collins and Mulcahy:

> The two legendary figures of the Dáil were Messrs Collins and Mulcahy. One had heard all sorts of stories about these two men during what is known euphemistically as 'the trouble' . . . Whether these and similar stories are true, I do not know. But they made me very anxious to see these two men in the flesh. Neither of them looks the part. Each, in a sense, is the antithesis of the other, but they both are very prosaic-looking individuals whom you never would dream of crediting with hair-raising exploits.
>
> Mr Mulcahy is one of the most interesting men in the Dáil. Mr Collins fairly oozes energy; he is what the Americans would call a 'kinetic' type. Mr Mulcahy, although he walks with a jaunty gait, is remarkable for his repose. I have watched him sitting for an hour on end in the Dáil while deputies raved at one another and half a dozen were on their feet at the same time. He never stirred. Sitting with his arms folded, he might have been listening to an interesting sermon in church. He has a very impassive face. It is deeply furrowed, and suggests a well-balanced mind, and his long nose gives him an almost aristocratic appearance. When he is speaking, he purses up his lips, and has a knack of using uncommon words, which he chooses with the utmost care. He always seems to be tracing something with his finger on the desk in front of him, and never raises his eyes. His speech in favour of the Treaty

was a remarkable utterance. He was virtually the only member of the Dáil whose words did not contain a trace of bombast. There was no sabre rattling or beating of drums. He ignored the 'gallery' and made his appeal to the intellect rather than to the sentiment of his listeners. I tried to think of some non-Irishman with whom Mr Mulcahy might be compared, but his type is very rare. Mutatis mutandis, he has much in common with Colonel Lawrence, of Arabian fame. If he wore silk socks, and were a Fellow of All Souls, the resemblance would be even stronger.

He then goes on to talk of Collins. He refers among other characteristics to his leonine energy, and his love of action which

> . . . makes him impatient and easily provoked . . . But he did his very best not only to restrain himself, but to induce his fellow-members to maintain the dignity of the Dáil.

Nichevo then brings us down a peg when he finishes on the rather mundane note that

> It is a pity that he [Collins] did not exert his influence to prevent the members from smoking; cigarettes and pipes should have no place in the vital councils of a nation.

Among many letters and telegrams Mulcahy received after Collins's death,[34] the following extracts are quoted. Frank Aiken, by September a prominent Irregular leader, wrote to my father after Collins was killed, expressing extreme sorrow on his loss. In his letter he states that it was particularly tragic because he believed that Collins was about to change his mind at the time of his death, realising that he was wrong in opposing the Irregulars. He would, according to Aiken, have stopped the Civil War and supported the republic:

> You alone now can save the nation! I think if you believed absolutely in the sincerity of the men opposed to you, you would stop the struggle. If that is true, I prove to you if you wish. I die in order to prove to you if you guarantee to me that you'll stop this civil war if I do so. For God's sake, Dick, agree to this and let one death end it all.

He signs the letter *Mise do naimhid agus do chara* ('I am your enemy and your friend').

This letter sums up both the tragedy and the poignancy of the Civil War, of the shattering and passionate break among those who fought side by side against the British, a break which was made all the more tragic because of the patent sincerity of those on both sides of the struggle. It also underlines the strange loss of realism among the Irregulars when such stalwart men as Aiken asked my father to stop the Civil War, when Liam Lynch, in November 1922, asked that all pro-Treaty supporters should be ostracised, and when, at the very end of the war, with only a few of his companions left with him in the loneliness of the Knockmealdown Mountains to fight the Free State army, Lynch seriously believed that victory was in his grasp.

It was also part of the Irregulars' propaganda after Collins's death to say that he had become disillusioned with the Free State and that he had been critical of the Four Courts attack, which marked the commencement of the formal Civil War. George Gavan Duffy wrote to Mulcahy on 23 September 1922, the day after Collins died:

> I have never known a man so great, with that combination of magnetic personality and dominating will and character, [and] far-seeing judgement. And to you, who were his intimate friend, the tragedy must be beyond words. But it is on you pre-eminently that the shouldering of his burden will lie, and your lead and your example must now be our beacon. I feel that you will turn to Eoin MacNeill as the one fitting counsellor left to you in the big things of life. I pray that our responsible men will smother in their own hearts the intense bitterness they must feel against the irregulars; there will be acrimony and recriminations enough anyway without any prompting from our propagandists; and your dignified address to the army was in the very note to strengthen the situation that was wanted. With your cool head to direct the military mind, I have no fear of the outlook there.

The telegrams Mulcahy received included such exhortations as: 'Trusting you will be spared to carry on his work to a finish, and may God spare you for a good cause' and 'Fight on for free Ireland in memory of our gallant commander-in-chief'.

Mrs Katherine Tynan Hinkson, in a letter in *The Times* after Collins's death, writes:

> Your Dublin correspondent, writing of the calamitous death of Michael Collins, said of Richard Mulcahy that he is 'handicapped by the temperament of a philosopher'. Well, he may have the temperament of a philosopher – though I should not call that a handicap in Irish politics – but he has also the temperament of a poet, without which no Irish genius is complete. I listened at the Dáil meetings last autumn to speech after speech which seemed to me, brought up on the traditions of Irish oratory, deliberately commonplace and dull. Then came Mulcahy and the whole thing was changed. He was not ashamed to put his emotions into oratory; listening to him one was back in the great days. His address to the army on the death of Michael Collins seems to me admirable as poetic prose. Nothing could be finer. There is no higher type of man in our history than the man who is at one a poet and a man of action, as witness the great men of the Elizabethan days. Ireland has suffered a terrible calamity in the death of our two leaders [that is, Griffith and Collins] but while such men as Richard Mulcahy, and the Brennans of Clare, lead her army, we may lift up our heavy hearts.[35]

ARTHUR GRIFFITH

Arthur Griffith was the founder of Sinn Féin in 1905, minister for economic affairs in the First and Second Dála, acting president of the First Dáil during de Valera's time in America, and president of Sinn Féin from 10 January 1922, after the ratification of the Treaty, until his death on 12 August 1922. Despite beliefs to the contrary, he was not a member of the Cabinet of the Provisional Government but was chairman of the co-existing Dáil Cabinet, a body which had become little more than a talking shop after the ratification of the Treaty. However, he kept in close touch with the members of the Provisional Cabinet up to the time of his death and became impatient with Collins and Mulcahy because of their reluctance to deal more quickly with the dissident Volunteers over the Treaty.

Griffith was an active member of the Sinn Féin standing committee during the 1917-21 period:

> From about 15 April 1919, after Griffith came out of Lincoln Jail, he systematically attended at all the meetings of the standing committee of Sinn Féin up to 15 October 1920, when he was arrested. He presided at most of these meetings, to the number of about fifty in all.[1]

Mulcahy makes many references to Griffith in his annotation, particularly in relation to his political role while de Valera was in America, and to his role during and after the Treaty negotiations. If Collins was Mulcahy's military hero, Griffith was his political hero and his philosophical mentor. Griffith's political philosophy, based on self-determination for Ireland but retaining a link with the Crown, and therefore with Great Britain, appealed to Mulcahy's pragmatic view of things. It was in keeping with the attitudes of the people in the early part of the twentieth century, and indeed right up to the Treaty, where the great majority did not conceive of or support the concept of an independent republic, and when Ireland was so close to Britain in economic, cultural, social and professional affairs.

Padraic Colum, in his biography of Arthur Griffith,[2] quotes Griffith as saying:

> Though I am a believer in the republican system of government, I am ready – as I believe is every other Irish Nationalist – to accept any form of native government in preference to alien rule.

My father admired Griffith for his political realism, his modesty, his lack of personal ambition and his firm adherence to the Treaty agreement. He was appalled by the treatment Griffith received after the Treaty negotiations, particularly as he had been reluctant to take part in these without de Valera. He was saddened by the bitterness and vituperation of the Treaty debates and by their impact on Griffith, and by Griffith's differences with Collins, when the latter was, in Griffith's perception, compromising the Treaty agreement later in

1922. Mulcahy was saddened too by Griffith's untimely death. His death, like that of Collins, in Mulcahy's opinion was an important destabilising factor during the difficult months of the Civil War. Griffith had a high opinion of my father as a young military and political leader with a part to play in the foundation of the new state, and supported his military policies. In connection with Griffith's attitude to de Valera, Mulcahy said:

> Both as a matter of principle and as a matter of full and voluntary agreement, Griffith [was] to maintain full confidence in de Valera. A story by Denis McCullough of a discussion in Gloucester [Jail] at a time when Griffith and a number of others were there under the German Plot arrests, epitomises Griffith's whole philosophy and attitude. The point he made there, when asked for his opinion after a long discussion on certain aspects of things that might be going to happen, was that, 'whatever de Valera does, I agree to that'.[3]

My father spoke as follows about Griffith, the Treaty and the Treaty negotiations:

> He had fully supported de Valera's election as President of Sinn Féin in October 1917. On one occasion, probably during the approach to the conscription issue in March 1918 (though it could have been shortly after April 1919, when the full Cabinet had been set up), I had occasion to go with Griffith to visit the Archbishop of Dublin, Dr Walsh. We went up by tram and, entering the gates to the Archbishop's palace on foot, Griffith was telling me that nearly all his life he had been looking for a young man to lead the political movement (in the early days no doubt he regarded Rooney as this), and he was expressing his great appreciation of the fact that, in de Valera, they had now got the kind of young man they wanted. It is possible that even in his great disappointment of having to face the London negotiations without having de Valera with him, and de Valera shouldering the responsibility of chairman of the plenipotentiaries, he still clung to his early hope and principle that 'whatever de Valera does, I agree with'. To the very end, I feel he [Griffith] relied confidently on Dev to lead, though quite

surprised and distressed that he declined to lead the plenipotentiaries.[4]

M. J. MacManus, in his book *Eamon de Valera*,[5] referring to details of the Treaty conference held in London at 3 o'clock on the afternoon of 5 December, reports:

> Lloyd George proceeded to deliver his hammer blow . . . The British could concede no more and would debate no further. The Treaty must be signed or else . . . Griffith surrendered. 'I will give the answer of the Irish Delegation at 9 o'clock tonight,' he said. 'But Mr Prime Minister I will personally sign this agreement and recommend it to my countrymen.' 'Do I understand Mr Griffith that, though everyone else refuses, you will nevertheless agree to sign?' 'That is so,' replied Griffith.

Mulcahy continues:

> The question arises to my mind as to whether these are not the most valiant words ever spoken in the course of Irish history. They were the words of a man who, in an unquenched gaiety of spirit, had suffered poverty and degradation and apparently fruitless labours for years, entirely devoted to the service of the uplift of the people in terms of spirit, economic well-being, social happiness, political strength.
>
> Pakenham thinks that, before he spoke to them, he should have got on the telephone to de Valera.[6] I don't know what Pakenham may have known about de Valera or the position of the others around de Valera in Dublin; or what he can have known about the mentality of Lloyd George and the circumstances around Lloyd George affecting his strength to do things or support for anything that he might want to do – support from his colleagues. There are some pages in *The Decline and Fall of Lloyd George* by Lord Beaverbrook[7] that give some idea as to what the difficulties there were in coming to and holding fast to a decision on anything like satisfactory Treaty terms. Griffith must have, by 5 December, been fully aware of the dangers that were inherent in the inconsequential approach of persons like Stack and Brugha, and he must have been fully aware of the internal difficulties among the most

important British members of the negotiating group. I cannot feel that, in his most wearied, his most frustrated, his most disappointed moment, Griffith would yield to any element of despair either personally or for the Irish people, but I feel that these words represent a supreme valour that in another might have to be called despair or recklessness.[8]

Later on the next page, Mulcahy states, speaking of the problems posed by de Valera and his Cabinet colleagues at home:

What we apparently have to do here is to examine their weaknesses, their pettinesses, and see to what extent they contributed to the circumstances that Griffith found himself in when he had to make such a declaration on the 5 December 1921.[9]

He went to London. He strenuously objected to being required to go there without de Valera. He had borne the burden of acting president of the Cabinet during de Valera's absence in America. He would always have regarded it as his duty to undertake the responsibility for partaking in such a mission as the London mission.[10]

I have already referred to the anomalous situation facing Griffith while de Valera was in America in relation to the difficulties and lost opportunities of negotiating with the British.[11] Despite Griffith's disabilities as regards initiating truce negotiations, Mulcahy had noted:

If in fact de Valera were able to do this, that is to go to America at that time without injury to our morale, it is a tribute to the character of Griffith and to his past, and the confidence that his work of the past had inspired in us, that we had a sound political approach for a people who had a strong national tradition and a warm fruitful culture to maintain. Given that Griffith was there, I didn't at the time feel any weakness in the situation. My position as the military head of the army probably suffered a diminution of importance politically, in that I had no head of government between whom and myself to sandwich the minister for defence.[12]

On the question of Griffith's attitude to armed intervention, in Padraic Colum's biography of Griffith, the old Fenian John O'Leary, in a conversation with Griffith, speaks of the prospect of Irish Freedom:

> **O'Leary:** You have too lofty an opinion of the people's fibre, Mr Griffith. They have been too long in slavery to exhibit the moral courage your policy demands.
>
> **Griffith:** I have great faith in the innate strength of the people's soul, sir.
>
> **O'Leary:** Don't you think it cannot appeal to a crowd; it touches no chord of patriotism or spirituality in contemporary life.
>
> **Griffith:** I am not concerned about today. Tomorrow will be ours. It has backers already among the intellectuals and with men and women of faith and vision. Their opinion will infilter the masses of the nation in time.

Colum refers to Griffith's commitment to a pluralistic society on page 95:

> The Union was hateful to him because it destroyed the consensus that the Irish Parliament was working towards, because it stratified diverse interests, and because, through placing the centre of normal political activity outside the country, it put the great deal of the apparatus for reconciliation beyond the reach of the Irish people. The educational system, which in other countries would bring young people of different creeds and classes together, in Ireland, through the stratification of interests, gave no such benefits. The constitution of 1782 was of importance to him, not as something ultimate, but as something round which a consensus could form.

And he refers to Griffith's views on the mutual dependence of capital and labour, and to the nation's responsibility to protect both. Speaking about Griffith's contribution to the economic advancement of Ireland, Mulcahy states:

> The fact of the 'Commission of Enquiry into the resources and industries of Ireland' is a monument to the vigour and the persistence of Griffith's purpose in the economic side of all his long years of teaching. It has to be remembered that this commission was set up in

the teeth of the suppression of the Dáil. To the people generally, and particularly to the type of people who were concerned with the economic situation in Ireland, the fact that this committee was working and getting the cooperation of many witnesses was a very great steadier and a contribution to the morale of the people.

It is little wonder that my father admired Griffith and his political philosophy, and that Griffith remained his political hero throughout his life. As early as 1905, Griffith had proposed the idea of a dual monarchy along the lines of the pre-Union Parliament, but for some years he remained politically suspect, on the one hand from the great majority of the Irish, who favoured Home Rule, and on the other from the very small number of radicals who favoured a republic. The 1916 Rising and the executions were to change all that. My father's sense of sadness at Griffith's disappointment because of the Treaty debacle is understandable, as is his despair that the man who inspired our first successful national movement was humiliated, berated and maligned by his anti-Treaty opponents during the Treaty debates. Griffith was a pragmatist and would gladly have accepted complete freedom where there would have been no inconsistency in full self-government and retaining the symbol of the Crown.

Griffith's death was attributed by some people at the time to a broken heart, but, with a little more realism, it was generally accepted that he had died from a stroke. The diagnosis entered on the death certificate was a subarachnoid haemorrhage (caused by an artery rupturing into the brain and its surrounds). He was cared for in the private wing of St Vincent's Hospital at 95 Lower Leeson Street by Oliver St John Gogarty, who signed the death certificate.[13] There is no record of a post-mortem examination but the history of his death was related to me by the staff of the hospital. His death was quite instantaneous and was consistent with a heart attack caused by coronary heart disease. We have evidence that he was a cigarette smoker; it was to take another fifty years to identify cigarette smoking as a major cause of heart disease.

Griffith and Collins died at the height of the Civil War. Their deaths were described by my father as the ultimate tragedy for the emerging young state, a tragedy which included what he described as the 'compound disaster' of the Civil War.

EAMON DE VALERA

Eamon de Valera first came to prominence as commandant of the Fourth Dublin Brigade in the Rising. He was elected president of Sinn Féin and president of the national Volunteer executive in October 1917 and remained in these positions until the ratification of the Treaty on 7 January 1922. Griffith was proposed but refused because of his support of de Valera. De Valera's presidency of the Volunteer executive was an entirely nominal position. He was Priomh Aire (first minister) of Dáil Éireann from April 1919 to January 1922, and was elected President of the Republic by the Dáil in August 1921. While my father had numerous meetings with de Valera during the years from 1917 to 1922, his relations with him appear to have been formal and in keeping with his position as head of the army in the presence of the head of state. There certainly appeared to be no sense of intimacy between them, and Mulcahy's description of some meetings presents de Valera as a rather patronising colleague – advising him to study economics and to read Machiavelli's *The Prince*, or asking the rhetorical question why, as assistant minister for defence, he did not attend Cabinet, but adding, before he got a reply: 'You are as well not to, you would be as bad as the rest of them if you did!'

My first main contact with Dev would have been about the end of August 1917 in the Keating Branch of the Gaelic League, when a small group of us, including Ashe, de Valera, Collins, Cathal Brugha and others – about eight or ten – met to consider the approach to the reorganisation of the Volunteers and the calling of a Convention. Dev would have been much more involved on the political side of things and in relation to the organisation of the Sinn Féin Convention. The next contact would be in connection with the holding of the Volunteer Convention in Jones's Road on 27 October; the next serious meeting would be when he and others came up to Fernside [Mulcahy's home] in April 1918 (I had lumbago), when the first real excitement about conscription began.

Dev was arrested in May 1918, and from that time until he returned from America on 24 December 1920, the only revealing contact I had with him was at 3 Fitzwilliam Square, before he went to America, that is to say, April or May 1919, when out of the blue, in a casual conversation for a few minutes in the hall of the house at Fitzwilliam Square, the president, soon to depart for the States, said to the chief of staff of the army: 'You are a young man now going in for politics, I'll give you two pieces of advice: study economics and read *The Prince*.[1]

My father became interested in economics in his later parliamentary years but probably never read *The Prince*. At least there is no copy of the book in his library. I do not think that Machiavelli's political philosophy would have appealed to him.

Two particular meetings with de Valera during the Truce were the Cabinet meeting with the GHQ staff on 25 October 1921, to discuss – and disagree with Dev on – the 'new army', and the meeting of the staff with Dev alone on 10 December, where, in answer to Dev's question, the members of the staff were to swear loyalty to him if he were to win the vote against the Treaty in the Dáil. Mulcahy had many casual meetings with de Valera during the post-Treaty period, but his only meeting with him during the Civil War was in Dr Farnham's house in September 1922. Dr Farnham was a gynaecologist and was a close friend and confidant of de Valera's. This meeting finished in a matter of a minute or two, when the two men were unable to reconcile their views on the Treaty and the acceptance of the people's decision on the matter.

Mulcahy appeared to think that de Valera made little contact with any other leader during the Truce and the run-up to the Treaty negotiations, and that his strategies were the result of his own initiatives and were just rubber-stamped by Dáil Éireann. De Valera may of course have discussed matters with Childers or other confidants, but certainly not openly with the other political or military leaders, nor at Sinn Féin, Cabinet or Dáil meetings. That Childers was particularly close to Dev is referred to by Mulcahy when, in a reference to Griffith's association with Darrel Figgis, who was joint secretary of Sinn Féin, Mulcahy said:

> Griffith kept up a very close working friendship with him [Figgis] but only to a very minute degree would he have been to Griffith what Childers was to de Valera.[2]

Mulcahy wrote of Dev's apparent lack of communication with others before and after the Truce:

> We are concerned with two periods of such communications. First, the approaches and the correspondence leading up to the actual acceptance of a truce position, and secondly, the considerations and the correspondence that led up to the taking of the decision which brought about at Downing Street on 11 October 1921 the first meeting of the peace conference that ultimately concluded the Treaty agreement. I get the impression from the story here that there is less personal contact for the discussion of these things between the principals, even between Collins and de Valera, than would have been possible and desirable.[3]

De Valera had four preliminary meetings with Lloyd George in July 1921, after the Truce. They lasted seven and a half hours in all. Although de Valera had a substantial group of others with him in London, including Griffith, he attended all the meetings on his own. Surely he was one to keep things close to his chest!

Under the title 'National Unity' in the tapes, Mulcahy excuses the members of the Dáil for their unanimous and uncritical support of de Valera's decisions:

> Was there anything unnatural in the show of 'national unity' that was made by the Dáil by the reserve of criticism? It can hardly be said, given the type of lead that de Valera was giving, with apparently the Cabinet supporting him, that there was anything unreasonable in the absence of criticism made in the Dáil: it was rather a demonstration of national unity and strength intended to give confidence to the leader and the Cabinet in facing up to the work that was going to fall on them. De Valera's proclamation to the people of Ireland dated 10 October 1921 was an appeal almost to the people to copper-fasten their mouths as a protection against division and in the maintenance of 'an unwavering faith in those who have been deputed to act in the nation's behalf'.[4]

It is also possible that the Cabinet itself merely rubber-stamped de Valera's decisions, at least if one is to go by the paucity of information in the Cabinet minutes during the war and the subsequent Truce. There is no doubt whatever that my father laid the primary blame for the Civil War on de Valera's shoulders, although his view of Dev's culpability was described by Valiulis as an obsession, with its pejorative ring. Perhaps it might be worth considering the matter in more detail by examining the basis of his views, which he has recorded in the annotation. Before quoting relevant passages, let me try to encapsulate what he thought in a few lines.

De Valera became the leader of the Irish separatist movement in October 1917, when he was elected president of the newly elected Sinn Féin executive and of the general executive of the Irish Volunteers. He received unswerving loyalty from all his colleagues from this time to the ratification of the Treaty in January 1922. This loyalty was extended to him despite the fact that he was absent from the country for two and a half years during the three and a half years between his election as president and the Truce of July 1921. This loyalty was, according to Mulcahy, copper-fastened by the desire to maintain unity and, despite some inconsistencies in his character and problems created by his actions during the time, he was accepted as a moderate who would best lead the country to independence. De Valera, in his initial contacts with Lloyd George after the Truce, proved to be a stubborn and difficult negotiator, but whatever understanding he had with Lloyd George which led to the Treaty negotiations, he was aware that the British would not yield on the Crown and that the inclusion of the six northern counties of Ireland with the twenty-six counties as an independent state was not a possibility. Indeed, partition was already a fait accompli since the Government of Ireland Act in 1920. At the time, de Valera was quoted by Collins as saying that only the extremists would oppose a settlement.

When the plenipotentiaries were appointed in October 1921, he refused to join them, despite objections by many of his colleagues, and more strenuous objections since. He did, however, ask the people of Ireland to trust them in their endeavours, to await patiently the outcome of their task, and he pleaded for reticence about the final settlement, at least until the terms had been discussed by Dáil Éireann.

On the question of the genesis of the Civil War, Mulcahy also believed that de Valera had betrayed the cause of democracy by his political ineptitude in failing to prevent a split in the army, despite the assurances from all the members of the GHQ staff, conveyed to him at a meeting on 10 December 1921, that, in the event of the Treaty being defeated in the Dáil, they would continue to support him as the army of the Republic. This support was qualified by both Mulcahy and Collins, who stated that, under such circumstances and because of their political commitment to the Treaty, they would have to resign their leadership positions in the army and revert to being ordinary soldiers. Everyone else said that they would stand as soldiers supporting the Dáil and the government.[5] Nine of the GHQ staff subsequently supported the Treaty, while four opposed it. De Valera, who attended the meeting with the staff at the suggestion of Griffith, stated: 'If he lost the vote on the Treaty, he would not stand for mutiny.'

This meeting with the GHQ staff was arranged because Griffith advised de Valera that he should consult the army if he intended to oppose the Treaty. The attitude of the army and its leaders facing a return to war needed to be ascertained in the event of the Treaty being rejected by the Dáil:

> If I was regarding myself as the brass hat responsible for the army, here now you have come to peace and we must not go back into war, and I must see what is going on about the peace. [If] I would have taken up that attitude, it would have been a reasonable attitude to take up because here you have de Valera in December after the Treaty was signed preparing to go back if necessary into the danger of war without consulting the GHQ at all about the matter.

De Valera's reputation as a moderate was shattered, as were his earlier pleas that any settlement should be considered dispassionately by the people until it was approved or otherwise by the Dáil, when, on the day after the terms were announced, he publicly rebuked Griffith and Collins, his colleagues in the Cabinet; and when two days later he published his opposition to the Treaty in the newspapers. It seemed odd to me that during the discussion of the Treaty in the Cabinet on 8 December 1921, where de Valera, Brugha and Stack stated their opposition to the Treaty, Dev should say at the meeting that he intended to announce their opposition publicly by writing to the newspapers. It was surprising that the other members favouring the Treaty – Cosgrave, Collins, Griffith, Barton and O'Higgins (who had no vote) – would have insisted that the Cabinet discussion should first be brought to the notice of the Dáil members, in view of previous undertakings by de Valera that the Dáil should be the first authority to consider the settlement.

In my father's opinion, de Valera's precipitate action had a disastrous effect on the army. It also had an adverse effect on the many people who would otherwise have accepted the Treaty, at least as a stepping stone to a republic free from the symbolism of the Crown. Mulcahy held that de Valera's intransigence provoked many of the inflammatory anti-Treaty speeches in Dáil Éireann, which had a further, and final, adverse effect on army unity. Finally, he believed that if de Valera had supported the Treaty, if he had joined in preventing the split in the army, and if he had not played a part in preventing an election immediately after its ratification, thus preventing the people from expressing their opinion about the Treaty, he would have brought the great majority of the Dáil with him, so that the more seriously disaffected members of the IRA would have had little chance of precipitating a civil war, and certainly not the prolonged and destructive war which occurred. De Valera admitted that the majority of people in Ireland favoured the Treaty.

Mulcahy particularly condemned de Valera because of his proclamation during the Civil War advocating a policy of assassination of pro-Treaty deputies and other prominent supporters of the Treaty. It was this act which led to the shooting of Deputies Hales and O'Malley, and to the government's illegal execution of four Irregular prisoners. It is a constant theme throughout all Mulcahy's writings that de Valera had failed as a leader during the vital four years from 1918 to 1922. He concludes that de Valera had a 'blind pride in seeking power'. Was this his Messiah complex, his proclaimed ability to be able to look into his heart and to know what was best for the Irish people?

Mulcahy's view of de Valera was shared by many of the pro-Treaty leaders, including William Cosgrave, Eoin MacNeill, Paddy McGilligan, Kevin O'Higgins, Michael Hayes, Desmond FitzGerald, Fionan Lynch and James Dillon.

Valiulis stated, speaking of Mulcahy's view of de Valera's culpability, that 'his obsession was to remain with him to the end of his life'. Undoubtedly, de Valera was never far from his mind in his last few years, when his cognitive functions had begun to deteriorate and when his deep-down conviction about de Valera's role in precipitating the Treaty split began to emerge, but, if one were to ignore his writings and recordings in the last years of his life, one would find little evidence of such an obsession, despite his acknowledged views about de Valera's culpability. Mulcahy never criticised de Valera during his many public lectures to the 1916-1921 Club, to Fine Gael groups, and to other organisations in his later years, nor did he ever discuss his views about Dev and the Civil War in his earlier years – unless on the rare occasions when he might have been questioned on the matter in private conversation. The various tape recordings of his public lectures are notable for the absence of any criticism of any colleagues, whether friend or foe, and his charitable sentiments about so many of them.

Mulcahy was of course appalled by the tragedy and the human, economic and political consequences of the Civil War, which he describes on tape as a 'compound disaster'. It is perhaps understandable that he was critical of those who fought against the new government, many of whom he admired for their contribution during the War of Independence. As a person dedicated to the democratic ideal, he could not understand how the anti-Treaty forces refused to accept the will of the majority. Mulcahy states that Griffith and Collins, while they reluctantly accepted the task of negotiating with the British without de Valera, believed that he was a moderate and that his influence would contribute to the acceptance of a compromise on the constitutional settlement agreed with the British. Apart from the fact that de Valera said that he was not a doctrinaire republican, Mulcahy had this to say to justify the faith that Griffith and Collins had in Dev as a moderate:

> On the question of the Treaty and the Crown: de Valera had, over his four meetings between himself and Lloyd George alone on the 14, 15, 18 and 21 July 1921, at least seven hours talking, with plenty of time in between for thinking and discussion. As early, therefore, as 21 July, he knew several very definite things:

That a Parliament had been established in Belfast to deal with affairs of the six counties and a government had been set up there. He knew that that would continue so to act, and in a subordinate position to the British Parliament, until those who had vested interests in that parliament were argued out of their position or persuaded or coaxed in some other way than by insult or arms or threats of any kind.

He knew that, in a scheme of definite order, as between representatives of the six counties and representatives of the rest of Ireland, the door would be open for the fullest and the most orderly discussions of whatever was involved by way of problem or otherwise that required conciliation or consultation or change.

He knew that the rest of Ireland was being offered all the power of a sovereign state, internationally recognised, and, as against any British interference, guaranteed and secured by four other dominions, of whom Canada was being pointed to as the prototype of the sovereignty that existed.

Nothing of this that he knew from his conversations with Lloyd George was undermined or pared down in any way by any references to 'empire' or anything else in Lloyd George's letter to him of 20 July 1921. It is not easily conceivable that, at any moment after understanding this or hearing this, de Valera could have envisioned his leading the Irish people or the Dáil into such a position that they would go back into a war situation with Great Britain.[6]

There is a fourth point that should be added to the three mentioned above as a thing which de Valera knew by 21 July following his four talks with Lloyd George, and that is that there was not the slightest doubt that as far as Britain itself was concerned, the British negotiators would resist, to the very last, any implied interference with the prestige, the mystique or the picture of the Crown as a linchpin idea in the constitution of Great Britain itself, of the individual dominions existing and its position as a connecting mystique for the Commonwealth group as a whole. On two headings he knew that there had to be some acceptance of the Crown: (1) on the aforementioned grounds and (2) on the holding, under any scheme, of any hope of giving a link of unity with the Northern counties.[7]

Mulcahy does not at any point mention the Dáil motion passed unanimously on 26 August 1921:

> That if plenipotentiaries for negotiations be appointed by the Cabinet or the Dáil, such plenipotentiaries be given a free hand in such negotiations and duly to report to the Dáil.

He recalled de Valera's proclamation before the negotiations started:

> In connection with these proceedings [the appointment of the plenipotentiaries] the 'proclamation to the people of Ireland' was issued by de Valera on the evening of 10 of October, which he winds up as follows: 'The power against us will use every artifice it knows in the hope of dispiriting, dividing, weakening us. We must all beware. The unity that is essential will best be maintained by an unwavering faith in those who have been deputed to act in the nation's behalf, and the confidence manifesting itself as hitherto in eloquent discipline. For this I appeal.'
>
> It remains to be considered whether he was asking for unwavering faith in those who had been deputed as negotiators and plenipotentiaries, or whether he was thinking of himself as 'those who have been deputed to act in the nation's behalf.'

Mulcahy also refers to de Valera's motion proposed at the Sinn Féin convention on 27 October 1921. It was a proposal to add to the constitution of the party the following clause, one which de Valera introduced after a preamble in which he emphasised that the declaration of the republic in 1916 was the basis of the independence movement:

> Dáil Éireann [is] the duly elected parliament of Ireland, in the exercise of all its legitimate functions and in all the steps it legitimately takes to maintain public order, to provide for national defence, to secure good government, and to ensure the general welfare of the people of Ireland.
>
> This amendment to the Sinn Féin constitution was discussed by the standing committee at a meeting earlier on the day of the Ard-Fheis. De Valera, who had proposed the amendment, had included the phrase 'and to the President and Cabinet of Dáil Éireann, the lawful Executives

of the State' after the words 'Dáil Éireann, the duly elected parliament of Ireland', but this phrase was eliminated by the unanimous decision of the members.

It was really an infamous performance on the part of de Valera, as the leader of the nation that he was appealing to, to issue this letter [the letter to the papers on 8 December] at this time. For all practical purposes, it was tantamount to his meeting Griffith at the boat at Dun Laoghaire and slapping him publicly across the face. For, although between the time he had received the terms of the Treaty, let us say the morning of the 7 December (in view of his preoccupation with Dante on the night of the 6), and his writing a letter on the 8 for publication on the 9, he must have had a session of the Cabinet with all members present; it cannot have been a session to consider in any kind of a reasonable way the terms of the document brought home.[i]

For political purposes, the slap in the face was administered from the time that de Valera met Griffith on his return. The contents of the letter can be examined from the point of hypocrisy, dishonesty, incitement, but it is the immediate effects of the publication of the letter that challenges examination with the whole nation's spotlight turned on him, the man who had been the leader of the country over the dramatic years announces monumentally a split in the government, and announces it in an explosive, irretrievable way. The fact that so many of us could not believe it probably made the happening all the more irretrievable.

As far as the people generally were concerned, they got the terms of the Treaty in the press on 7 December, and the president's letter in the press on 9 December, with the information that a public session of Dáil Éireann was being summoned for Wednesday 14 December. The Dáil meeting that day did nothing but add to the confusion, and emphasise how disorderly and impassioned the split in the Cabinet was going to be made. The public silence of the Dáil from 14 until the meeting on Monday 19 December added to the public distress and confusion. The reports of the Dáil meetings on 19, 20, 21 and 22 helped to make the

[i] The Cabinet minutes of 8 December were not available to Mulcahy when these notes were written. The minute (CPs 8 December 1921) is exceedingly brief and simply records the voting intentions of the members in relation to the Treaty and de Valera's proposal to write an immediate letter to the press announcing his opposition to the agreement with the support of Brugha and Stack. There is no record of any discussion.

position in the country worse. The vote in support of the Treaty on 7 January and the election of Griffith on 10 January as President of the Dáil caused a kind of a pause for breathing and for hoping, but the main thing looked for in the hope, was not to come – that is, peace.[8]

I have said already that of the two sides to the national movement from 1916 to the end of 1921, the military side of the movement, the Irish Volunteers, had completely discharged their function under the direction of the GHQ staff by 11 July 1921, when the people had been able to declare with unexampled strength and unity of voice, in the general election of May 1921, that they then stood for, and continued to stand for, what they took for in the general election of 1918, as a result of which they established Dáil Éireann in 1919.[9]

The following are some extracts of Mulcahy's views on the subject of de Valera's sojourn in America as recorded in his annotation of Béaslaí's biography of Collins. These views were recorded in the early 1960s. The first ten pages of his commentary on Volume 2 of Béaslaí's biography contain some interesting notes about de Valera's stay in America, which extended from May 1919 to December 1920:

> Béaslaí records that within eighteen months of his going to America, Dev had brought about a split, leaving two open organisations and two rival Clann na nGaedheal [sic] bodies. The original Clann na nGaedheal was the associate of the IRB and it was the organisation which stood in our minds in our early days for Irish organisation in America.
>
> Clann na nGaedheal, in the person of John Devoy,[i] meant for us the accumulation of tradition [of] mind and men that from the Fenian time had found refuge in America to develop organisation and purpose directed towards Irish freedom.
>
> The old Clann, as well as being closely connected with and helpful to the Rising of 1916, had in the circumstances ranging from 1916 to 1919 mobilised public opinion in favour of Ireland by a number of race convention meetings. The new open organisation, established as a result of de Valera's activities, was the American Association for the

[i] John Devoy was a veteran Fenian. After a long and eventful career as a separatist, he retired to the United States, where he spearheaded American support for the cause of Irish independence.

Recognition of the Irish Republic, which was launched on 16 November 1920.[10]

That Dev's absence in America had no effect on us – the sentries – was no doubt due to the fact that we had been accustomed to do without de Valera and to see the situation in Ireland developing and going along without him.[11]

His going to America after his release from Lincoln and the setting up of the full Dáil Cabinet in April 1919 was a very great surprise to us – and in many ways a disappointment. However, again the position was that we had no experience of having him with us, there was nothing in particular we wanted him for, except that we must have been looking forward to a situation in which the head of the government would be in the country.

Looking back now, it might appear a very remarkable thing that the national leader would leave the country immediately after the parliament had been set up and before the discussions that had taken place in the parliament had formulated for the people the lines upon which the parliament was going to conduct itself and endeavour to effect national, social and economic policy, while making at the same time its case for representation at the Peace Conference and making there the case for its freedom.[12]

And in referring to de Valera on his return from America on Christmas Eve 1920:

De Valera was back early that morning. I saw him at Farnham's at about 8 o'clock AM. In the back return room, without sitting down – in just a stand-up conversation – his line to me almost directly was, after just a mere word of greeting, something along these lines: 'Ye are going too fast. This odd shooting of a policeman here and there is having a very bad effect, from the propaganda point of view, on us in America. What we want is, one good battle about once a month with about five hundred men in each side.' That was the essence of our talk.[13]

Coming back after a long absence, you would feel that he disparaged our military efforts – at any rate he had no words of compliment or praise to give to it; our 'shooting of odd policemen' was bad from the propaganda point of view, and theirs in America; he had nothing more to say of any detail, of the type of resistance that had been carried out over the year 1920 from the beginning of the offensive on police barracks; he had an idea that we could have spectacular encounters with five hundred men on each side.[14]

And in his address to Dáil Éireann in January 1921, after his return from America, he advocated a less active military policy:

All Ireland had was the power of moral resistance. They ought to make up their minds to hold out, they should not seek a decision. This policy might necessitate a lightening off of their attacks on the enemy.[15]

According to Mulcahy, the Dáil had no sympathy for such an attitude. The military's view at the time is expressed in the following paragraph:

As far as we were concerned, the circumstances outside made the pace for us. It demanded all our attention and all our energies. We were involved in a machine and in work that had developed and had gone on without him. There was no particular assistance that he could give us except by leaving us alone and encouraging us; for all his prestige and power in America he had done nothing to get even a small supply of arms from there – Collins was to try and do something about that from America; Collins was to patch up the broken unity that he had left behind him in America; Collins was to get American government policy on the right path in relation to the League of Nations when Harding became president in March 1921.[16]

There must have been a great distortion of mind and balance in this particular matter arising out of the length of time and the absorption of de Valera in the US and the effect that had on taking the eyes of those in Ireland off the diplomatic and the negotiation side of things in Britain.[17]

De Valera was absent in America from May 1919 to December 1920. Previously he had been in a British prison from March 1918 to March 1919. From October 1917, he was the acknowledged leader of the Sinn Féin separatist movement. He adopted the mantle of authority with ease, and his leadership received the most complete support from all his political and military colleagues. His actions seemed to be never questioned and later he was accused of having a Messiah complex because of his failure to discuss his actions and motives even with his closest colleagues. Mulcahy believed that Dev's prolonged absence, particularly in 1919 and 1920, created a political vacuum at home which seriously militated against any possibility of peace negotiations with the British earlier than July 1921. He believed the prolongation of the War of Independence, with the increasing bitterness engendered during the last months of 1920 and the first six months of 1921, created an atmosphere which increased the likelihood of political polarisation and the development of more radical aspirations in relation to the eventual constitutional settlement. My father and Páidín O'Keeffe, in discussing the factors which caused the delay in reaching a truce with the British, underline Dev's absence in America, and Griffith's reluctance to adopt the mantle of leadership in his absence. Griffith replaced de Valera as acting president of Sinn Féin while the latter was in the United States. Despite Griffith's seminal contribution to the separatist movement, and despite the high regard in which he was held, particularly by Mulcahy and Collins, he never had, nor wanted to have, any ambition to supplant de Valera's authority in such a crucial area as negotiating with the British.

Of Dev's absence to America my father commented:

> . . . but while all kinds of conventions and meetings and all that kind of thing had been contacted in the US by de Valera personally . . . it would appear that no contacting of any kind had been done in either Great Britain or in the North of Ireland or among the Unionists here in Ireland to prepare for the day when such contacts as close to negotiation points would have been made as Craig, Derby, Smuts. As far as de Valera was equipped in the matter, he was apparently relying entirely on the heart and the eyes of Childers . . . While Griffith was left with the responsibility as acting president from the time de Valera went to America in May 1919,

he was overshadowed on the one hand by the leadership of de Valera and the glorified diplomatic level at which the leader had elected to go to work. The companionship of Collins on the Cabinet was very supporting and dynamic in its effects, but may have operated to close Griffith's mind to the desirability of trying to see what diplomatic contacts could be made in Britain. It was possible that the circumstances of the times here were such that he or nobody else could risk that. But there must have been some element of impulse in that direction on his part, when P. Moylett was doing his probing – apparently shortly before Archbishop Clune came over here.[18]

The following conversation took place between me and my father after I had read the above paragraph:

> **RM:** Are you making this point that, because de Valera was away so long and so far away, and because of the quality of the people who made up the Sinn Féin Executive at the time, that there was virtually nobody in the country who could explore possible peace plans at diplomatic level except Griffith, and that Griffith himself was under a serious disadvantage in this regard because he wasn't in fact the leader, that the leader was 2,500 miles away from him and that any contacts he might make might lead to trouble between himself and de Valera or trouble in the Sinn Féin organisation generally? What I'd like you to do is to summarise this aspect of de Valera's going to America, and being so long away that you think it created serious difficulties in establishing diplomatic contacts from the point of view of establishing peace feelers and eventually of establishing peace.

> **R:** Yes, and as a matter of fact I don't think that anybody here – Griffith or Collins or Brugha or anybody else – was in a position to get feelers or enquiries going in Britain leading up to a kind of preliminary diplomacy getting some kind of an idea under what headings a peace could be arranged with de Valera over on the other side, because Dev had been put to such a high level and he had got so completely away from the situation here, completely above as the leader and the final

power, that Griffith or any of these could easily find themselves in the powerless position of Father O'Flanagan, when Fr O'Flanagan in his blundering way came out in the open.

RM: In other words Fr O'Flanagan took on the mantle of leadership and he in fact created embarrassment for every body.

R: If, in an underground way, Griffith or anybody else were trying to make contacts or to have feelers set abroad, they might easily feel that they were weakening the situation.

RM: Cathal Brugha and Stack hadn't sufficient stature and sufficient sense of responsibility and sufficient poise as political leaders to have helped Griffith there or to have taken over themselves in the matter?

R:. They wouldn't have thought of it for a moment because Cathal Brugha or Stack would not take the position of acting president when Griffith went into jail in November.

RM: Were Griffith and Collins the only two with any real sense and feeling of leadership whilst de Valera was away?

R: On the Cabinet, yes.

RM: And all this crowd in the Sinn Féin Executive had none at all – none of them showed any promise of leadership in any way apart from Collins and Griffith?

R: No. And to some extent they were handicapped even in lifting or moving Griffith to the point of decision or to the point of initiative by reason of the fact that Dev was away.

RM: What about Eoin MacNeill or Plunkett? Had they any influence approaching that of Griffith at all?

R: Plunkett – none in the world. MacNeill would always be a man whose counsel would be appreciated very much, but he wasn't in the position of power nor was MacNeill attempting to use any power at all.

RM: Reading the histories of the time you get the impression the Clune negotiations and the general negotiations of that time broke down because of a certain amount of dishonesty on the British side in eventually making it a condition of truce that the Irish Republican Army would have to give up their arms, and the impression you get is that the truce idea broke down then because of this single demand by the British. Is it possible that, if Dev were in Ireland at that time and had been in Ireland for some months before that, the Clune negotiations would have succeeded?

R: It is possible that it would. I wouldn't have any strong views one way or another about it.[19]

In my opinion, the Truce of July 1921 could have been secured in December 1920 at the time his Grace Archbishop Clune endeavoured to mediate, but the opportunity was lost through the too-precipitate action of certain of our public men and public bodies. The actions taken indicated an over-keen desire for peace, and although terms of Truce were virtually agreed upon, they were abandoned because the British leaders thought those actions indicated weakness, and they consequently decided to insist upon the surrender of arms. The latter circumstance – the British last minute insistence on the surrender of arms – was clearly brought out by Collins in his *The Path to Freedom*.[20]

Mulcahy, in his conversations with Páidín O'Keeffe, raised the question of why the truce was delayed. O'Keeffe stated that he had no idea, but in his response said that Dev had been approached towards the end of his stay in the United States and told by the British consul there that the British were anxious for a truce. The British consul urged him to return to Ireland where he would be granted immunity from arrest. Perhaps Dev's presence was not that essential to achieving a truce. My father may have been exaggerating the influence of Dev's absence although clearly if Dev had remained in the country and had actively sought some accommodation with the British, a truce might have been easier to achieve at this early stage. Father O'Flanagan[i] and the Galway County Council were the agents who precipitated the breakdown in negotiations.

The Cabinet did discuss the possibility of a truce on two occasions in late

---

[i]Father Michael O'Flanagan was a teacher in Sligo and was vice-president of Sinn Féin. He retired from his church duties for a long period during which he was active in Sinn Féin. He opposed the Treaty and remained a committed republican well into the 1930s. His intervention in the Clune episode was considered to have encouraged Lloyd George in the view that the IRA was a beaten force. He eventually retired from politics and resumed his ministry.

autumn 1920. A Mr Henderson apparently wished to explore the possibility of peace but was refused an interview without first securing the release of Griffith from prison.[21] Two weeks later the subject was again discussed[22] and it was decided to leave the matter in the hands of Arthur Griffith. It appears that the Cabinet at the time had little concern with the Clune intervention and that the affair was largely in the hands of Griffith and Collins. Lloyd George terminated the negotiations with the remark 'we have murder by the throat', implying that the army would soon defeat the rebels. The increasingly bitter war, which continued for the six months following the Clune negotiations, was also a factor leading to the intransigence of those who opposed the Treaty.

CATHAL BRUGHA

Brugha was born in Dublin and was the owner or manager of Lawlor's, the candlestick makers in the city. It was generally believed that his father came from England but his son, Rory, claims that he was descended from an old Carlow family. Brugha was an active separatist long before 1916. He was seriously wounded during the Rising. He had been a member of the IRB, and was opposed to Griffith's concept of a dual monarchy. He was an Irish speaker and member and one time president of the Keating branch of the Gaelic League, whose members generally were active in the IRB and later in the Volunteers.[i]

Mulcahy gives an interesting account of Brugha's activities in the few years before 1916. As early as 1912, before the Volunteers were established in November 1913, Brugha and some of his colleagues in the IRB had organised rifle practice. Páidín O'Keeffe describes how he, with Brugha, Eamonn Kent and Sean MacDermott (the latter two were to be signatories of the Proclamation of the Republic), practised regularly on Sunday mornings at the old Greenmount Oil site at Harold's Cross Bridge. The owner or manager of the site allowed them to use the area and gave them a present of a gun. On one occasion he presented a prize of five pounds for the best shot. It was won by Cathal Brugha who, according to O'Keeffe, 'made a bull's eye every time'. Brugha was the first to encourage the reorganisation of the Volunteers in the

[i] Brugha's biography, *Cathal Brugha: a Shaol is a Threithe*. Dublin: Dublin, 1969, was written by Tomás O'Dochartaigh.

autumn of 1916, when he was approached by two members of the IRB, Diarmuid O'Hegarty and Sean O'Muirthile. He was elected to the executive of Sinn Féin and appointed chairman of the resident executive of the Volunteers at the two conventions in October 1917. He was appointed temporary priomh aire of the Dáil from January to April 1919 in the absence of de Valera, and minister for defence from April 1919 until the ratification of the Treaty in January 1922. He was implacably opposed to the Treaty and died from gunshot wounds sustained in the early days of the Civil War.

Mulcahy, in his capacity as chief of staff, had very close contact with Brugha during the War of Independence. His recollections of Brugha are included in considerable detail in various parts of his annotation on Béaslaí's life of Collins, and in his tapes. Brugha continued to manage his candle-making business up to the time of his death. My father met him for the first time and then only casually at the Keating branch of the Gaelic League. Brugha played an active role in the 1916 Rising. Because he had suffered severe gunshot wounds during the Rising, he was not arrested nor was he deported by the British. He emerged from the Rising as a heroic figure.

Brugha subsequently played a leading role in bringing the threads of the shattered Irish Volunteer movement together again after the Rising, so that there was a nucleus of Volunteer activity when the deportees and surviving leaders later returned to Ireland between Christmas 1916 and June 1917. My father writes about this early reorganisation of the Irish Volunteers by Brugha and a few IRB members, and he describes the setting up of the Volunteer executive in October 1917.[1]

Referring to relations with Brugha during the War of Independence, Mulcahy said:

> Cathal I don't think ever clashed with us, Collins or myself, in any aspect of the positive [army] policy that was being pursued. Beyond the one element of clash between himself and myself, when he challenged me about some violent action that took place between some Volunteers, including Tom Hales, in the Bandon area, and the RIC in respect of which he said he would call the volunteer executive together for the

purpose of dealing with whoever was responsible for it, there was no other occasion of any other complaint of this kind; and although both Collins and myself disagreed with Cathal's impulse to go on an assassination expedition to England, we not only did nothing to impede him in any way, but I provided, from the country and Dublin, the volunteers to go on that work, and others to intimate that they would be ready to go on that work if wanted.[2]

He adds:

None of us on the staff appreciated at all the idea of Cathal's mission to London [to assassinate the British Cabinet ministers]. I got the volunteers who were to go with him. Collins was here putting him in touch with an IRB contact in Liverpool who supplied more men there. He was there for quite a number of weeks. I think that I had the feeling that we were glad that Cathal had something to concentrate on and occupy him, leaving us free to feel and act about the situation in Dublin and in Ireland as we wanted to do on our own.[3]

There is a rather oblique reference in the Cabinet papers of 6 November 1920 to some plan Brugha had in relation to Britain which may have had a connection with one of his two sorties to go to London to assassinate British ministers. He was advised to discuss it with the president, who was still in America. Brugha did stay away for some weeks on such a mission – but fortunately nothing came of it. My father as head of the GHQ staff kept in close touch with Brugha, who was the minister for defence. These visits kept Brugha informed of Volunteer activities and provided an opportunity to discuss matters relating to military policy. Apart from such discussions, Brugha played no part in military activities, did not attend staff meetings (despite Béaslaí's description of him as chief of staff), and at no time did he have any conflict with the policies initiated by the staff, except in relation to one or two minor occurrences. It was not until the end of 1920 or early 1921, after Dev's return from the United States and when rumours of Truce were in the air, that Brugha began to become more involved in army affairs.

Neither did Brugha appear to be much occupied on the political side until

MICHAEL COLLINS, M.P.

RICHARD MULCAHY, M.P.

Special note is to be made of these men's features by all ranks & if they are recognised it should be reported at ANY officer at the earliest opportunity. If no officer available to Civil Police

'Special note is to be made of these men's features by all ranks and if they are recognised it should be reported at ANY officer at the earliest opportunity. If no officer available to Civil Police.'

Richard Mulcahy after the Civil War

Irish Volunteers, Coosan Camp, Athlone, summer 1915. L to R: William Mullins, Richard Mulcahy, Sean Lester, unidentified, Donal Barret, Terency McSwiney, John Griffen, Liam Langley, Pierce McCann, Austin Stack

Thomas Ashe after the Rising

At the time of theTruce of 1921. L to R: Sean McEoin, Richard Mulcahy, Sean Moylan, Eoin O'Duffy

'General Headquarters Staff, July 1921' by Leo Whelan, now in the posession of the National Museum of Ireland. Seated L to R: Michael Collins, director of intellligence; Richard Mulcahy, chief of staff; Gearoid O'Sullivan, adjutant general; Eamon Price, director of organisation; Rory O'Connor, director of engineering; Eoin O'Duffy, deputy chief of staff; Sean Russell, director of munitions; Sean McMahon, Quarter Master General. Standing: J. J. O'Connell, assistant chief of staff; Emmet Dalton, director of training; Seamus O'Donovan, director of chemicals; Liam Mellows, director of purchases, Piaras Beaslaí, editor of *An tOglach*

The commander in chief with officers in Kilkenny during the Civil War

With 'Min' at Lissenfield, 1922

Richard Mulcahy at the hustings, before the 1923 elections (from a front page report of a German newspaper)

Michael Collins and Richard Mulcahy at Arthur Griffith's funeral, August 1922

The last of the Dublin of Parliament days – the funeral of General
Michael Collins, 29 August 1922

L to R: Neillí, Richard Mulcahy, Risteárd, Min, Elisabet in 1948

Mulcahy meets Éamon de Valera in Dingle, *c.* 1950

Richard Mulcahy meets old comrades in 1968 to discuss the genesis of the Civil War. Seated, L to R: Michael Brennan, Richard Mulcahy, Peadar McMahon, Joe Sweeney. Standing: Sean MacEoin, Liam Archer

Min and Richard Mulcahy with
Seán Lemass in 1963

Sean T. O'Kelly, member of
Fianna Fáil cabinet, 1932–45;
President of Ireland, 1945–59
and Richard Mulcahy's
brother-in-law

Richard and Min Mulcahy's Golden Jubilee, June 1969, at
Temple Villas. L to R: Padraig, Elisabet, Risteárd, Maire,
Neillí and Seán

Dev returned. He attended the Cabinet, although whether he did so regularly is not clear. He did not attend the standing committee of Sinn Féin and he refused the acting presidency when Griffith was arrested in November 1920. Mulcahy states that, after his return from America, de Valera and Brugha were intent on wresting power and influence from those – like Griffith, Collins and himself – who had led the struggle while he was away. It was about the time Dev returned from America that Brugha's antipathy to Collins began to manifest itself. This antagonism had become a major cause of discord by the time of the Truce in the autumn of 1921, when Mulcahy found himself the object of Brugha's antagonism also. There is no doubt the effect of Brugha's antagonism to Collins and Mulcahy contributed to the political and military split after the Treaty. According to Páidín O'Keeffe, Brugha was also antagonistic to Griffith for a much longer period – probably from the early days even before 1916. This antagonism was probably based on Griffith's Sinn Féin policy advocating a dual monarchy as part of the constitutional settlement with Britain, which did not appeal to Brugha and the more separatist IRB members. Mulcahy, however, states in response to O'Keeffe's assertion that he had never noted any animus between Brugha and Griffith.

Despite being sacked by Brugha twice during the Truce, and despite Dev's demand for a 'new army' in November 1921, Mulcahy remained chief of staff until he resigned the position after the ratification of the Treaty in January 1922 in order to become minister for defence in the Dáil Cabinet. He had this to say to Páidín O'Keeffe about his sacking:

> Mind you, I had a job of my own to stick to, too, and it did you no good to be suspicious of people or to be questioning them. You had to go along . . . Actually I was sacked twice by Cathal from being chief of staff during the Truce, but also I thought that a very strange thing, you see . . . and you thought it would make me suspicious and difficult, but you didn't mind it. You simply went on and you felt you had trust in everybody . . .

Brugha's antagonism to the two military leaders continued up to the ratification of the Treaty, when Brugha opposed it and resigned his ministry.

Mulcahy refers to Collins's attitude towards Brugha during these bitter times of discord when he confirms that Collins retained his admiration and affection for Brugha; and he did not appear to show animosity or resentment at any time (nor did my father), despite his difficulties with Brugha during the latter days of the War of Independence and the Truce. A definite element in Collins's make-up was that, no matter what was developing even up to the worst moment between Dev and Cathal and himself, he had an established, sneaking regard for whatever good was in them. He had a particular affection for Cathal in the same way as one would have for a difficult but natural child.[4] He refers to Brugha's brusque and impetuous character:

> Cathal Brugha was a very intense person, but he never sat down to any working councils of ours. My impression is that from the setting up of the GHQ staff in March 1918, he took no part in the discussion of any matters that could be regarded as purely staff or military matters. And that would almost refer even to the development of policy. I kept in the most constant personal touch with him; visiting him at his working office in Lawlor's – the candle makers' place – at Ormond Quay, or at his own home in Upper Rathmines Road. Normally, talking to him was never a great pleasure. You were never sure when some intensity of mind on his part about something or another was disturbing his atmosphere. But in the developing of the situation, our appreciation of it was very much a common one and my experience of him was that, as we progressed in policy from one step to another, his agreement flowed naturally and readily with us.
>
> He was naturally blunt and frank and was no more tending to intrigue than he was to diplomacy. I had a couple of experiences of his brusqueness, but in the light of his broad agreement, and his tendency not to interfere in any way in the absence of some intenseness about something on his part , I found it easy to discharge my duty of keeping in touch with him. And there was never any necessity on my part or on the part of the members of the staff to feel that we were not in all matters pursuing a policy entirely approved of by him and by the government. Béaslaí's phrase, 'He was hopelessly out of touch with our army and the realities of the situation',

means nothing. If it did mean anything, it would mean that I, who was assistant minister for defence as well as chief of staff, was out of touch with Cathal or keeping things from him – that is not so. And that Collins, who was his colleague on the Cabinet as well as being deep in very responsible work in the army, was likewise neglectful.[5]

On the question of agreement on policy it can be said: our whole approach to the aggression and reaction period pre-September 1919 was one on which there was entire agreement between the staff and Cathal. Our approach to the attacks on barracks [at the end of 1919], begun as a result of my discussion with the Cork people, had his entire approval. The natural development subsequent to the evacuation and burning of barracks and the development of columns was similarly agreed on; similarly with regard to the shooting of spies and detectives.

He describes Brugha as 'tending to crush both communication and manners' and he was not 'a *tête-à-tête* man'.[6] Unlike others, Brugha would not allow himself to be captured without putting up a fight. Griffith is quoted as describing Brugha being 'as brave as a bull and as brainless'.[7]

Mulcahy describes the night he spent with Brugha after they had met with Collins and Dick McKee (O/C of the Dublin Brigade) to discuss the shooting of the detectives in November 1920, the night before Bloody Sunday. Mulcahy was on the run at the time and, rather than cross the city to one of his haunts on the south side at such a late hour, he decided to stay the night with Cathal at a haunt of the latter's near Mountjoy Square. Apparently because of the military activity following the shootings of the British officers, they stayed on into the following morning. At one stage when there was a particular commotion – probably when the military were arriving at the nearby Croke Park where the Bloody Sunday atrocity was to occur – they must have felt threatened. And

> . . . what does Cathal do but went up to his room, pulled up the window, pulled over a chair alongside it, pulled out two revolvers and put them on the bed beside him, and took off his boots! . . . Now, my tactics would have been entirely different. I would have [had] my bicycle

out and been out of the gate at the back, and I would have been off up
Drumcondra; but, noblesse oblige, I had to sit alongside my minister on
the side of the bed there, praying at whatever was going to pass.

Mulcahy quotes, as appropriate to Brugha, a comment by Pope John XXIII:

In the daily exercises of our pastoral office we sometimes have to listen
– much to our regret – to voices of persons who, though burning with
zeal, are not endowed with too much sense of discretion or measure.

The circumstances surrounding Brugha's death in 1922, and his reaction to
possible British interception on the night of 21 November 1921, would
support this view of his personality. Brugha indeed died 'as brave as a bull' on
19 June 1922, when he refused to surrender to Free State forces at the start of
the Civil War. He died as he lived: impetuous and passionate and a victim of
his own idealism. He was a symbol of those who were committed to the
immediate attainment of a political ideal which had not yet been demanded
by a pluralistic Irish society. He died 'full of passionate intensity'.

Mulcahy writes of Brugha and his sacrificial death:

Cathal Brugha – who considered in 1917 that, because a policeman was
killed in Cork, somebody was irresponsibly bringing destruction on the
people and ruining the country; and who could in March 1921 be
sending one of our most brilliant sustainers and leaders of the people
generally to do a Japanese act of self-sacrifice in assassinating a British
minister[i] – was throwing away his own life in O'Connell Street to stain
our work in blood.

Whether my father spoke about Brugha with resentment or with
compassion is hard to say, but he often spoke of him to me with sympathy
and respect. When he was invited by the 1916-1921 Club to speak about
Brugha in 1965, he refused on the grounds that he did not wish to be seen to
be critical of him. He felt that Brugha, like many others who opposed the
Treaty and fought against it, had been misled by de Valera and had been
influenced to take up arms against the democratically elected government of
the Free State. Whether it really was Dev's influence that incited Brugha and

---

[i] Brugha wanted Sean MacEoin, the renowned Volunteer leader from Longford, to go to London to lead a party
to assassinate British Cabinet ministers – a proposal which my father refused to countenance.

other anti-Treaty forces cannot be confirmed; but it might be considered unlikely in view of Brugha's rather uncompromising character. Indeed, could Brugha have influenced de Valera, when Dev showed such anger towards Griffith when he first met the public at the Dante Exhibition on the evening after the terms of the Treaty were announced?

What might have transpired between Brugha and Dev when, just after hearing of the settlement, the news of which was received by Dev in Limerick with a noncommittal verbal nod, they travelled alone together by train to Dublin on 6 December? I would be tempted to exchange my worldly goods to have a transcript of their conversation in that railway compartment. Mulcahy had been in Clare, Limerick and Galway reviewing the troops with de Valera and Brugha at the time of the Treaty settlement. But, as a matter of courtesy to Stephen Rynne, who was accompanying them, he travelled back to Dublin in the compartment next to Dev and Brugha's. Apparently neither man made any comment in Mulcahy's presence about the negotiations which were then taking place in London, nor would my father ask any questions.

It seems typical of my father's perception of his relationship with the political leaders that he would not feel it proper to question them on such important political matters. It was equally typical of Dev that he would not discuss any political matter, however topical or related to the military situation, with the head of the army. His only comment when he heard the news of the settlement was to say 'I did not think that they would settle so soon.'

ERNIE O'MALLEY, DICK MCKEE, LIAM LYNCH AND OTHERS

While most of his references were to those who had leading roles in the struggle and its aftermath and who are well-known in the history of the time, Mulcahy recalls his contact with many of his less prominent colleagues in his conversations on tape and in his annotation. Typical are his references to Frank Teeling, Ernie O'Malley and Simon Donnelly:

> An interesting thing about this general Kilmainham episode is the fact that after three successive nights of frustration and the attempt to escape,

then failing by reason of the rope breaking; Teeling, O'Malley and Donnelly, without any outside assistance, succeeded in escaping on the following night. There is plenty of room for story telling here and Simon Donnelly is still alive. He was a great 3rd Battalion man, would be very loyal to de Valera because of that, and his association with Stack in relation to police matters pre-Truce copper-fastened him on the irregular side. He is mentioned here [on page 189 of Béaslaí's biography] as becoming the commanding officer of the 'Dublin Republican police' [during the War of Independence]. I always regarded him as being, as it were, the chief commissioner of the republican police. I may have correspondence to indicate that. If he wasn't, then Stack had done nothing to put a headquarters top to the direction of his police and it shows how much the matter of police work was being left on the shoulders of the Volunteers.

Teeling was a rather interesting and very definite type of the fighting man, quite fearless and concentrated but with no flamboyancy.[1]

ERNIE O'MALLEY

From the time Ernie O'Malley was with me in Tyrone he must have been engaged as an organiser with the Volunteers. We will find his tracks in the documents relating to many areas. At a time when the Black and Tans had established a headquarters at Inistiogue in Kilkenny, a county where there had not been any great sense of aggressiveness or resistance shown, I sent O'Malley down there lest the presence of the Black and Tans would reduce the Kilkenny men too much. I found him in Dublin about a week or so after I thought he had gone down, but I could find excuses for that. In his book however, he appears to have criticised the Kilkenny people with the result that for a number of days in the Irish Press at one particular period, they ran a long series of articles on O'Malley and his doings in Kilkenny. At one particular part they seem to suggest that he did a lot of sitting by the fire and reading, mentioning *Mr Britling Sees it Through* as one of his guide books. He was apparently always very much at home with the South Tipperary men, Seamus

Robinson and Co, but over a fair part of the midlands, Limerick, South Tipperary, perhaps North Cork area, he did a good lot of work. When the Treaty division came there was no particular reason why he should be against the Treaty . . . [H]e was one of a group talking in [Paddy] McGilligan's house in Leeson Street, and is recorded as saying that 'there would be nothing to do for a fellow like him in Ireland now after this Treaty, that there would be no more fighting and people like him would have to go off to India or some place like that.' The idea was that he could do fighting there.[2]

In fact, O'Malley joined the Irregulars, was in the Four Courts with O'Connor and Mellows, but escaped when they were captured by the Free State forces. He became one of the leading members of the Irregulars during the Civil War. He wrote one of the earliest and most popular books on the War of Independence (*On Another Man's Wound*).[3]

O'Malley was in prison after the Civil War and was one of the last to be released in 1924. He went to America where he did much writing and married Helen Roeloff, a sculptress and a wealthy American who had two children by him and who was to become devoted to Ireland and to Irish culture. Ernie O'Malley's son, Cormac, has done much to remind us of his father's writings and letters and his contribution to the Irish revolution.

In another part of the annotation Mulcahy writes of Florrie O'Donoghue, the Cork IRA leader and biographer of Liam Lynch: 'I placed him as one of the impeccables without whom the Civil War could not have arisen.'

DICK MCKEE

Dick McKee was a member of GHQ from its foundation, and my father placed him second only to Collins in the struggle against the British. He was head of the Dublin Brigade, a position he inherited from my father. As head of the Dublin Brigade he provided invaluable support to Collins and to the Squad. He was also held in great esteem by some of the country brigades, which he had visited and left his mark on, as director of training. Mulcahy quotes Liam Deasy, the IRA leader, who remembered McKee organising a training camp in Glandore, County Cork, speaking of the camp as an event which

> . . . was to have far-reaching and decisive results. This was the six day training camp at Glandore under the command of the late Dick McKee who was then O/C of the Dublin Brigade. In all about fifty officers attended that camp. For six days an intensive course of training under the most rigid discipline was given under the stern command of Brigadier McKee. It is hard for me to attempt after such a lapse of time to tell in cold words what Dick McKee meant to those of us who were chosen to undergo that course of training.

The cumulative effect of Dick McKee's training and leadership was evident in the fighting record of every unit of the 3rd Cork Brigade in the succeeding two years when attacks, raids and ambushes were carried out with a verve and competence that would have done credit to the elite corps of any army in the world. In Dick McKee the fighting men of west Cork had found a mentor worthy of their metal. Mckee was captured on the night before Bloody Sunday, and was killed that same night while 'trying to escape'. No other loss during the War of Independence affected my father more than the loss of McKee. He was highly regarded by those who came in contact with him and who knew him best. As director of training on the GHQ staff, he played a vital role in organisation, particularly in those parts of the country where the army was to prove most effective.[4] He carried out a number of brilliant operations, including the raid on the military airfield in Collinstown, when seventy-five rifles and six thousand rounds of ammunition were captured and sent to some country units which were seriously short of arms.

After the foundation of the Irish Free State, the army headquarters on the Navan Road was called after McKee, a measure of how my father regarded McKee and of his role in the War of Independence.

Liam Lynch

In the annotation,[5] Mulcahy writes about Liam Lynch, the commandant of the 1st Southern Brigade; he mentions in the context of the west Cork activities the later establishment of the Southern Division of the IRA, which was formed at the later stages of the war. He describes west Cork as the 'O'Donovan Rossa country', after the great Fenian patriot who was born there. This part of the country had a special place in my father's affections, since it was there that he had spent two years in Bantry as a post office learner and where he first heard of Griffith. There he first became immersed in Irish culture and nationalism; and it was there he attended the 'university' of Siobhán an tSagairt in Ballingeary. He was also aware that west Cork was the birthplace of some of his Volunteer colleagues, including Collins, Seán O'Muirthile, Gearoid O'Sullivan and Diarmuid O'Hegarty. Mulcahy thought Lynch was the most competent, reliable and inspiring of all the southern leaders. He appeared to have a special sense of trust in and admiration for Lynch, which made it all the more difficult for him to understand why Lynch proved such an implacable opponent of the Treaty:

> It was Liam Lynch's leadership and work in the north Cork Brigade number 2 that I found most impressive and orderly.

He also found it hard to comprehend how Lynch's apparent fanaticism in support of the Republic, as chief of staff of the Irregulars, led to his futile and lonely death in the Knockmealdowns after the struggle was obviously long since lost – to all except Lynch himself.

Mulcahy's confidence in Lynch's maturity and good sense was such that, just before the assault on the Four Courts, when Lynch was already under arrest, he was released on my father's specific instructions. He believed Lynch would have a moderating effect on the recalcitrant Four Courts garrison. He was to be sorely disappointed, however, when Lynch joined the Irregulars after the Four Courts attack and proved to be the most implacable opponent of the Provisional Government. It was Lynch who wrote to Dad, shortly after the signing of the Treaty on behalf of many of the southern volunteer leaders, stating that the Treaty was unacceptable to them on the grounds of the oath (they wanted an oath to the Commonwealth and not to the King) and because of the retention of the ports by the British. They also stated that partition was not acceptable to them, although it was by then a fait acompli for nearly two years.[6] It was the early adverse reaction to the Treaty by Lynch and his west Cork colleagues which prompted Maryann Valiulis and others to believe that even de Valera's acceptance of the Treaty would have made little difference in terms of the subsequent army split.

Speaking of Lynch's outlook on the Treaty, Mulcahy said:

> . . . as an outlook that would perhaps not reasonably have led him into the fighting of the Civil War or into any development like it, if the reaction of de Valera to the Treaty had been different or even if de Valera had stopped short of approving of the use of arms by the Irregulars, whether after the Four Courts or before it.[7]

This is a further example of Dad's prevailing view that Dev's immediate, unexpected and trenchant reaction to the Treaty was a major factor in provoking others to oppose the Treaty.

> Liam Lynch, who had been a lion of the resistance movement in the heart of the supreme British effort against the people, had left to serve with Cathal Brugha, whom on 6 December on pre-Treaty grounds he had declined [to serve with], [and] to become, by August or so 1922, a person so bedevilled with his position that he was telling de Valera that he [Lynch] would have to look in future to Childers as his leader . . . dying deserted on the Knockmealdowns.

I assume what Mulcahy meant here was that by August 1922 even Dev was not extreme enough in his opposition to the Provisional Government to satisfy Lynch. Lynch would have to look to Childers, the leading anti-Treaty propagandist, as his political leader. And Lynch was literally deserted when he died on the Knockmealdown Mountains; by the capture of many of his republican colleagues and the retirement of the rest as they saw their cause was lost. But even at the end, when Lynch was holding out on his own, he believed that the war would be won by the republicans. This unrealistic optimism was a feature of the irregular campaign during the later days of the Civil War, and is alluded to by Mulcahy. Only a very passionate and frenzied person could throw his life away under such circumstances. His death, like that of Brugha, was the ultimate reminder of the futility of civil war.

A book entitled *Guerrilla Days in Ireland* was written by his comrade Tom Barry after he died.

FURTHER FACTORS IN THE GENESIS OF THE CIVIL WAR

I have already referred to my father's view about de Valera's influence in causing the split in the army and the resulting Civil War. I have also referred to the failure of the Clune Truce initiative in November 1920. A further delay in reaching a truce is referred to by Sturgis in his diaries.[1] He states that from de Valera's return from America in December, when there were continuous efforts to reach a truce agreement by Fr O'Flanagan and others, and when there were numerous feelers from Dublin Castle, it was impossible to get a direct response from de Valera, although Dev was aware at the time that he was under the protection of the British administration. There is no doubt that an earlier truce would have avoided the later and most bitter months of the War of Independence and the animosity that gathered between the two sides before and after the Truce in July 1921.

It is evident that the attitude of the rank and file of the Volunteers towards the Treaty was largely determined by their leaders. An important factor in creating the split in the army was the intractable attitude to the Treaty on the part of the Cork leaders who had been so active and successful during the War of Independence. They had achieved a military success in the south-west which was sufficient to clear the police from the largest part of the province. They may have been sufficiently isolated in their region to be unaware of the political realities of the country in general – where the great majority of the people wished or at least had no objection to maintaining some link with Britain and the Crown. They may have thought that the great majority of people in Ireland, apart from the Unionists, were in favour of an independent republic. It is likely that the independent spirit of the Cork IRA and the rigid attitude of the Four Courts group were important factors in finally causing the split in the army. A further factor affected the attitude of the Cork Volunteers: it appears, from Mulcahy's account, that the prisoners were particularly badly treated by their British captors during the truce, and that the liaison officer appointed by GHQ had great difficulties in dealing with the British forces. According to Mulcahy, the bitterness between the republican prisoners and their captors was an important factor in alienating the Cork Volunteers.

The failure of those who took up arms against the Treaty to accept the democratic decision of the people may be difficult for us to understand and accept, but a devotion to democracy may have been less strong then, particularly among people who had only a short history of participating within such a political system. A number of the IRA leaders who opposed the Treaty, some of whom fought against it, were clearly aware that the majority of the people favoured the settlement.

> In view of subsequent events it is well to remind ourselves that Dan Breen, South Tipperary; Tom Hales, West Cork; Humphrey Murphy, Kerry; and Sean O'Hegarty and F. O'Donoghue, Cork City, made public their awareness that it was admitted by all sides that the majority of the people of Ireland are willing to accept the Treaty and that it should be possible to have an agreed election: with the result being a government that would have the confidence of the whole country: and that this would secure army unification.[2]

The leaders referred to in this quotation by Mulcahy were united in their opposition to the Treaty; but to my knowledge none of them took part in the Civil War. Their willingness to await the will of the Irish electorate was in contrast with the uncompromising attitude of Rory O'Connor, Liam Mellows and the other leaders of the Four Courts garrison.

Mulcahy goes on to discuss other aspects of the army split and the effect of the Treaty debate on the army's attitude:

The effect of the [Dáil] proceedings since its first assembly on 14 December 1921 to discuss the Treaty, following Mr de Valera's repudiation of them on 8 December, had been to spread confusion and dismay through the country as a whole. The vast majority of the people were completely in favour of the Treaty. They were appalled by the fact that de Valera challenged it, and by the way in which he did it in his statement to the people generally, before the Dáil met, and in the manner in which he did it in the Dáil. They were shocked and frightened by the obvious development of disorder and strife. There was nothing, however, that the great majority of people could do about it – only talk, and develop opinions, and wait.

The Volunteers, the army generally, was in a very different position. They had heard from the highest possible level that the plenipotentiaries had, as it were, behind the backs of de Valera and other members of the Government, broken their word in London and had done something that they should not have done; with the implication that they would not have been allowed to do it if, having obeyed what were alleged to be their instructions, had they consulted their colleagues at home before taking action. They were told that in future they would be the King's army, and that the King himself or his Governor-General in Ireland would be the person who would permit and sign all their commissions; and that, while the British Army could go out now, it had every legal right to return where and whenever it pleased. They had painted to them by a person who knew all about the King and the inside of British Government working [Erskine Childers, who had been in the British civil service and army], and he was supported by de Valera and other members of the Cabinet and other members of the Dáil, the contention that the King had power over every scrap of legislation in Ireland and that his power could be decimal pointed in its effect by the use of the telephone. The binding and immobilising influence of the oath to the Republic was pressed home on them; and the inflexibility of any possible interpretation of that word in practice, except in accordance with some brainwave of de Valera's or some aspect of de Valera's conscience, was pushed home. The eyes of their dead comrades were turned upon them, and the eyes of important people like Stack and Sean T. O'Kelly etc. who were ready to sacrifice their lives, either deliberately or in terms of a bet, against the idea of de Valera ever doing wrong. (Stack had said that he would commit suicide if he thought Dev would do anything wrong.)[3]

As far as the general rank and file of the people were concerned with the challenge in all this, all they could do was think and pray and wait for the opportunity of saying what they thought, when they could go to the polls. For the army it was different. They were being challenged to stand to attention and in the face of all this, to humiliate themselves by acquiescence, or to take active steps to prevent, in one way or another, at the polls or otherwise, the bringing about of such a situation as would impose all these indignities on the country. With the varied experience of the days in which they were struggling against the British, the situation offered and suggested very many varied types of opportunity to various types of people for obstruction, incitement and aggression towards the new 'Dublin Castle Government'.[4]

My father also expressed the view to me that the Volunteers in Cork, who were so successful in clearing the British police and the British presence from that part of Munster, were particularly influenced by the commitment to a republic and to a total break with Britain. In their isolation, induced at least to a degree by their successful campaign, they may have had an inflated conception of the Volunteers' military success in the War of Independence; and perhaps nurtured the prospect of continuing the war to a successful conclusion if hostilities were to resume. They may have been unaware of the obstacles to achieving a republic in a country where the majority wished to accept the Treaty and to retain some link with Britain and the Commonwealth. They were also unaware of, or at least indifferent to, the reality that partition and the Northern settlement was no longer a negotiable issue. It is historically understandable that, in resisting parliament by arms, they were less committed to the principles of democracy which we so readily accept today. No doubt, they shared the opinion of de Valera that 'the majority had no right to do wrong'!

Mulcahy includes in his annotation a number of the statements made in the Dáil by the anti-Treaty deputies which he considered to have had an inflammatory effect on the army:

> The King representing the British Government or the Governor General will have power to give or refuse assent to Irish legislation.
>
> Every act of legislation done by Ireland will be read in the light of that inflexible condition that Ireland is virtually a protectorate of England, for under this Treaty she is nothing more.
>
> What the King means is the British Government, and let there be no mistake under the terms of this Treaty, the British Government is going to be supreme in Ireland.
>
> Pass that Treaty admitting the King to Ireland, or rather retaining him as he is in Ireland now, retain him while recognising him, recognise the British Government in Ireland and your rights and independence are lost forever.
>
> And the King and the Government behind the King would be barely two hundred miles away and capable of exercising immediate control over what is done in Ireland.
>
> Every Commission held by every officer in the army of the Irish Free State will be signed either by His Majesty or by his deputy in Ireland.
>
> Are we, by our own act, to abandon our independence? I hold that is impossible. I hold this assembly neither will nor can do that.
>
> That document makes British authority our masters in Ireland.
>
> I say they are subverting the republic. It would be a surrender which was never heard of in Ireland since the days of Henry the Second; and are we in this generation, which has made Irishmen famous throughout the world, to sign our names to the most ignoble document that could be signed?
>
> I regard the Provisional Government as Dublin Castle for the moment – as Castle Government.
>
> We are now in the position of Grattan and Flood. If Grattan had not permitted the Volunteers to be disbanded, the Act of Union would

never have been passed. Now you cannot – this government of the Irish Free State cannot control the Army of the Irish Republic.

They never saw one Treaty signed by England with Ireland that England did not dishonour. Have they any assurance that this Treaty will be honoured either?[5]

These rather bizarre statements were made by Erskine Childers, de Valera and Sean MacEntee.[i] Mulcahy considered that Childers's inflammatory attack on the Treaty was an important factor leading to the intransigence of the IRA, and may have particularly influenced those members of the army in Munster. Perhaps it is little wonder that the leaders of the Provisional Government were so bitter about Childers's intervention and his subsequent publicity campaign on behalf of the Irregulars in the Civil War. Childers, MacEntee and other speakers might have had little influence with the army, but these statements, if conveyed to the army from Dáil Éireann, would undoubtedly have influenced the soldiers. At least, that was Mulcahy's opinion.

If Dev had supported the Treaty, he would have been joined by most of the leading anti-Treaty TDs; including subsequent influential Fianna Fáil members such as Jim Ryan, Sean Lemass, Frank Aiken, Sean T. O'Kelly and Oscar Traynor. A number of these were reported to have responded initially in a favourable way to the terms of the Treaty. Mary Josephine Ryan, my mother, was a member of the Ryan family of Wexford, a family intimately involved in the Sinn Féin movement. She was a member of Cumann na mBan and was close to the political leaders. In her recollections on tape she states that her family, including her brother Dr Jim Ryan and several of her sisters – as well as many others who opposed the Treaty – responded enthusiastically at first to its terms; but were later influenced (most likely) by de Valera's outspoken opposition or by Sean T. O'Kelly, who married my mother's sister Kate Ryan and later her younger sister Phyllis.

It is hard to believe that a section of the army could have effectively opposed the Provisional Government or prevented an election on the issue of the Treaty if a substantial majority of the Dáil had accepted the settlement. It is highly unlikely that the type of contributions to the Treaty debate by Erskine Childers

[i]Sean MacEntee, born in Belfast, was a member of the Volunteer Executive during the War of Independence, but I have no record that he was active militarily. He was a founding member of the Dáil and later of the Fianna Fáil Party. He and his family were well known to us when they later lived in Leeson Park. Socially he was gracious and soft spoken – but he had a sharp political tongue and was active in the Dáil as a hatchet man on behalf of his political party.

147

and others, which served to inflame the anti-Treaty section of the army, would have taken place if the politicians had accepted the Treaty as an important step towards a republic. In such an event, it is equally unlikely that the hardcore anti-Treaty members of the IRA, such as O'Connor and Mellows, and the hard-line politicians, such as Brugha and Stack, would have had sufficient support to resist the Provisional Government in arms, or at least to create a resistance of the magnitude of the Civil War.

If Mulcahy appeared to be unrealistic in saying to Dev in September 1922 that he could stop the war by writing a letter to the *Evening Mail* (as is suggested by Prof Murphy in his review of the Mulcahy biography), he meant that even at that late stage of the Civil War, if Dev had called for a truce and proposed an amnesty, it was likely that the war would have ended earlier and with less bitterness and less political and material damage to the country. And certainly the later and disastrous assassination policy promulgated by de Valera and the Irregulars, which intensified the retaliatory execution policy of the Provisional Government, would not have occurred.

Perhaps the most important questions are: to what extent did Dev's early and outspoken antagonism to the Treaty ensure that 'a section of the army was determined to revolt', as asked by Mulcahy's biographer? And to what extent did he thus influence leading anti-Treaty politicians who might have otherwise supported the Treaty? How could a more substantial majority in the pro-Treaty camp have influenced the more ardent republicans to accept the Treaty as a stepping stone? To what extent did the more inflammatory contributions to the Treaty debate encourage so many members of the IRA to oppose the new Free State in arms, when the supporters of the Treaty were dubbed as traitors to the country?

My father, in answering those questions, was speaking as the person most intimately associated with the army, and close to all the political and military leaders. He was convinced that there would not have been a split serious enough to lead to Civil War if Dev had not started the devastating chain reaction of aggressive opposition to the Treaty, before it had even been discussed by the Dáil. By the time the Treaty was ratified one month after its signing, and all had spoken: it was too late for Dev or anybody else to influence the dissidents in the army. By then the damage had been done; and anyhow Dev's continued equivocation merely served to further confuse the situation, and certainly did not help to maintain unity in the army. Tom Garvin wrote that

> Irish people have always sensed that a great disaster occurred between the signing of the Anglo-Irish Treaty on 7 December, 1921, and its ratification on 7 January 1922.[6]

I questioned my father on several occasions about the divisions between the army leaders and some members of the Cabinet which developed during 1921. He would not agree that the differences between de Valera, Stack and Brugha on the one hand, and Collins and himself on the other played any significant part in the disagreement about the Treaty. However, I cannot believe myself that the circumstances which existed in 1921 were not at least significant factors in the split. Brugha's increasing interference with the army, his less than proper recognition of and consultation with the chief of staff on matters of the military's responsibility, his open antagonism to Collins on apparently trivial matters, his later antagonism to Mulcahy, his longstanding antagonism to Griffith and, in addition, Stack's implacable hostility to Collins, must have sown the seeds of the later political and military divisions. These tensions among some of the leading participants in the national movement cannot be ignored when studying the genesis of the Civil War.

In a paper I read to the Army Club at McKee Barracks on 22 March 1996, I spoke about my father's views about the genesis of the Civil War. In describing the war as a 'compound disaster', he attributed many of the political, economic, social and psychological problems which faced the new state to its consequence. In particular, he states that the Civil War had a disastrous effect on Craig's attitude and on possible Northern conciliation.

Professor J. J. Lee, in his history *Ireland 1912-1985: Politics and Society*, reminds us of the deterioration of Ireland's economic status, compared to Britain and other European countries, which occurred after we had gained our independence.[7] Apart from the senseless destruction of lives and property, there were other reasons for the adverse economic change, but it must have been largely caused by the divisive effects of the Treaty and the subsequent civil war.

Few of our politicians after the foundation of the Free State had a strong and enlightened interest in the economic and social progress of the country, when much of the energies of our leaders was dissipated in the prolonged and bitter divisions that followed the Civil War; nor would those interested in such aspects of politics have been easily heard above the cacophony of acrimony and recrimination.

I am struck by the extraordinary polarisation which occurred among intelligent and responsible people in relation to the Treaty and the tragic consequences of their irreconcilable differences. It was particularly poignant to hear my father talk about the internees in the Curragh who were so loud in their cheering and jeering when they heard of Collins's death.

I wonder whether we should be studying conflict as a human problem, one which is so evident in the world today with all the civil and military conflicts which are taking place everywhere. How otherwise will we ever achieve a state of universal peace and security? The language, opinions and abstractions that surrounded the concept of the Republic, in the light of the pluralistic nature of southern Irish society and of the Northern dilemma, created problems that transcended even the tragedy of the Civil War. In practical terms what was needed was to achieve concrete objectives which would grant full Irish self-determination, the ability to change our constitution when and as we wished, and the opportunity to exist in peace and harmony with our neighbours – to the mutual advantage of both countries. Surely this was all granted in the Treaty, as was proven by subsequent events. The tragedy lays in the baleful influence the Treaty divisions and the Civil War had on our relations with the North and on our own political, social, economic and psychological development. It also may have created a political vacuum which allowed the Catholic Church to exert too much political and social influence on the citizens of the Free State.

Clearly, the Civil War had a multi-factorial origin, and it would be difficult to quantify the influence of each factor – although there are some which were more significant than others. According to Mulcahy, the outstanding factors were the strait jacket of the republic imposed by the policies and rhetoric of the Sinn Féin movement, and de Valera's immediate reaction to the Treaty. Some of these have already been dealt with.

THE STRAIT JACKET OF THE REPUBLIC

Without the gathering commitment to a republic, the Civil War would not have taken place. The proclamation of the republic by the signatories in 1916 left a relic for the succeeding political movement which nurtured the republican ideology, rather than the achievable reality of a constitution encompassing self-determination and the will of the majority to retain some connection with Britain and the Commonwealth. The pre-1916 view of 99 percent of the population was either in favour of retaining the status quo or, for the most part, limited Home Rule. The myth was sustained from 1917 to 1922 by the rhetoric of the leaders of Sinn Féin. Mulcahy discusses the stated republic of 1916 and the notional republic of the IRB. He believed that few participants during and immediately after the War of Independence had any real concept of the final constitution of a free Ireland. Michael Hayes, a close friend and political associate of my father's, refers to the concept of the state's future constitution as perceived by the many participants in the freedom movement. His views correspond closely with my father's, whose views on this subject were also shared by other leaders. Michael Tierney, in his biography of Eoin MacNeill,[8] quotes MacNeill as follows:

> For my own part, as well as being a Gaelic Leaguer, I am a Nationalist in politics. My politics are very simple and amount to this, that the less connection we have with Great Britain the better for us in every way. Still I do not believe in carping and finding fault with those who are trying to gain us a limited but effective amount of self-government. In theory I suppose I am a separatist, in practice I would accept any settlement that would enable Irishmen to freely control their own affairs, and I would object to any theoretical upsetting of such a settlement. If the truth were known, I think that this represents the political views of ninety-nine out of every hundred nationalists.

In a letter, Griffith advised that it would be unwise (in November 1920, while he was in prison) to define the constitutional position of the new Irish Free State. At this time of the Clune intervention, he may have been concerned about the possible consequences of a commitment to the republican ideal which was the stated policy of Sinn Féin. There are several comments in Valiulis's biography implying that Mulcahy was lukewarm about the Treaty and that his motivation to support it was largely based on his loyalty to Collins. I must confess that I am surprised by the suggestion that he might otherwise have been lukewarm about the Treaty. Nothing in his early or subsequent political outlook, and nothing in the nature of the man, would suggest to me that he could be anything but enthusiastic about the terms of the Treaty. Although a separatist by conviction, he was a pragmatist by nature; and on several occasions, in discussing the circumstances of the Treaty settlement and the unhappy outcome, he told me that despite the notional republic promulgated by the Dáil and the army during the War of Independence, the driving force behind his separatist ideals was self-determination. He claimed to have had only a superficial idea of the final constitutional settlement that might be achieved. He was, apparently, no doctrinaire republican; nor did he think that the doctrinaire republicans were anything but a small minority of the Irish population. He had a great regard and admiration for Griffith, and would expect him to put matters of practicality and common sense before matters of ideology. He was greatly influenced by Griffith's political philosophy, particularly by his early proposal for a dual monarchy. I believe that Mulcahy, like Griffith and MacNeill, would always put matters of practicality and pragmatism first. He was not the kind of person that could be easily drawn into polarities on issues that could be solved by simple compromise.

It was Mulcahy's opinion that many of his colleagues who were active politically and militarily during the War of Independence were especially vague about their vision of a constitutional end-point. I believe that he was totally committed to the Treaty from the beginning by personal conviction, and that it embodied all the criteria for self-determination to which he aspired; including the capacity to evolve constitutionally in any direction the democratic electorate might decide. His speech to the Dáil during the Treaty debates has received particular praise.

If at any time during the spring and early summer of 1922, when he was entirely dedicated to preserving a unified army, he gave an impression of being lukewarm about the Treaty, I would argue that it was in the interests of diplomacy and as a means of mollifying the increasingly vitriolic anti-Treaty faction of the army. Apart from seeming ambivalent about the Treaty in his tenuous relationships with the more recalcitrant members of the army, there is no evidence, of which I am aware, to suggest that he was anything but enthusiastic about the settlement.

Speaking of his election campaign in December 1918, when he was a candidate for the post-war election, he said:

> The whole of my election comment was based on the self-determination principle, and not until MacEoin and I were required to nominate de Valera as President of the Irish Republic at the Dáil meeting in August 1921, did I ever in a public speech refer to the Irish Republic in any way.[9]

I do not believe that his later influential role in pacifying the more radical members of Cumann na nGaedheal, despite the perceived anti-republican policies of the first Free State Cabinet, was evidence of an inherent republicanism, as is suggested by Valiulis. Nevertheless, it is evident in his tape recordings that he was more committed to Irish culture, language and traditions than many of his political colleagues – with the exception of Eoin MacNeill and possibly Ernest Blythe. I believe that he was as committed to the Treaty as Cosgrave, O'Higgins and the other Cabinet members. That he was less identified with their 'pro-British' policies was largely due to his military role prior to the Treaty, because he was no longer a member of the Cabinet after the Army Mutiny, and because of his fluency in Irish and his chairmanship of the Gaeltacht Commission in 1927.

Certainly, his detachment from mainstream political power following his resignation in 1924 distanced him from much of the pro-British accusations and opprobrium the Cabinet attracted at the time. In my view, Mulcahy would have approved of the Treaty as a permanent settlement with Britain – subject to such modifications as the taking over of the ports and the eventual achievement of unification, subject to the democratic agreement of the North. In 1944 his views about Ireland and the Commonwealth were crystallised when, in his first address to Fine Gael as their newly elected president, he pledged his party's intention to remain in the Commonwealth. Ireland's departure from the Commonwealth in 1948 – a decision made without consulting Mulcahy – was announced by Jack Costello, Taoiseach of the first Inter-Party Government.

It might be useful to remind ourselves of the people elected to the first Dáil in December 1918. Sixty-eight Sinn Féin deputies were elected; each of them chosen not by the democratic will of their constituents, but instead by Michael Collins, Harry Boland and Diarmuid O'Hegarty, and then ratified without question by the standing committee of Sinn Féin. These deputies, representing seventy-three constituencies, were all members of Sinn Féin or the Irish Volunteers, although not all of them were doctrinaire republicans. There were six Parliamentary Party and twenty-six Unionists elected. In the second Dáil of May 1921, 121 Sinn Féin deputies were elected without contest, including almost all of the ones elected to the first Dáil. The rest were chosen nationwide by the local Sinn Féin cumainn, with a strong influence from the army.[10] The second Dáil ratified the Treaty in January 1922 by sixty-four votes to fifty-seven – a narrow majority.

Put simply, the second Dáil was not representative of the Irish people. Voters across the country who desired self-determination had no choice but to vote for Sinn Féin. By May 1921, the Parliamentary Party was completely discredited and did not even put forward any candidates. The Labour Party had not contested the 1918 or 1921 elections, by agreement with Sinn Féin in order not to split the nationalist vote. No other party went forward on a platform of self-determination that could be described as being less radical than the predominant republican ideology of the time. It is therefore not surprising that, while the Dáil only passed the Treaty by a slim majority, the Irish people approved it by a very substantial one.

Because of the non-representative nature of the second Dáil, it was probably inappropriate for de Valera to invoke the republican claim in an interview with the *Irish Bulletin* in the spring of 1921 when he was challenged by his interviewer about the moral right of the Volunteers to fight the War of Independence. Dev makes the point that this was the army of a government legitimised by the people in the 1918 elections; and that, because of the sacrifice of the republican leaders of the 1916 Rising, the republic was mandated by a grateful nation. Under the circumstances, Dev's response was understandable, even if it was not based on the facts of the matter. Dev's argument, however, must have been most convincing to the people, particularly to those who failed to realise that the less radical members of the public were deprived of the opportunity of voting because neither Labour nor the Irish Parliamentary Party had put candidates forward at the election. It is not surprising that many members of the army in Cork and Kerry, who were removed from the political goings-on in Dublin, were so committed to the republican ideal when the Treaty issue arose; particularly when they would have been aware of de Valera's opposition to the Treaty. It was also perhaps naive – if not disingenuous – of de Valera when, two days after the Treaty was signed in London, he wrote to the newspapers rejecting the settlement:

A chairde Gaedheal,

You have seen in the public press the text of the proposed Treaty with Great Britain. The terms of this agreement are in violent conflict with the wishes of the majority of this nation as expressed freely in the successive elections during the last three years.

I feel it my duty to inform you immediately that I cannot recommend the acceptance of this Treaty, either to Dáil Éireann or the country. In this attitude I am supported by the Ministers of Home Affairs and Defence. A public session of Dáil Éireann is being summoned for Wednesday next at 11 o'clock. I ask the people to maintain during the interval the same discipline as heretofore. The members of the Cabinet, though divided in opinions, are prepared to carry on the public services as usual.

The army, as such, is, of course, not affected by the political situation and continues under the same orders and control.

The great test of our people has come. Let us face it worthily without bitterness and, above all, without recriminations. There is a definite constitutional way of resolving our political differences. Let us not depart from it, and let the conduct of the Cabinet in this matter be an example to the whole nation.[11]

When discussing the genesis of the Civil War, Mulcahy also mentions the failure of the politicians to support the efforts of the military leaders to prevent a split in the army. Despite his strenuous efforts, and those of Collins and the more moderate elements on the republican side, no agreement could be reached between January and June 1922 to prevent it. Attempts at reaching an agreement failed chiefly because of the recalcitrance of O'Connor and Mellows, and their colleagues who subsequently occupied the Four Courts.

Mulcahy records the failure to reach decisions about working the Treaty by Sinn Féin at its Árd Fheis in March 1922, and in May he complained to the Dáil about the politicians' failure: 'This is the forty-seventh time we have discussed the issue without any prospect of agreement or compromise.' He muses at length about the influences which caused Dev, Brugha and Stack to oppose the Treaty so vehemently, and describes in great detail the negotiations to prevent the split between January and June 1922.

In a conversation I had with my father, we discussed the hypothetical situation of what might have happened if the Treaty had been defeated by the Dáil. We concluded that it would have created an anomalous situation where the majority of the people would not support their parliament and where perhaps the British government would adopt the role of supporting the people against its own elected representatives. We speculated that a number of the deputies who voted against the Treaty through lack of moral courage would have voted otherwise had they believed it would be defeated. This is a valuable and detailed exposition of Mulcahy's opinion of Dev's and other politicians' failure to provide leadership at that crucial juncture in Irish politics.

Post-Treaty and the Army Mutiny

Perhaps one of most difficult and frustrating periods between 1916 and 1924 for my father was after the ratification of the Treaty, when he and Collins made the most strenuous efforts to prevent the army division and the Civil War. Between January and June 1922, he devoted his time and energies to reconciling the opposed factions of the army while, as he complained, the politicians squabbled. In their efforts to mollify their opponents, he and Collins at times came dangerously close to offending the supporters of the Treaty, although this does not mean that they were not fully supportive of the Treaty themselves. In retrospect, it seems that their efforts were never likely to overcome the intransigence of the anti-Treaty factions.

The first step leading towards the army split happened shortly after the ratification of the Treaty by the Dáil. Jim Donovan, who was bitterly opposed to the Treaty, had been appointed to the GHQ staff as director of chemicals about six months before the truce. In January 1922, he wrote to Mulcahy, who then had been appointed minister for defence, on behalf of IRA leaders opposed to the Treaty. Donovan demanded a meeting to set up an army executive, including both pro- and anti-Treaty IRA members, which would be independent of the Dáil. In the letter, Donovan proposed a convention with the following terms:

> That the army re-affirms its allegiance to the Irish Republic. That it shall be maintained as the Army of the Irish Republic, under an Executive appointed by the Convention. That the Army shall be under the supreme control of the Executive, which shall draft a Constitution for submission to a subsequent Convention.

Mulcahy's view of the army's crucial role in safeguarding Ireland's democratic institutions is clear in his reply:

> In reply I have to say: (1) That the Dáil as a whole is the elected Government of the Irish Republic and that the supreme control of the army is vested in it, and (2) that the proposal contained in the resolution to change the supreme control of the army is entirely outside the constitutional powers vested in the Dáil Executive by the Dáil.

We are further reminded by many other sources of Mulcahy's commitment to democracy; and particularly by Tom Garvin who, in his 1922 book *The Birth of Irish Democracy*, writes 'as founders of Irish democracy, Cosgrave and Mulcahy have been profoundly underrated'.

Collins and Mulcahy were not alone among those who did everything in their power to prevent the split in the army. Indeed, a number of leading moderates on the anti-Treaty side were involved in searching for an amicable solution. Tragically, the army failed to remain united and the Civil War, and its ghastly consequences, became inevitable. Many of the anti-Treaty Volunteers were opposed to civil war, but the Four Courts Garrison, led by Rory O'Connor and Liam Mellows, refused all compromise.

Mulcahy had great pride in the army he had helped to build and command; it was an integral part of his brand of ideology and nationalism. He believed it held the key which would ensure Ireland's emergence as a free, prosperous, Christian and pluralistic democracy, with a culture encompassing both the Gaelic tradition and the Anglo-Irish community. His ideal extended beyond the function of the army as a military force alone and he believed an army training would prepare young men to be better citizens. Even at the height of the Civil War he was already laying down plans – with his brother-in-law, Denis McCullough, and John Larchet, professor of music at University College

Dublin – to establish an army school of music. John Larchet and his family were close friends of my parents, and it was he and McCullough who travelled to Germany in late 1922 or early 1923 to find a bandmaster to organise the school.

In a speech to the Free State troops on 8 October 1922 during the Civil War, Mulcahy thanked the army for its excellent work in restoring the roads and railways, and bringing a state of peace and normality to many parts of the country. He said:

> In the same way [we look] forward to making the army a national institution through which the young men of Ireland [would] pass to be much better men and citizens.

Well before the Civil War ended, they had engaged Fritz Brasé, one of the ex-Kaiser's bandmasters, to head up the army school of music. Mulcahy's stated objective in setting up the school was to train musicians who would continue in a musical career after discharge from the army, and who would enhance the musical traditions of the country. A short history of the Army School of Music has been published.[1]

As early as October 1923, the first army band, under the baton of Fritz Brasé, gave its first public concert in the Gaiety Theatre to a crowded audience, including W. T. Cosgrave and members of the Executive Council. Mulcahy, as minister for defence, and the members of the Army Council, occupied a special box in the theatre. It must have been a proud moment for my father, particularly as the band played the Mulcahy March, composed by Fritz Brasé, for the first time in public. However, the aftermath may have proved embarrassing because of his decision, supported by his army colleagues, to remain seated during the national anthem. He had already proposed to his ministerial colleagues that, the war with Britain being over, the bellicose tone of the national anthem, 'Amhráin na bhFiann', was no longer appropriate. He proposed instead 'O'Donnell Abu' (the words of which, in my opinion, are equally bellicose, though perhaps less topical) and it was to make this point that the minister and army leaders decided to sit out the anthem. I suspect their action misfired, and may have given an undesirable impression of arrogance to the audience; and ultimately I believe Mulcahy was embarrassed by the incident. In the same tape he criticises Dev for 'dipping his dirty fingers' into the Irish version of the anthem to name his new party – Fianna Fáil – in 1926.

Mulcahy also had ideas for a peacetime army. He believed the soldiers, after demobilisation at the end of the Civil War, should be employed in reafforestation and other public works. Whether such projects were practical at the time is questionable. Similar proposals were made to the Cabinet as early as September 1922 but received little or no support from his colleagues. Because of the overriding effects of the Civil War and the grim political situation, such economic policies had low priority. The major political problems associated with demobilisation, which led to the Army Mutiny and Mulcahy's resignation from the ministry, put paid to such high minded plans.

He resigned from the army in May 1923 at the end of the Civil War, and decided to devote his life to politics. He retained his position as minister for defence in the Cabinet and was returned to the fourth Dáil in August 1923 with a whopping 22,203 votes, a figure which has not been reached by any Irish candidate before or since, and which was surely a powerful mandate by his Clontarf constituency and an endorsement of his previous military career. The *Irish Times*, on 22 September 1923 wrote:

> General Mulcahy has cast aside the sword, to resume once more the legislator's toga. He, too, has been through the fires within the past twelve months, and, if one does not notice such a marked change in his personality, it is because he is a philosopher. He was a wise head long before its time and today he is the same curious mixture of gentleness and relentless purpose, the same strange amalgam of dreamer and man of decisive action and one of sympathy, and compelled our respect when first he stood up in the Mansion House, a frail and somewhat pathetic figure, and spoke in lyric phrases about Cúchulainn at the ford.[2]

Much was written in the national and international press about my father and his dominant role during the period of 1922-1923, and after the Civil War had ended. He was even described as 'the most interesting man in Europe' by a correspondent in *Colliers Magazine*.[3] The correspondent went on to say

Michael Collins was the bold charging front of the rebellion: Mulcahy was the organising and planning brain. When I learnt of Collins's death, it seemed to me that he rather than Mulcahy should have been killed. The task in hand required a Mulcahy type.

The correspondent writes at length about the organising of the Free State army and asks,

What was Mulcahy's task? [He] was a man with a hand of steel who offered the volunteers uniforms and regular pay in return for unceasing drill and absolute obedience.

The years 1916-1924 in my father's military career ended with the Army Mutiny and his resignation from the Department of Defence ten months after the Civil War ended. I interviewed him about the circumstances leading to the mutiny and the role of the IRB in the army at the time. The mutineering officers were acting on their perception of renewed IRB activity among senior Free State army officers, believing that the IRB members were being retained and promoted while they, the 'Old IRA', were being discharged despite their service during the War of Independence. These officers were disaffected for various reasons, perhaps mainly over jobs and internal politics, and were critical of certain aspects of the army's activities and policies – and they found a sympathetic ear in Minister Kevin O'Higgins.

Kevin O'Higgins was Mulcahy's colleague as minister for home affairs, and the presence of renewed IRB activity was one of O'Higgins's main complaints about the army at the time. Although I seemed to do most of the talking on the tape, my father managed to deal with some important matters in his responses. He talks about the relationship between himself and O'Higgins before, during and after the Treaty; and in particular his contention that O'Higgins and the Department of Home Affairs interfered to an unacceptable degree with the army beginning at the end of 1922. He also names some of the army officers who were in contact with O'Higgins, but who were unknown to him at the time. O'Higgins's increasing criticism of the control of the army during the Civil War and its aftermath caused Mulcahy considerable (and justifiable) irritation. While he never showed any personal animosity towards

O'Higgins, he said that neither O'Higgins nor any other member of the Cabinet knew anything about the army and the difficulties it faced during the Civil War and its aftermath.

O'Higgins's complaints included a charge that venereal disease was rampant in the army and was not being properly dealt with. Mulcahy denied this and spoke of the high standards of the medical services in the fledgling army; staffed by medical professionals who later distinguished themselves in Ireland's medical services. Mulcahy mentions the names 'Pops' Morrin, Tom O'Higgins and Matt O'Connor as a few of his medical officers: Morrin became a well-known surgeon at St Vincent's Hospital and had been trained as a trauma surgeon in the British army during the First World War; O'Higgins, Kevin O'Higgins's brother, was later appointed chief medical officer of County Meath; and O'Connor became the pathologist to the Richmond Hospital.

It is likely that, despite the high ethical and disciplinary standards to which the leaders of the Free State army aspired, it was impossible to mobilise such a new and raw army and pursue a difficult military campaign without *some* lapses in discipline and control. Indeed, it seems almost miraculous to me that the army succeeded in maintaining such high standards under the impossible circumstances of such a bitter and prolonged civil conflict, against adversaries who did their very best to reduce the country to a state of chaos. Yet O'Higgins and his friend, Paddy Hogan, the minister for agriculture, became increasingly critical of the army's conduct during the Civil War. O'Higgins further accused Mulcahy and the army of a lack of discipline among the ranks, and he complained about atrocities in Kerry. He also claimed that the Civil War was allowed to continue for too long and without reason – and notably argued and that there ought to have been more executions as a deterrent against Irregular activity.[4] According to Mulcahy, O'Higgins actually undermined troop morale because of his contact with officers who kept him apprised of army activities without the knowledge of Mulcahy or the Army Council.

O'Higgins's criticisms of Mulcahy and the army continued well after the Civil War, when Mulcahy had the formidable task of demobilising forty thousand or more troops in an effort to establish a professional, peacetime army. Mulcahy's attempts to ease the problems of rapid demobilisation, by finding jobs for those who were discharged from the army, received, according to him, little sympathy or support from the Cabinet. The problems and disturbances associated with the task of transforming what had been an insurgent army into a peacetime force created tensions between Mulcahy and those of his military colleagues who were no longer suited to the discipline of peacetime duties. The processes of demobilisation led to disturbances among the soldiers, culminating in a serious episode in 1923 when a large number of officers defected with weapons from the Curragh.

Mulcahy's relationships with his Cabinet colleagues are discussed in detail in his papers.[5] He writes about his unsuccessful efforts to convince Cosgrave and the other Cabinet ministers to solve his demobilisation problems by providing discharged soldiers with extra employment in housing, road building, forestry and other public works; although he does admit elsewhere that he could have made greater efforts to consult Cosgrave. As early as September 1922, at the height of the Civil War, he raised this issue with the Cabinet. It would appear, then, that he had some foresight of the difficulties that would be involved in the army's demobilisation. These difficulties led to the mutiny and its aftermath, and to a serious rift in the Cumann na nGaedheal party – all of which posed serious threats to the new and fragile government. In making the point about consulting Cosgrave, Mulcahy may have been implying that Cosgrave might have had a restraining effect on O'Higgins and may have had greater sympathy for the Army Council at the time of the mutiny.

In response to my question about the government's poor efforts to accommodate the demobilised soldiers, my father answered: 'I fell down in not forcing them to realise that better'. He remarks about the stultifying effect on the Cabinet of being confined to government buildings during the early months of the Civil War, and their neglect of economic and social problems while the Dáil debated the new constitution and indulged in a 'gossipy' type of atmosphere during the autumn of 1922. According to Mulcahy, their continued preoccupation with newspaper accounts of the disturbances in the country had the effect of cornering their attention, so that they had nothing better to do than criticise the army as it was trying to defeat the Irregulars.

When I questioned him about a possible breakdown of relations between himself and the Cabinet during and after the Civil War (highlighted by Valiulis as a factor leading to the mutiny), he did not deny this. But he did maintain that he was too preoccupied with pursuing the war to spend time sitting around talking politics with his Cabinet colleagues.

Despite difficulties for himself and the Army Council, Mulcahy states that he did not let these interfere with his personal relations with his colleagues. One of the stated reasons for the tarnishing of Mulcahy's reputation, as suggested by Valiulis, was his draconian command during the Civil War. He never expressed any regrets about the illegal executions of the Irregulars Rory O'Connor, Liam Mellows, Richard Barrett and Joseph McKelvey in November 1922 in response to the shooting of Deputies Hales and O'Malley. However, he did state that he regretted having to adopt such severe measures and blamed the proclamation by de Valera and Lynch in November 1922 which advocated the assassination of members of the Dáil and other leading pro-Treaty figures. He and the members of the Army Council had ordered the executions, although Kevin O'Higgins suffered the greatest opprobrium subsequently. Indeed, O'Higgins was the last member of the Cabinet to agree to the extreme proposal and apparently only did so reluctantly.

He deplored Dev's support of the policy of assassination and he believed that democracy in Ireland was under imminent threat because of it. He believed the executions of the four prisoners – as did the executions of Childers and many other Irregulars who were caught with firearms – and the threat of further executions, brought a sudden, cold sense of reality to his opponents. There was serious public reaction to the shootings of the prisoners. From a distance of almost ninety years it certainly seems they may have been extreme in their reaction. Like most others, I believe the execution of the four prisoners – as well as the prolongation of the execution policy into the spring of 1923 – was unnecessary. But it is difficult to assess now the necessity of these actions at that critical time.

Mulcahy includes a note about the reasons and circumstances under which he proposed the execution policy and the military courts to the Cabinet in September 1922; and also why he agreed with the decision to execute Erskine

Childers in November 1922. As a member of a well-known Anglo-Irish family, Childers had been in the British civil service and the British army, fighting in the Boer War and later in World War I. He became passionately committed to the republic, and masterminded the Howth gun-running episode in July 1914. Childers also made certain inflammatory and misleading statements during the Treaty debates which were taken by my father and others to have provoked many of those who took up arms against the Treaty. His bitter Civil War propaganda, circulated widely at national and international levels, made him particularly disliked by the Free State leaders. It is easy to understand why Cosgrave and his colleagues did not want to make an exception for him.

According to Terence de Vere White, Diarmuid Coffey asked Cosgrave to grant a reprieve to Childers. Cosgrave apparently did so the evening before his execution on the condition that Childers would remain out of politics.[6] It is alleged that Childers refused the offer on such conditions. However, Déirdre McMahon has told me that she has found no reference to such an intervention in her examination of the Childers papers.

Frank Holland was a private in the Free State army in 1922 and had been active during the War of Independence. He was the soldier assigned to guard Childers after his arrest, and was with him constantly until his execution. Holland described the extraordinary courage of Childers facing his executioners: he thanked his executioners, expressed forgiveness to his opponents and refused to be blindfolded. In fact, he actually did eventually agree to a blindfold when the ranking officer explained that it would cause undue distress to the firing party if his eyes were not covered. The order to fire was signalled by dropping a handkerchief instead of the usual verbal command.[7]

There is a graphic account of the Childers execution on Mulcahy's tapes. He was housed in a large shed in Beggar's Bush Barracks, where he exercised three times a day by walking one measured mile inside the shed. Between his walks he would sleep for a few hours, and spent the rest of his time writing. There was maximum security to prevent his rescue, either by outsiders or by members of the army. Paddy O'Connor, the officer in charge, informed Childers of his execution. Childers thanked O'Connor, and, according to Holland, the information did not seem to cost him a thought. At midnight he asked to see Bishop Gregg of the Church of Ireland, who arrived promptly and spent the night with him. The bishop, according to Holland, wept at times.

There were fifteen men in the firing party, but only five had loaded rifles. O'Connor arranged secretly that the five loaded rifles would be given to World War I veterans, ostensibly because of their superior marksmanship. The execution took place in the early morning, at first light, and was arranged so that Childers was placed at the end of a shed where part of the roof had been removed, leaving him in the light. The firing party were in the dark where they could not be easily seen by Childers. His death was instantaneous and the marksmanship, apparently, very accurate. Only a man with a profound belief in his principles could have behaved as Childers did; and he died a martyr to his cause. The tragedy of Childers's death is a sad reminder of the consequences where principle conflicts with pragmatism, where passion overcomes all sense of realism, and where a man will die for what others perceive to be an empty formula.

The continuation of the policy of execution for arms possession and other crimes into the early months of 1923 has often been criticised, even by supporters of the army. While there is justification in such criticisms, one must appreciate the state of the country at the time, where the war had deteriorated into widespread vandalism, murder, robbery, arson and intimidation, and where in many places law and order was difficult to uphold. Perhaps it was felt that the possession of arms by the Irregulars, who lacked a central military command, was the primary reason for the continuation of the conflict, and that draconian measures were required to discourage the perpetrators.

There is a taped conversation between my father, mother and myself on various aspects of the circumstances leading to the Army Mutiny, and about his relations with his Cabinet colleagues. During this conversation, Mulcahy said:

> The situation I was dealing with, the circumstances and, if you like, the technique or the absence of technique that I had to adopt not to increase the area of conflict or to inflame that contact which was there, [meant] I never attempted to enter into detailed dissection of [the] O'Higgins

mind . . . It wasn't my makeup to try and examine what kind of a man Joe McGrath was, what kind of a person Kevin O'Higgins was, what kind of a person Paddy Hogan was . . . There was developing in the army evidence that Hogan and people like that were out to undermine the position of myself at any rate and others in the General Headquarters staff . . . As far as the Cabinet was concerned I relied on Cosgrave to handle any Cabinet situation that was there, and I didn't either discharge my feelings by analysing O'Higgins or by analysing Joe McGrath and I didn't even discuss with Cosgrave, perhaps to the extent which I might, the developments of antagonism to us in the army.

Mulcahy and O'Higgins had much in common. They were both dedicated to democracy and to the survival of the new Irish Free State; they both felt impelled to adopt a draconian approach to the Irregulars as the turmoil of the Civil War disrupted the nation; and each projected a public persona of dedication, austerity and perhaps stoicism. O'Higgins differed from Mulcahy, however, in his propensity to the sharp and wounding retort, and to a certain intolerance of others' views – attributes which must have affected his foes more than Mulcahy's more measured approach. O'Higgins was also perceived to be committed to retaining an association with the British in his last few years and, to the rank and file of the party and perhaps to a wider national audience, he was less 'nationalistic' than my father.

Mulcahy continued as minister for defence in the Cabinet following the 1923 election, and remained in that position until the Army Council was sacked by the government after the mutiny. He resigned in protest, but O'Higgins maintained that he would have called for Mulcahy's resignation if he had not first resigned. Apparently the only Cabinet minister to support his defence of the Army Council was the minister for fisheries, Fionán Lynch. There is little point in outlining the details of the mutiny and its genesis. Valiulis's account in *Almost a Rebellion*[8] gives a definitive account of this episode, as does her biography. The Mulcahy papers and the report of the government's commission of enquiry are housed in the UCD archives and provide a comprehensive background to the affair. There is a detailed discussion about the mutiny on tape. The following conversation was recorded:

> **RM:** To what extent was this increasing intrigue and conflict between these two groups of the military movement [the IRB, alleged to be the Army Council, and the Old IRA, by which the mutineers described themselves] affecting the army during 1923 and 1924? If you had decided to oppose O'Higgins it is very likely that you would have had a serious bloodbath. Is that true?
>
> **R:** Oh you could have had a burst-up but you couldn't have controlled it. I couldn't have controlled a situation in which you have McGrath on the one side and a section of the army on the other, opposed by McGrath, and [another] section of the army supported by O'Higgins. Any kind of reasonable attitude by me other than what I did, I would have been simply squeezed between two very disruptive forces.
>
> **RM:** There were three sections in the army . . .?
>
> **R:** . . . and the IRB was not one of them. You have the pure Volunteer spirit that was just serving and serving in the traditional spirit . . . There was no clash between an IRB section and any other section. It was a figment created by the Tobins and these, and used by O'Higgins.

Mulcahy believed that Tobin was the main instigator of the mutiny.

There is no evidence that attempts by senior officers to revive the IRB had any sinister significance, or that it was related in any way to the demobilisation. However, it is clear from a conversation between Sean MacEoin and Mulcahy on other tapes that some of the senior officers in the army were interested in reviving the IRB 'to further the national and cultural aspirations of the country'; although it is not clear what is meant by this. It is apparent that Mulcahy as minister for defence was not aware of these plans, but he was probably naive to think the IRB was moribund at that point in history. On the other hand, he was certainly correct in believing that the IRB's influence in the army was of little significance, and that it had no further military aspirations. Nevertheless, he did seem a little embarrassed when he learned that Sean McMahon, chief of staff of the Free State army, was the head of the

IRB in 1923, and that Sean O'Muirthile, the quartermaster general, was its treasurer.[9]

Tobin, Dalton and the other leaders of the mutiny had been part of Collins's group during the War of Independence. I believe they resented having to serve with another leader, and that they never reconciled the death of Collins. Talking about their lack of discipline, Mulcahy said of Tobin and Dalton

> . . . that even Collins, who didn't always require people to be disciplined around him, had pushed the two of them out of Dublin in the early stages of the Civil War to be out of his way.

This statement about the old Collins group is confirmed by an extract from the Report of the Army Enquiry Committee in 1924:

> That the organisation, which brought about, and many members of which joined in, the late mutiny, was in existence at least in embryo, before the outbreak of the Civil War, and that many of the officers who mutinied and of those who encouraged and abetted them had become a problem to General Collins before his death in August, 1922.

In response to my question about O'Higgins's knowledge of the army and its problems during the Civil War and to Mulcahy's secret meeting with de Valera in late September 1922, he said that O'Higgins 'was blindly ignorant of the problem that my mind was up against and that the army command was up against'. Mulcahy had been pressured to meet de Valera in late September during the Civil War with a view to reconciliation. The priest who persuaded him to do so maintained that Dev was 'a changed man'. With the approval of Eoin MacNeill, Mulcahy met him reluctantly despite an earlier Cabinet decision that no talks would take place with the Irregular leadership without the Cabinet's knowledge and approval. Mulcahy's remarks can be summarised in his view that he 'didn't give a damn' who ran the country, as long as the government conformed to the democratic will of the people. Dev's response was to say 'some men are led by faith and some men are led by reason. Personally, I would tend to be led by reason, but as long as there are men of faith like Rory O'Connor taking the stand that he is taking, I am a humble soldier following after them.' The meeting lasted less than two minutes. When the episode was later reported to the Cabinet by Mulcahy, O'Higgins was not pleased with his initiative.

The latter half of the tape deals with my mother's account of Mrs Cosgrave's visit after my father's resignation from the ministry:

> **MM:** When that was going on before the [mutiny] enquiry, Máire was born at that time and I was up in my room in bed and Mrs Cosgrave described that he, her husband, had retired with illness. The doctor said he wasn't to go out. She came in to see me in a great [state] – I was in a bit of a state myself but I wasn't as bad as that about this whole thing. Dick came home one night and told me he was out of everything.
>
> She [Mrs Cosgrave] said ' . . . it is just the same with Willy [Cosgrave], he's there and O'Higgins wants him to resign'. He wants Cosgrave to resign, she told me, and that he was to take over the whole thing. She told me that, I remember that. She said he is a terrible man. I didn't know what to say to her, I had enough on my own mind. I don't remember what I said about Cosgrave, whether he had to stand down or else. She thought that time that Cosgrave was going to resign. She said you'd be afraid of this fellow.

One might naturally assume that the Army Mutiny and its aftermath, and Mulcahy's resignation from the ministry, would have left him feeling bitter and frustrated. However, when I questioned him about the event and speculated about other outcomes that might have spared him some personal loss, he replied that it was only by the grace of God that the compound problems faced by the government from 1922 to 1924 ended as peacefully and as well as they did. His only expressed regret was that the mutiny caused irreparable damage to the Government and to the Treaty supporters in general, contributed to the failure of the Boundary Commission and to the near-failure of the government in the election of 1927. He may not have approved of the Free State government's treatment of the Army Council in 1924, but I suspect he understood their dilemma caused by the demobilisation conflicts at the time. It is also likely that his resignation and the dismissal of the Army Council members may have been accepted by his colleagues in the Cabinet and Dáil, who may have been motivated by the need to maintain the stability of the Free State government. Mulcahy's own views concerning the genesis and effects of the Army Mutiny are recorded, and they are supported by Michael Tierney in his biography *Eoin MacNeill: Scholar and Man of Action, 1867-1945*,[10] when he writes:

> In the long run the episode of the so-called 'mutiny' did immense damage to the cause of the government. In November, [Joe] McGrath[i] and eight of his adherents resigned from the Dáil, precipitating a series of by-elections which were described as 'a miniature general election'. Of the five seats contested, the government lost two, but the number of seats was less important than the general feeling of depression which the incident created. Thousands of ex-officers and ex-soldiers scattered up and down the country [and] brought with them a message, no longer of revolution, but of vague disappointment and discontent. On the Treaty side of the division which the Civil War had made permanent, courage and determination gave way too often to cynicism and disillusionment. The only beneficiary of the whole sad episode was de Valera.

---

[i] Joe McGrath had been a minister in the first Free State government and was sympathetic to the mutineers: he resigned from the Dáil because of their dismissal from the army. He subsequently pursued a very successful career in the business world and was best known as the organiser of the Irish Sweepstakes which gave such significant support to Irish hospitals.

The Years 1924-1932

Political Wilderness

By resigning the Department of Defence, Mulcahy pre-empted Kevin O'Higgins's apparent intention to demand his resignation. O'Higgins accused Mulcahy of collusion with the IRB and of incompetence, accusations which were subsequently struck down by the Commission of Enquiry that followed the mutiny. Compared with his prior prominent and influential role in the military and political affairs of the new State, he found himself suddenly cast into the political wilderness as a back bencher. Despite his protests in the Dáil over the treatment of his officers, he received little support from his political colleagues. Their attitude is perhaps understandable considering the necessity of preserving a united Cabinet and a stable government at such a critical juncture. He did, however, receive many private expressions of support. Furthermore, if one is to judge by the collection of letters in the UCD archives, there were many expressions of regret over his departure from the Cabinet and a genuine appreciation of his service record and his spirited public defence of his officers.

Bishop Fogarty of the Clare diocese wrote to my father:

> I write now, not so much to utter the deep sympathy I feel, but to express my admiration for the public spirit and most edifying and gallant patience with which you have met a situation and a set of circumstances that are surely hard to bear. It is like you and worthy of your distinguished past, and is sure to bring its reward sooner or later.

I wish all others had the same public spirit. There is widespread sympathy with you personally and a fixed conviction that you will soon be back again in the government where you rendered such eminent services to Ireland.

In his reply to the Bishop he wrote 'I feel confident that the line of action which I have taken in recent circumstances will be all for the best generally . . . '[1]

Another correspondent wrote:

Please accept my sincere sympathy on the sorrow and sadness and hardship received through the scant courtesy – or total want of it – given you by our present government. You fully gave your work, your whole, your very life for Ireland. While you live you still will be a creditor no earthly power or government can repay. I feel there is still a greater future for you in Ireland's cause . . .

His uncle John Slattery wrote of the pain the news caused him personally, but also of the delight and pride he and his family felt:

. . . because of the high standards of honour you have always maintained in your position. You may rely on it that the country will not be slow to remember and recognise who it was who saved the Free State, and upon whose honour and integrity they can always place their entire trust.

The many other tributes follow the same themes – his services to Ireland, his defence of the army, the country's need for his continued services, his integrity, his lack of personal ambition and his equanimity in the face of adversity.

Eoin MacNeill, in his speech to the Dáil following Mulcahy's resignation, had this to say about him:

If there is a man in this assembly whom I would like to call a friend, if there is a man whom I would be proud to call my friend, if there is a man whom I would hope in the future to call my friend, and who, I hope, will be my friend, it is the ex-minister for defence. There are few men in this assembly who know and are able to appreciate what this country owes to General Mulcahy. I doubt if but for General Mulcahy it would now be possible for us to be discussing the conduct of General Mulcahy. I remember when there was a price upon his head and we remember the extraordinary difficulty when he was covered with every obloquy that hostile minds could think of, and I do not think there is a man alive, and I think there are very few men dead, to whom Ireland owes more than it owes to Deputy Richard Mulcahy, and I think the members removed from positions in the administration of the army as subordinates have also in their time deserved well of the country.

After 1924, Mulcahy drifted out of mainstream affairs. He spent the months after his resignation preparing his submission to the Army Mutiny enquiry set up by the government. This proved to be an unsatisfactory affair, largely because many of the crucial witnesses who had participated in the mutiny refused to testify. Like many similar enquiries since, the setting-up of the Mutiny enquiry served mainly to quickly defuse a critical situation at the time. In preparing his submission to the enquiry, my father had access to all his and the army's Truce, Civil War and post-Civil War papers in Portobello Barracks. He removed them to his home at Lissenfield at the time and retained them afterwards. They now form an important part of his papers in the UCD Archives.

Mulcahy continued to attend the Dáil during 1924 as a backbencher. Details of the 1924-1927 period of political isolation are described by him in his tape recordings. Although apparently outside the main corridors of power during these years, he continued to support the government from the back benches and played an active role in the affairs of the Cumann na nGaedheal Party, among whose members his prestige remained undiminished. Mulcahy confirmed that, from the end of the Civil War in April 1923 until the assassination of Kevin O'Higgins in August 1927, he travelled throughout Dublin and the country freely and without protection. During this time he was never molested or threatened by anybody, (apart from the Irish in America), nor was he ever conscious of being at risk of assassination himself, despite receiving several anonymous threatening letters.

From the time I dropped the uniform after the Civil War and went up for the 1923 election, even after that I went to every part of this country [where] I wanted to go, unarmed and unattended . . . I never got a belt in the mouth.

In response to my question about O'Higgins's vulnerability, he said 'It was not what he did but by his disposition that perhaps made him more vulnerable.'

It is extraordinary that the man who directed the Civil War – and who was most closely associated in the public mind with the draconian measures adopted by the Free State army against the Irregulars – was able to walk the streets of Dublin and visit the four corners of Ireland from 1924-1927 without guard or weapon. The bitterness remaining after the Civil War left many violent dissidents who probably thought it their moral duty to eliminate the architect of their defeat, and a traitor to the republic! After the O'Higgins's assassination three years later, guards were provided for members of the Cabinet; and in fact from 1922 we had guards in our house, contiguous to the Portobello Barracks. The guards were housed in a large galvanised hut under the old beech trees close to the avenue in our family home in Rathmines. This hut was built by the army in the early twenties to house the men assigned to Mulcahy's protection. They were welcome company to us as children and we could take many liberties with them (although they wisely never allowed us to handle their Thompson submachine guns). During the Civil War the house was attacked by the Irregulars but they were fought off by the guards, and one of the intruders was killed. To the best of my knowledge, no other attempt was ever made on Mulcahy's life.

Sometime later, perhaps in the early 1930s, the army guards were withdrawn and replaced by a police car manned by two detectives. Mulcahy insisted that he did not need protection and stubbornly refused even to recognise their presence. He asked the Department of Justice to have the escort withdrawn, without success. The police car was not permitted to enter the grounds of the house, and for several years the car remained parked on the roadway, always manned by the detectives. We all thought he treated the detectives rather badly, deliberately dodging them and ignoring their presence when he passed them on his way to the tram. It is difficult to understand his motives in treating them the way he did, but it may have been that he wanted to avoid the perception that he might be the recipient of Fianna Fáil's patronage.

He describes on tape his two-week journey around Ireland on board the *Murchú*, the first naval and fishery-protection vessel acquired by the new government, shortly after his resignation. He was a guest of Minister for Fisheries Fionán Lynch, who, according Mulcahy, was the only minister to support him in the Cabinet at the time of the mutiny. Later, in 1925, he represented the government at the Inter-Parliamentary Union Meeting in New York, accompanied by the Chairman of the Dáil, Michael Hayes, and Thomas Johnson, the leader of the Labour Party. Here he received the accolades of the Treaty supporters, but also the more vocal abuse and vituperation of anti-Treaty Irish-Americans. He and his two colleagues were actually attacked by an aggressive crowd of protesters when they disembarked from the ocean-liner at Hoboken Pier in New York. The detailed newspaper report states:

> As the baggage inspection was in progress, a group of men rushed at the General [Mulcahy]. One struck him in the face and another kicked him in the legs. The General was nearly swept off his feet.

His companion on the pier who was leading him was then knocked down by a blow to the jaw. The report goes on:

> General Mulcahy was pummelled with fists and pelts [*sic*] with eggs and tomatoes but he stood his ground until the arrival of the police. When General Mulcahy and his party started to leave through the gate they were showered with rotten eggs. One of his aids was struck on the eye by a stick hurled at him.

The placards carried by the protesters carried such slogans as:

> *If Emmet had not been executed in 1803, Mulcahy would have executed him in 1923*, and *Mulcahy murderer, Mulcahy perjurer, Mulcahy traitor!*

The following resolution was passed at a meeting of the St Brendan's Society in Boston:

> [Mulcahy's] hands are dripping with the blood of his former comrades, as an enemy of liberty and American ideas and principles.

I have already referred to the division which existed among Irish Americans after de Valera's visit. John Devoy and his long-established Clann na nGaedheal supported the Treaty, unlike de Valera's break-away group, the American Association for the Recognition of the Irish Republic, who opposed it as a betrayal of Irish national aspirations. It was supporters of this latter movement who demonstrated against Mulcahy at various stages of his visit to America. For this and certain other reasons, it is reasonable to ask if the influence of Irish-America did more harm than good to post-Treaty Ireland. He spent five weeks in the United States and Canada.[2] He was greatly impressed by the United States and its people, and by President Calvin Coolidge, and his regard for the United States was to last his lifetime:

> I was never in a more cheerful and hospitable nation than this, which I consider the first ranking democracy on earth.

On many occasions later in life he prophesied to me that the United States would play a major role in maintaining world peace and in creating a rational world society. I think differently, believing that America's more recent mix of fundamentalism, materialism, foreign policy and neglect of the environment is a recipe for disaster.

The year 1926 was spent largely in parliamentary and party work. Towards the end of the year, Mulcahy asked Cosgrave if he would reinstate him in the Cabinet if the government won the election and if the party returned to power. The election was due to take place in the spring of 1927. He gives a detailed account on tape of his further strategy from the moment in the autumn of 1926 when Cosgrave, in response to his enquiry, dismissed the idea of reappointing him. On being refused by Cosgrave, he put his name forward for a forthcoming election to the Cumann na nGaedheal Comhairle Ceanntar, stating in his submission that he was doing so based solely on the issue of his reappointment to the Cabinet. He was supported by a large majority of the party members, indicating considerable support for his return to the Cabinet. Cosgrave soon yielded to pressure by some of his colleagues, including Kevin O'Higgins and Paddy Hogan, to avoid a serious division within the party.[3]

Paddy Hogan apparently informed Michael Hayes, who was chairman of the Dáil from 1922-1932, that he and O'Higgins regretted having forced Mulcahy to resign at the time of the mutiny. The fact that O'Higgins supported the move to re-install Mulcahy in the Cabinet before this election lends support to that. Despite his rebuff and apparent lack of sympathy for my father, Cosgrave was served with great loyalty by him until Cosgrave's retirement in 1944. He describes how the various differences which existed between himself and some of his political colleagues during these years, and the ensuing crises, did not materially affect his personal relations with them. Nor did he ever waver in his support of the government. It may be, however, that his implied withdrawal of support for the government after the approaching 1927 election if he was not offered a Cabinet post, was an added factor in influencing Cosgrave to accept his nomination. Whether or not he would have actually resigned from the party and withdrawn his support if he had not been included in the Cabinet is a moot point; but I very much doubt if he would have done so. He maintained that a failure to include him in the Cabinet would have destabilised the government. I have little doubt that he was correct in this view, bearing in mind the increasing difficulties facing Cosgrave after 1924. In fairness to Cosgrave, Mulcahy was offered a parliamentary secretary's appointment some time after his resignation from the military in 1924, which, he states, he 'naturally' refused.

Mulcahy would have considered that his full-time occupation as a parliamentarian from 1922-1961 was his single most important contribution to Ireland and its welfare, even if it contrasted in terms of notoriety and public recognition with his earlier military role. Despite his diminishing profile with historians and some newspaper correspondents, he continued to play an active and effective role in parliament and his party.

CUMANN NA NGAEDHEAL

Maryann Valiulis, in her paper *After the revolution: The formative years of Cumann na nGaedheal,*[1] underlines the considerable stresses which existed within the Cumann na nGaedheal Party from 1923-1927. Many of the party's members, who were still committed to the Treaty and vehemently opposed to de Valera, believed that the government, and particularly the Cabinet, was failing to satisfy the more nationalistic aspirations of the revolutionary movement. According to the dissidents, the government, in strictly adhering to the spirit and the letter of the Treaty, was maintaining the power and privileges of the wealthy Protestant minority; and was retaining the institutions of the British regime while neglecting the needs of their own supporters, who had fought for the freedom of Ireland and had supported the Treaty. My father, as one of the leaders of the party and the pro-Treaty group, as well as being outside the Cabinet, was in a unique position to act as the honest broker between the two conflicting groups. On a few occasions he played a role in mediating between the government and the dissidents. Valiulis highlights the party's difficulties up to 1926, and the Cabinet's conservative approach to party organisation and its limited efforts to formulate a national grass roots system of support, as some reasons for the government's failure to maintain public support from 1927 onwards.

Her analysis of the evolution of Cumann na nGaedheal during the 1920s makes interesting reading and is based on the party's minute books and on the extensive papers in the Mulcahy collection. However, Valiulis fails to mention the difficulties which were created for the government and the pro-Treaty group by the constant public opposition and sniping by defeated republicans: whether it was sneering at the ministerial top hats and fraternising with British ministers, accusations of being traitors and West Britons, or shooting the odd policeman. One is reminded that had it not been for the common enemy of the anti-Treatyites, the Cosgrave government might not have survived for long after its formation in 1923. It was perhaps fortunate for the Treaty supporters that the Cosgrave government did survive until 1932. Without the assassination of Kevin O'Higgins in August 1927, and the second election after his death which gave the government a more stable majority, the government might have been defeated much earlier. Despite the fact that the Treaty was supported by more than 80 percent of the people in the 1922 election, the Cumann na nGaedheal Party won only 47 out of 153 seats in the first election in June 1927. It continued in government because of support from other groups and the absence of the forty-four Fianna Fáil deputies who had not yet entered the Dáil.

However, the government only survived by the chairman's casting vote when Fianna Fáil were forced by a new electoral act to enter the Dáil in August 1927, after the O'Higgins death. Six of the Fianna Fáil deputies refused to join Dev in entering the Dáil. Otherwise the government would have been defeated after the second election in September 1927. The government was to survive another five years, although it was far from being stable during this period. By 1927 the government and Cumann na nGaedheal had lost much of its support to other parties, including Labour, the Farmers' party, the Nationalist League, a large number of independents, and even to Fianna Fáil. In 1930 Cosgrave was defeated in the Dáil and promptly resigned, but he was forced to continue because de Valera refused to form a government.

Mulcahy speaks at length about the inexorable decline and fall of the Cumann na nGaedheal government. It was suffering the political consequences of the Army Mutiny and of the government's neglect of the army after the mutiny: a situation which, he states, was compounded by the lack of interest and sympathy of the two ministers of defence who succeeded him, Hughes and Desmond Fitzgerald. He thought that Hughes, who replaced him as minister for defence shortly after his resignation, was particularly unsuitable for the post and had no qualifications for the position. He believed that Desmond FitzGerald, who replaced Hughes after he was defeated in the first 1927 election, was out to 'destroy the army'. He describes the disillusionment of the soldiers and the many who supported the government during the difficult times of the Civil War. He believed the government had alienated itself not only from the army following the mutiny, but from the spirit of the IRB, the Irish language, and other symbols of the national movement.

The failed Boundary Commission was another factor in the party's decline. Mulcahy reminds us that Michael Tierney, in his biography of MacNeill, attributes the Boundary Commission's failure to ambiguities in Article 12 of the Treaty.[12] Perhaps most of all, the Cabinet's lack of sympathy for and cooperation with its own supporters in Cumann na nGaedheal inevitably aided its own decline. Cumann na nGaedheal would also lose the support of the Labour deputies by 1927 because of its stinginess in dealing with the poorer members of the community, taking a shilling off the old age pension and, later, a shilling off the school teachers'. The Labour leaders believed that the government was more sympathetic to the rich and consequently to the old establishment. This apparently was the principal reason the Labour party changed its allegiance to Fianna Fáil. The government was also accused of favouring the small and privileged Protestant minority. There was some truth in that assertion, but it was a result of Griffith's agreement during the Treaty negotiations that the Free State would not victimise them.

Mulcahy was critical of the party's organisation and policies for several other reasons. He regretted its failure to retain the Sinn Féin name and he believed it had alienated itself from the economic policies of Arthur Griffith. He makes no reference to the part that the execution policy during the Civil War and the prolonged war itself may have played in alienating some of the party's supporters. Despite the fact that he received a huge vote in the 1923 election immediately after the end of the Civil War (confirming the electorate's approval of his role in bringing the war to an end), the government did poorly, and even at this early date was already showing significant signs of waning support. Most of all, as indicated previously, the party lost support because of the Cabinet's poor relations with its own rank and file and because of its total neglect of constituency-level organisation; and all this at a time when Fianna Fáil was setting up its efficient network of cumanns across the country. Mulcahy had apparently been critical of the party because of its neglect of an efficient electoral machine and particularly its public-relations failures. Constituency organisation depended largely on the impulses of local TDs, and in general was patchy or nonexistent. For example, virtually all of the Fine Gael TDs in 1944 were veterans of the early state and had grossly neglected their constituencies. Compared to Fianna Fáil's well-oiled machine, the Fine Gael organisation (and its precursor, Cumann na nGaedheal) was clearly ineffective in most parts of the country.

Michael Hayes, the chairman of the Dáil and the closest to Cosgrave, believed that Cosgrave was more interested in the health and fate of the country than the Cumann na nGaedheal Party. This view is supported by Cosgrave's anxiety to encourage the democratic process by forcing the Fianna Fáil deputies to enter the Dáil, even though their entry was certain to be a serious threat to the survival of his government; and further supported by other aspects of his tenure of office, including his insistence that the attorney general should be independent of government and a policy of avoiding all forms of political patronage.

The party's policies of refusing political patronage is encapsulated in the following paragraphs from my father's memoirs and was, I believe, a major reason for the defection of many supporters. My father's commitment to this policy is evident from the following paragraphs.

Included in the 1927-1932 ministry papers are numerous letters from supporters and others seeking his support for members of family and friends who were seeking jobs in the public services. His responses to these letters almost invariably underline his inability or unwillingness to help because of structures which had been put in place by the government to ensure that such appointments were made based on merit and not through political influence. The Local and Civil Service Appointments Commissions were specifically set up by the Cumann na nGaedheal Government in 1926 to ensure that there would be no nepotism in public appointments. By being direct and blunt with favour-seekers, he undoubtedly confirmed his reputation for integrity. However, the following letter noted in the archives was not likely to enhance my father's popularity with his supporters. It was in response to a letter he received from a supporter in Cork, who wrote to Mulcahy on behalf of a public health nurse seeking a job, claiming the support of the Bishop of Cork:

> No, the Bishop of Cork did not write to me . . . and, in any case, it wouldn't be any use in this case. The appointment will be filled as a result of a selection committee examining all possible applicants, and their general experience and qualifications . . . without any marks for

religion or changes of religion. Besides, too, there really is a ministerial function to be exercised and it could not be exercised by anyone telling people what nurses should be appointed, and what workmen, and what carpenters, and what engineers, and what doctors, etc etc. So please . . .[3]

One wonders at times if it is possible to remain for any length of time in office without political patronage. The same concern for country over party may be characteristic of the Cabinet in general, and may be one reason for their increasing unpopularity during their tenure. It is said that a politician is someone who looks forward to the next election, while a statesman is someone who looks forward to the next generation. I have often wondered about the definition of 'statesman'. My Random House dictionary defines it as 'a man who is experienced in the art of government or who exhibits great wisdom and ability in affairs of government'. I would add to that integrity, and in this sense Cosgrave certainly deserves the title; as indeed do many of his colleagues in the first Cumann na nGaedheal government.

In her examination of the evolution of the Cumann na nGaedheal Party during the 1923-1932 period, Valiulis refers to the government's disdain for the ordinary workings of the organisation and its failure to appreciate the need of having strong grass roots support. She writes:

> . . . at a party meeting discussing an appeal which was to be made for funds, Richard Mulcahy, former minister for defence, suggested that President Cosgrave's name would be a more effective fund-raiser than that of Eoin MacNeill, president of the organisation and the proposed signatory on the circular. The indignant reply of Kevin O'Higgins testified to the type of disdain felt about this kind of activity. O'Higgins rejected Mulcahy's proposal and rather contemptuously added that he hoped that they had not yet reached the point where it was necessary for the president to appeal for funds.

Mulcahy made other comments about the party's woes in the late 1920s. He regretted the departure from politics of his friend, Eoin MacNeill, following the Boundary Commission debacle. He thought Joe McGrath's resignation in

1924, at the time of the mutiny, was a major loss to the government despite the fact that McGrath had supported the army mutineers and was opposed to Mulcahy. J. J. Walsh's defection from the party in 1927 was also a big loss considering his interest and proactive outlook on economics, his pragmatist disposition, his attributes as a good organiser, and his strong nationalist outlook (my mother even described him as an early Seán Lemass). Walsh's entrepreneurial attributes were recognised as early as November 1921, when the Cabinet awarded him a grant of £2,000 to assist in Ireland's participation in the Olympic Games in Paris. Mulcahy believed Walsh pulled out of the second election because of his disillusionment with the Cabinet's conservative economic policies, perhaps feeling that he could be better occupied elsewhere. Mulcahy believed the rest of the Cabinet, with the exception of Paddy McGilligan, had lost some of the nationalist spirit engendered by the War of Independence and the setting up of the first Dáil.

Mulcahy saw in O'Higgins, Blythe, Fitzgerald, John Marcus O'Sullivan, Hogan and to a lesser extent Cosgrave, a group that lost its support in the country because of their reactionary economic policies and their gradual distancing from the economic, social and nationalistic policies of Griffith. When he was critical of Liam Burke, the party secretary, for his lack of interest in grass roots activities, John Marcus O'Sullivan, the minister for education, accused Mulcahy of 'being out after Burke'. Despite this charge, both Burke and O'Sullivan were close friends of my father's at the time and remained so afterwards. The sixteen years in opposition beginning in 1932 can also be attributed to organisational neglect. According to Denis Burke of Clonmel,[4] as early as 1934 Mulcahy was advocating involvement in local politics but was clearly unable to bring any great enthusiasm for it to the party, or for more active constituency involvement, until he replaced Cosgrave as president in 1944. His first act as president was to insist on more constituency-level activity and to bring fresh talent into the ailing party. During the twelve years of opposition before he assumed the presidency of the party in 1944, he may have had the right ideas about party organisation, but he must have lacked the influence or energy to have them accepted by Cosgrave and his colleagues. I expect that he did not push his views on constituency organisation in order to avoid conflict with his front bench colleagues. However, from 1944 onwards the party assumed a much more active role, both at grass roots level in the constituencies and in opposition in parliament. The party's subsequent revival bears testimony to the success of this previously much neglected initiative.

THE IRISH LANGUAGE

Perhaps Mulcahy's most important contribution during the period 1924-1927, when he found himself in something of a political wilderness, was to chair the Gaeltacht Commission. This appointment was made despite the opposition of some of his colleagues, including Ernest Blythe, minister for finance, who, more than any other Cabinet member (besides Eoin MacNeill), shared with him a strong commitment to the revival of the Irish language. This opposition was surely a reflection of the residue of animus towards Mulcahy by some members of the Cabinet, no doubt the result of their guilt at causing his earlier resignation. It was an unpaid appointment, but one which he accepted with enthusiasm because of his lifelong dedication to Irish language and Irish culture. While he was in the Cabinet he had already suggested a commission to investigate the extent and viability of the Gaeltacht, and also influenced the Cabinet to set up a manuscript commission. At a meeting celebrating the ninetieth anniversary of the first Dáil, Michael D. Higgins referred to the Gaeltacht Commission and thought it a remarkable and comprehensive contribution to our knowledge of the Gaeltacht areas.

Ernest Blythe was a Northern Protestant and was minister for finance in the Irish Free State government. He and my father, who was then minister for local government and public health, were both excellent self-taught Irish speakers, and were enthusiastic about the Irish language revival. Both were responsible for the establishment of Coláiste Mhuire, an Irish speaking secondary school in Parnell Square; and Mulcahy was also involved in converting the Model boys and girls primary schools in Marlborough Street to Irish speaking schools. It is my understanding that Eoin MacNeill joined him in this initiative.

It was characteristic of Mulcahy – and perhaps an indication of his wishful thinking – that he was confident the Irish language would be successfully revived by the policies adopted by the government in the early years of the state. Michael Tierney was pessimistic about its revival in an article in *Studies* in March 1926.[1] Mulcahy, in a following article,[2] replied that it could be restored as the functional language of Ireland. He pointed to the examples of Greece before the time of Aristotle, Finland after the Swedish hegemony had ended, and the survival of French as the functional language of the Canadian province Quebec. We might wonder why, despite the efforts of two prominent ministers who were devoted to the Irish language and its propagation, the Irish language movement failed to gain much ground, and why the Gaeltacht has since undergone slow and inexorable decline. The reasons are numerous and complex, and, as is common with matters of language and religion, rational discussion on the subject is easily impaired by emotion and prejudice. Irish could only be revived by stimulating an esteem and love for the language and its culture: it could not be revived by financial incentives, by the deóntas (money in return for speaking Irish in the Gaeltacht areas) and the greed they induced, or by compulsion. Sadly, public policies copper-fastened the widespread indifference to the language among the people and contributed to resentment and cynicism of it, instead of the esteem which this beautiful language deserves.

Many of Mulcahy's political colleagues had a perhaps more realistic opinion about the prospects of revival; and many others were entirely indifferent, caring little about the language's revival as a cultural or political factor in the future of the state. By 1922, English had long been the functional language of Ireland in every aspect of life – social, cultural, economic, professional, scientific and academic. Even ignoring Ireland's close ties with Britain and the United States and other English-speaking countries, the rapid, global spread of English (particularly in business and the sciences) made it increasingly likely that the revival of Irish as a functional language would not happen.

The 1916 Rising and subsequent political events could not easily or effectively reverse the trend away from Irish towards an anglicised culture among the people, particularly in our urban areas. The heavy emigration of Irish to English-speaking countries during the last ninety years was an added disincentive. The effects of the Civil War were still evident into the late forties and early fifties, when Mulcahy was minister for education, at least among politicians. To get rid of compulsory Irish in schools at that time might have been correct practically-speaking, but might also have been politically disastrous, allowing the ultra-nationalistic Fianna Fáil to portray my father as being pro-Britain, and hence condemn him as being anti-Ireland. This was part of the realpolitik of the 1940s and 1950s. With the powerful cultural effects of the Celtic Revival in the late nineteenth and early twentieth centuries, which embraced all classes and denominations, we might argue that its influence was more successful in reviving Irish, even if it were deemed to be an elitist rather than a functional language. Despite the best and noble ambitions of its leaders, the 1916 Rising effectively put an end to this important pluralism, and the baleful effects of a more extreme and rigid nationalism were compounded by the Civil War, distracting the country from the cultural revival.

For these and other reasons, it is not surprising that the Irish language revival policy of the last ninety years has not succeeded, at least in terms of its revival as a widely accepted spoken language. But the rot of compulsion, hypocrisy, cynicism and the deóntas-mentality may have had its beginnings even before the Civil War. The early Dáil Cabinets had a minister for Irish (Sceilg, an Irish-speaker from County Kerry) and at least a notional department. It also had an assistant minister, paid £400 annually, £50 more than the assistant minister for defence and chief of staff! Yet, despite 115 meetings of the Cabinet from March 1919 to December 1921, there is scant mention of Irish or its minister. One of the rare references to Irish was to consider granting a sum of $25-50,000 to establish an Irish-language bookstore in New York and possibly in Chicago.[3] Whether or not the plan was implemented is unclear. Another was to award fishing associations who agreed to conduct their work in Irish a 20 percent grant on any loan they received from the government.[4] On the latter date the minister for Irish was asked to approach the Gaelic League to formulate a policy aimed at the revival of Irish. Otherwise, the Irish language received no attention from the Cabinet, and one wonders what occupied the minister and his assistant who were both in full-time positions, at least in terms of salary.

The questions of general education policy after the foundation of the State, and specifically of the Irish language policy in the schools, are raised a few times in Mulcahy's tapes. He refers to the residual effects and political distractions of the Civil War. As in the case of other nationalist aspirations which might have evolved after the Treaty, the Civil War and its aftermath destroyed much of the country's interest in Irish language revival. The general cynicism that was the product of the war spilled over to the language, with one side claiming to be 'more Irish' than the other, the other side being naturally defensive about this.

The Oireachtas, too, can be blamed for the failure of the revival. Political leaders were quick to make Irish compulsory for an indifferent people, while making little attempt to adopt the language as a functional part of legislative proceedings. Logically, they should have made a good, working knowledge of Irish an essential qualification for Dáil and Senate candidates, having already insisted that the same condition be applied to most public and educational appointments. It was surely a reflection on the Oireachtas that only a handful of members over the years of self-rule could speak Irish well enough to use the language in Dáil and Senate proceedings.

The great majority of Cumann na nGaedheal and Fianna Fáil deputies cared little about the revival of Irish, whatever lip service they may have paid to the subject. Mulcahy complains about the lack of sympathy for the language and the lack of cooperation shared by some of his colleagues in the Cumann na nGaedheal Cabinet. He singles out John Marcus O'Sullivan particularly, who succeeded Eoin MacNeill as minister for education in 1925 and who made little effort to solve some of Mulcahy's difficulties in maintaining Scoil Muire and Scoil Colmcille as Irish-speaking primary schools. The Irish language provided the emerging state with its most prolific source of cynicism and cant.

In 1963, Mulcahy spoke at length about the Department of Education as he found it on taking office in 1948. It took him six months to realise the nature and extent of the malaise he found there, a malaise which was then being further aggravated by a six-month teachers' strike.

There was no sense of initiative, vision or power; no cerebration. The reason was that there had been no ministerial function in the department for years and that Derrig[i] was simply a bluebottle on a window there. The department did not believe in the policy they were operating for [compulsory] Irish and they had no idea of the attitude to the language of the native speakers in the Gaeltacht, where the language was in progressive decline. There was no policy for primary or secondary education, and university education was neglected by both the department and the universities themselves.

I asked him if he had had confidence in the compulsory Irish policy. He answered, 'I hadn't but I was caught for a way out.' And he added later,

I often feel ashamed of myself to think I was in the Department of Education for two periods of office . . . I ask myself, 'what did I do there?'

Aside from his perceived failings as minister for education, Mulcahy complained on several occasions that the then-minister for finance, Paddy McGilligan, was not only excessively stingy in giving money to the Department of Education, but was almost impossible to even contact. McGilligan was frequently absent from Cabinet meetings, usually for health reasons, and it is my belief that his wife was over-protective, and looked after him with consummate care. (Incidentally, her ministrations were obviously effective, for he lived to the reasonably advanced age of ninety.) On the other hand, the difficulty of contacting him was no doubt an advantage to a finance minister who was likely to be perceived by his colleagues the gate-keeper of a bottomless pit of money. This might explain Mulcahy's financial problems as minister. Despite his frustrations with McGilligan, my father nevertheless had a high opinion of McGilligan's abilities, and they and their wives always remained close friends.

Paddy Lynch, who was a confidante of Costello's during the first Inter-Party Government and became Ireland's first 'spin doctor', told me that the Department of Education was treated with near-contempt by other ministers and departments. From discussing and reading other accounts of Inter-Party affairs, I feel that Mulcahy, as minister, was also treated with little respect and

[i] Thomas Derrig had been the longstanding Fianna Fáil minister for education for the party's entire administration from 1932 to 1948.

that his seniority in the Cabinet counted for little. I do not think that even as early as 1948, when he first became minister for education, he showed any sense of innovativeness about the inert movement for language revival; he was happy to accept the status quo. Compulsory Irish remained a volatile, though sleeping, movement; carefully watched over by both post-Treaty parties, lest one be accused of being less patriotic than the other. I expect that my father, like his other political colleagues, did not wish to stir the dormant passions which can bedevil a language movement; and neither was he likely to welcome the political implications of confronting such a controversial issue. Even in 1948, Mulcahy and his colleagues on both sides of the political divide must have known that the compulsory Irish policy was not succeeding and was not likely to succeed in the future without radical and effective changes in policies and public attitudes.

Mulcahy's conservatism, most evident in his later years, was symptomatic of his civil servant mentality and training. If a political mentality requires a propensity to challenge of the status quo and a willingness to adopt new ideas, then Mulcahy was hardly suited to a political role, at least during his later years in parliament. I think the day Mulcahy handed over the de facto party leadership to Costello marked his last contribution to Irish politics, except for his later vigorous and successful campaigns against two of de Valera's proposals to abolish proportional representation.

Mulcahy did, however, set up a council of education to advise the government on the function and curriculum of the primary schools. This decision was approved by the Cabinet on 21 March 1950. The council reported to his Fianna Fáil successor in 1954 and its recommendations are summarised by Dr John Coolahan:

> It called for no fundamental or radical changes though it did urge the inclusion of drawing, nature study and physical education as compulsory subjects, and it called for a more generous scheme of scholarships for pupil participation in secondary education.[5]

Few of these recommendations were implemented. In 1954 the council undertook an appraisal of the secondary school curriculum and provided its report in 1960, which was published in 1962. Coolahan points out that 'It identified the dominant purpose of the schools as the inculcation of religious ideals and values.' It too made certain recommendations, but had little effect on general education policy – until Donough O'Malley introduced free, universal secondary education in 1967. The 1960 report had concluded that free secondary education was an 'untenable' and 'Utopian' ideal.[6] Politics is rightly described as the art of the possible, but O'Malley, for one, showed that sometimes the impossible is possible, even in a highly conservative society.

The Irish language and Gaelic culture were the keystones of Mulcahy's sense of nationality. Although proficient in Irish himself and maintaining an Irish-speaking household, his thirty-five years in parliament and six years as minister for education did not appear to encourage him to promote policies any more progressive than those of successive governments. Whatever his exact thoughts on the subject might have been, I cannot recall any criticism by him of compulsory Irish in schools or of any other aspect of Irish language policy; nor can I recall his expounding any innovative ideas on the subject. It seems that during his life he never showed any real initiative to alter affairs unless he had a specific role to lead, rather than simply participate, in public service. Indeed it is remarkable how a patently unsuccessful language policy gave rise to so little public comment or concern over so many years. The entire Irish programme was by and large an ineffective and poorly-executed exercise – truly successful only in alienating the people. As Eoin MacNeill wrote:

> You might as well be putting wooden legs on hens as trying to restore Irish through the schools alone.[7]

And yet it is ironic that it was MacNeill, as minister for education, who in 1924 introduced compulsory Irish in the primary schools and a compulsory subject for the intermediate and leaving certificate examinations. There was some resistance to the Irish revival policy by academics like Michael Tierney. But I believe that, while a few ministers – including Mulcahy, Blythe and perhaps MacNeill – sincerely believed in the programme, the real cause behind such an unsuccessful approach may have been the damage the Rising and the rhetoric of the republic did to the pluralistic legacy of the Celtic Revival. Irish children were subjected to compulsory Irish in the schools from the early years of the state, but they were poorly taught in most cases, certainly in terms of learning Irish as a spoken, functional language. This situation remains despite the success of the Gaelscoil movement. Many teachers were unfit to teach the language, either because of their ignorance of the tongue, or because of their training; while other teachers were simply cynical about the revival of Irish and about the utility of the revival programme. And when the children went home and into the outside world, they found that English was the only language spoken.

1932 AND AFTER: OPPOSITION AND THE INTER-PARTY GOVERNMENTS

After his resignation from the Department of Defence in 1924, my father's public life and his full-time commitment to politics continued without interruption until his retirement as president of Fine Gael in 1959. It is true that, in the public perception, his stature as a national leader was gradually overshadowed by events and by his successors. That is not to say, however, that he did not continue to contribute to the advancement of the country. During the thirty-seven years from 1924-1961, Mulcahy was one of the most active and diligent parliamentarians in the Dáil and for two brief periods in the Senate. He devoted his time fully to the affairs of the legislature and to his own political party. In his full-time capacity as a parliamentarian, he held many briefs and acted as a watchdog for his party in the Dáil and in the country in general. He was undemonstrative by nature, both in his public and private life, and did not use the histrionic techniques employed by some politicians to attract public attention. His speeches were described as long and boring, and this was certainly true of his later years. In his last few years his letters began to resemble his speeches, such that on one occasion in commenting on one letter, I wrote:

> It is a most perfect example of his tortuous and parenthetical writing which was a feature of his last years.

Another stated that, following his acknowledged contribution to the State up to 1924, he failed to give any further worthwhile service. It is certainly true that he was an unsuccessful politician, in terms of his personal fortunes and as measured by political advancement and material acquisition, but we might ask what success really means in politics. I suspect it would depend on whether one viewed politics as a career or a vocation. He would have been satisfied that his own long contribution to parliament and to the democratic process, unspectacular as it may have been in the perception of our present day media, was the type of success to which he would consider it proper to aspire.

Mulcahy remained in the Dáil until 1961, with two short breaks in 1937 and 1943 when he was defeated in two elections. He was fortunate that both parliaments lasted only one year, and was returned in 1938 and 1944. He retired from the Dublin North-East constituency in 1944, to take up Gerry Ryan's seat in Tipperary South Riding. Dublin North-East was a three-seat constituency, with four 'big guns': Jim Larkin, the well-known labour leader, Alfie Byrne, the long-standing lord mayor of Dublin, Oscar Traynor, the Fianna Fáil minister, and Richard Mulcahy. Mulcahy, as leader of the Fine Gael Party in 1944, probably thought it more prudent to move to a safe seat in Tipperary South Riding. I recall the numbing shock in the household in 1937 when he first failed to be elected. A blanket of gloom settled on the family and on many of his supporters. The only person who remained calm and serene, at least externally, was the failed candidate himself.

The Fianna Fáil electoral success in 1932 must have been a sore disappointment to Mulcahy, his family and his colleagues in Cumann na nGaedheal; although he found some consolation in the fact that the army was entirely loyal to the new administration, so recently its opponent in war. Fianna Fáil's success in the 1933 election must have been an even greater disappointment, particularly as Cumann na nGaedheal lost nine seats and Fianna Fáil gained an overall majority. I recall the 1933 election because of the serious disturbances, caused by Fianna Fáil and IRA supporters, which occurred at the Cumann na nGaedheal public meetings. I remember being present at a large meeting where my father, Mrs Collins O'Driscoll and other candidates were attempting to address the public at the Parnell Monument in

O'Connell Street. The speakers could not be heard because of continuous, loud interruptions; and shortly after the meeting started, the platform was rushed, and the meeting broke up in disorder. It was a serious complaint among Cumann na nGaedheal supporters that the Guards made little effort to control the mob. These and earlier disorders, and the inability of the police to control the crowds, were largely responsible for the birth of the Blueshirt movement and its precursor, the Army Comrades Association. The ACA was first organised by ex-army officers in early 1932 to ensure that the new Fianna Fáil Government did not purge the army after its anticipated success in the 1932 election. By 1933 it had adopted the role of protecting the democratic right to free speech, which was perceived to be under serious threat with Cumann na nGaedheal platforms being attacked by Republican and Fianna Fáil mobs. Mulcahy speaks of the setting up of the Blue Shirt movement. Members of the ACA met around July 1933 at the Cumann na nGaedheal headquarters at 5 Parnell Square to decide on a uniform for their organisation. Both blue and grey were considered, but Mulcahy was the only person present to favour grey. A subsequent convention, attended by a large number of ACA members in the Hibernian Hotel on 22 August 1933, was held to elect a successor to Dr Tom O'Higgins, who had been head of the ACA but who was prevented from continuing because of his full-time post as chief medical officer of County Meath. Both Mulcahy and O'Duffy were proposed, but Mulcahy refused to go forward, saying later that 'I had no fancy for that particular type of thing at all.' When I questioned him about O'Duffy, he said that he was on good terms with him in the army, that he was an excellent organiser, and that later he was considered a 'spectacular and colourful' figure. Although, he added, O'Duffy was 'a bit of a prima donna'. O'Duffy later replaced Cosgrave as head of the party and the other parties, including the Farmers' Party, which joined them to form Fine Gael. He soon became more bellicose and his leadership was short-lived, being terminated after the Blueshirt organisation was banned by the government. Whatever about his merits as a senior army officer and as a highly regarded head of the emerging police force, he proved disastrous as a political leader.

At no time during the turbulent days of the 1933 election did the Fianna Fáil leaders condemn the disturbances and riots. I recall it as a disorderly and dangerous time when there were fears that the government might take Civil War-like, draconian measures against the Opposition. The government, however, was restrained by many factors, including the presence of the standing army and the fact that many important families – such as my mother's, the Ryans of Wexford – had strong support and influence on both sides of the political divide. No doubt a strong middle class was another safeguard of Irish democracy.

Mulcahy was active in the Blueshirts when it was led by Eoin O'Duffy, but his commitment to O'Duffy must have been short-lived. My father was, of course, totally opposed to the fascist concept of a corporate state, and so too were the rest of his colleagues in Fine Gael. However, there was a great feeling of respect and admiration among the Irish for Mussolini and the tremendous advances he had made in the Italian state and in the enhanced prestige of Italy during the 1930s. De Valera was one of many to express their admiration for Mussolini's successes and the widespread rejection of Mussolini's regime was largely retrospective among the Irish.

In her epilogue, Valiulis states that, after 1924, Mulcahy no longer occupied the centre stage in Irish affairs. Certainly his star began to wane as he occupied himself almost exclusively with party work and settled down to the life of an active parliamentarian. In particular, his role as one of the founders of the State was gradually forgotten, especially as his own contemporaries began fading from the scene and as he became more involved in the mundane, low-profile work of party organisation. Although he remained president of Fine Gael from 1944-1959, his public image faded further during Costello's tenure as Taoiseach in the two Inter-Party Governments, with the perception that Costello was the de facto leader. I suspect that the circumstances of the relationship between Mulcahy and Costello bear an analogy to his earlier relationship with Michael Collins: Mulcahy was the *de jure* head, but Costello was perceived to be the 'real leader'. This circumstance did not bother my father in any way, and indeed, with his deference to Costello's capacity as leader of the government, he probably contributed to his own overshadowing.

About this time Aknefton, in the *Irish Times* on 5 September 1953, wrote about the leadership of Fine Gael:

> . . . so John Costello became Taoiseach. But Mulcahy is the power behind Fine Gael. This role of Machiavelli behind the throne is nothing new to Richard Mulcahy. The same old story repeats itself time after time. Rory O'Connor, Michael Collins – these men and many others were celebrated in song and story; yet the chief of staff, the man who accepted military responsibility for the whole campaign against the Black-and-Tans was Richard Mulcahy. In this man you find cold, ruthless logic, a master mind, if you like, but not the popular appeal which will bring the mass of voters to the polls shouting 'Up, Mulcahy' as they would be prepared to shout 'Up, Dev'.

I think the writer takes a rather oblique view of my father when he invests him with the attributes of 'the Prince', as Dev once described Machiavelli to my father. I would think of him more as being a backroom boy who had an unusual gift for organisation and a strong dedication to achieving his goals, but who lacked the vanity which can only be satisfied by the approval of others. I suspect that he was too self-effacing to be Machiavellian, and while Aknefton might be correct in describing Mulcahy's previous role in the army and politics, he certainly was not the power behind the throne in 1953, although without him the throne would remain empty.

While he was a dedicated worker for Cumann na nGaedheal and its successor, Fine Gael, and its principal watchdog in parliament during its long years in opposition; he failed to make an impact on the country as a political innovator or as a political controversialist. His six years in the Department of Education (1948-51 and 1954-58), during which time he buried himself in the work of the department, further removed him from the public eye. He was also not by temperament a person born with a desire for the mantle of leadership – he lacked the thirst for power, and he lacked the mystique and detachment from the the people which attracts the loyalty, admiration and adherence of others. But, when he was thrust into leadership, as he was from 1918 to 1924, he did not shirk the responsibilities of his office. Any success he had as a leader was based almost entirely on his organisational ability, on his

197

diplomacy in dealing with difficult situations and colleagues, and on his dedication to the ideals of his own political creed.

During World War II Mulcahy represented the Fine Gael Party on the National Defence Conference, a body set up to advise the government on general wartime policy. Fine Gael's request to have a national government at the beginning of the war was refused by de Valera, so the Conference was established as an alternative. Mulcahy attended meetings regularly but was totally disenchanted by its proceedings, claiming that Dev paid only lip service to its deliberations and recommendations. Just as he did during the Treaty days, Dev kept things close to his chest. Nonetheless, Mulcahy did appear on the same platform as Dev and his ministers during the recruitment campaign in the early years of World War II.

Mulcahy had been leader of Fine Gael since 1944, and had seen his party recover during his first ten years as leader from a parlous state of decline, with only thirty seats and a general state of demoralisation to fifty seats in the 1954 election. He led the party into a new spirit of enthusiasm and confidence, inspired by a fresh influx of post-Civil War youth and talent. He retained the leadership of the Fine Gael Party during the two Inter-Party Governments of 1948-1951 and 1954-1957, although the perception of his leadership role was blurred by Costello's appointment as Taoiseach on both occasions and by Costello continuing as leader of the Opposition from 1951-1954 and 1957-1959. Mulcahy's presidency of Fine Gael continued from 1944 until he retired in 1959, nominating James Dillon as his successor. He apparently preferred Costello as his successor, but Costello refused to take the presidency in a full-time capacity. This caused my father to nominate Dillon and to say, rather harshly, about his close friend Costello that he had 'reneged on his leadership'.

In his letter on 26 October 1959, refusing the leadership of the party, Costello finished with a warm tribute to my father:

> Your selfless and unselfish devotion, indomitable courage, and tireless energy have ever been an inspiration to me, and sustained us all in the work that we were doing, and in the conviction that we were working not merely for party but for Ireland. Not only have you never looked for

reward or thanks – you never even thought of it. If your recompense is not here it will be hereafter.

And T. J. O'Farrell, writing at the time of my father's retirement, finished by saying:

> I admired your very quiet, unassuming demeanour for a man with such a national record. That has been your attitude ever since in a period of national stress and storm and peril. You are one of those who helped to build this state at the same time as you defended it, in circumstances that were at times as fantastic as they were baffling and perilous. You have made history that will last long after you and I have passed to other realms. Thanks for what you have done.

Stephen Barrett wrote from Cork:

> I would like you to know that many people share my personal conviction that your time in public life has done more for the country than almost any living being.

Before his resignation from the presidency of Fine Gael, he fought a vigorous battle against de Valera's proposal to abolish proportional representation and to create single-seat constituencies without a transferable vote. He saw Dev's proposal as a move to perpetuate the hegemony of Fianna Fáil and as a threat to the democratic system as a whole. His other colleagues in Fine Gael were equally committed to resisting the move, as were all other political parties – except, of course, for Fianna Fáil. Despite objections by Fine Gael and the other opposition parties, the government insisted on holding the necessary referendum on the same day Dev was opposing Sean MacEoin for the presidency of Ireland. Dev was elected fairly comfortably, but the opposition parties were vindicated when the proposal to abolish proportional representation was defeated equally comfortably.

To me it seemed that, with this new threat to democracy, my father's leadership qualities and energetic responsiveness rose briefly from the ashes. During the entire campaign leading up to the referendum, Mulcahy was singularly committed to opposing his old foe, Dev. A second attempt a few years later to achieve the same constitutional change was again resisted vigorously and was again defeated.

Valiulis refers to Mulcahy's problems when he took over the leadership of Fine Gael. Apart from himself, who had always regularly attended at the Dáil and who was the only member of his party to fully devote his time to political work, attendances by his colleagues in 1944 were only sporadic. The poor level of political participation by the politicians themselves was symptomatic of a demoralised and flagging political party and general opposition. Support for Fine Gael country-wide was gradually waning, and there was talk of the party's early demise. His worries about the party's survival were aggravated by his failure to get candidates to stand for four of the five by-elections in December 1945, and for one later by-election. Fine Gael won none of the ten by-elections during the 1944-1947 period, the time in which Seán MacBride's Clann na Poblachta came to prominence.

Mulcahy's worries were further aggravated when Liam Cosgrave, the son of William Cosgrave, who was elected to the Dáil in 1943, announced his intention to resign from the party. Liam was one of the few young post-Civil War deputies in the party and was highly thought of as a promising politician, an excellent constituency worker and a potential future leader. By attending carefully to his constituency of Dun Laoghaire/Rathdown, Cosgrave was one of the few members of the party to realise the importance of grass roots support. His constituency work was reflected in the strong support he received in successive elections. Mulcahy believed that his resignation would have had a disastrous effect on the party's image. Fortunately, however, despite Cosgrave's misgivings about the party's future, he was persuaded to remain. He was eventually to be Parliamentary Secretary to the Taoiseach in the first Inter-Party Government and minister for external affairs in the second. He was appointed head of the party after Dillon resigned and was Taoiseach in the 1973-1977 coalition government.

Mulcahy had always favoured a more active political machine and much better attention to constituency organisation, similar to Fianna Fáil's policies. As soon as he took over the leadership of Fine Gael, he threw himself into the task of restoring the fortunes of the party by building a more effective organisation, through more active participation by the deputies in the Dáil and by mobilising more active constituency support throughout the country. After the 1943 election, when Fine Gael lost a further ten seats bringing it down to thirty seats, it was widely believed that the party was in the last throes of decline. However, the 1948 election marked the turning point of the party's fortunes. Although the number of elected TDs remained pitifully small, with an increase of one member only, the former drift was reversed at least and, most important, there were seven new, young and ambitious TDs elected who promised to reinvigorate the party. My family and I can recall my father's strenuous and dedicated work to restore the party's fortunes during the first four years of his presidency. Without a car, he travelled the four corners of Ireland on an autocycle – a heavy bicycle with a 100cc engine to propel the front wheel. He carried two heavy leather panniers on the back carrier, and a heavy leather coat protected him from the elements. He had told his party members that he was available to travel to any constituency in the country and was thus almost always away at weekends. As leader of the party, he did not have the use of a car until the start of the general election campaign in 1948.

Valiulis gives him full credit for reviving the fortunes of the party through his dedicated organisational work, the constant pressure and encouragement he exerted on his colleagues to be more active and visible in opposition and in their constituencies, and his seminal role in forming the two Inter-Party Governments of 1948 and 1954. Fine Gael was never a party to uphold a 'hall of heroes', but his colleagues in the 1940s and 1950s would certainly acknowledge the important part he played in restoring the fortunes of his party, and as a family we were well aware of his unique contribution. Prof. John Murphy, in his review of Valiulis's biography, states that she is too generous in crediting him with the reversal of Fine Gael's fortunes in the 1950s. While acknowledging the important encouragement to the party provided by participation in the Inter-Party Government (an institution which was Mulcahy's brainchild), I know of no other factor which may have contributed to the turnaround apart from his tireless encouragement and emphasis on the importance of constituency work during his first four years as party president. We might also note that in his Thomas Davis lecture about the party system in Ireland from 1945-1951,

Murphy makes no reference to Mulcahy, either in relation to Fine Gael's revival or to the formation of the first Inter-Party Government.

THE INTER-PARTY GOVERNMENTS

The thrust of Mulcahy's proposal for an Inter-Party Government was based on his desire to oust the Fianna Fáil government, which had been in power for sixteen years. He was not motivated by personal ambition. That his desire to oust Fianna Fáil transcended any sense of personal ambition is confirmed by his willingness to support Jack Costello as the new head of government. He was a great admirer and colleague of Collins and never resented Collins's public reputation or his frequent incursions into the domain of the chief of staff. Nor, having a similar close relationship and admiration for Costello (which Costello reciprocated), did he resent Costello's rise to prominence in 1948 when he became the head of the Inter-Party Government and subsequently remained leader of the Opposition when out of power until Dillon took over the presidency of the party in 1959. In the first case he was satisfied that Collins was playing a unique and vital part in the army and Sinn Féin during Ireland's struggle for independence. In the second case, Costello's work was a major factor in keeping so many disparate groups and individuals together in the two Inter-Party Governments; and thereby forcing Fianna Fáil and de Valera from office. Mulcahy believed Costello's public leadership would be an excellent compromise. After a brief moment of uncertainty and doubt over his capacity to serve as Taoiseach, Costello was convinced to accept the nomination by Mulcahy and by his legal colleague and friend, Arthur Cox.

I have often thought that my father's dedication to public service was his fundamental attribute. Perhaps he needed a leader to whom he could devote his service and his sense of loyalty to Ireland's institutions. At no time did my father speak to us about leading the government, nor did he express such an ambition. Any effort to actively promote himself would have been uncharacteristic, particularly as he was aware of the fragile nature of the political structure he was proposing. Indeed, I am of the opinion that he may have been relieved that he was not faced with the responsibility of leading such a disparate coalition of politicians. Clearly, ending the Fianna Fáil hegemony was his only concern, and his goal had been reached.

My father speaks about his relations with Costello at the times of the Inter-

Party Governments, and of 'Costello's remoteness from his ministers'. Mulcahy's own remoteness in the Department of Education was even more remarkable. In the same tape he describes his reaction to Costello's declaration of a republic in Canada in 1948.

At this juncture, it might be worth noting some of the political events that dominated the first Inter-Party Government of 1948-1951, of which Mulcahy was the architect. Controversy still exists over the manner in which Costello announced the intention of his government to rescind the External Relations Act 'to take the gun out of Irish politics' and to declare a twenty-six county Republic of Ireland. This was in September 1948. Controversy also exists about the wisdom of the constitutional change. Mulcahy discusses Costello's premature declaration of the Republic during a visit to Ottawa, Canada, at length on tape, where he defends Costello. It has been suggested that Costello made the decision on the spur of the moment and in response to some slight he received from the Governor General or the authorities there. Costello denied this, and implied that the decision to declare the Republic had already been made with the full knowledge of his Cabinet colleagues.

On the Sunday morning following his announcement, when the subject was first reported in the newspapers, I was breakfasting with my father. The *Sunday Independent* arrived with front page banner headlines announcing the proposed constitutional change. Although my father said little at the time, it was clear that Costello's statement came as a surprise to him. He intimated that he had no knowledge of its being discussed in Cabinet and that the announcement in Canada was unexpected. In fact, the first mention of the repeal of the External Relations Act at Cabinet level was on 11 October 1948, six weeks after Costello had returned from North America. Mulcahy would have been too loyal to Costello and too protective of the Inter-Party Government to show any disagreement. But I often wonder what he really thought of the wisdom of leaving the Commonwealth when one recalls that only four years earlier, in 1944 when he became president of Fine Gael, he announced as part of his party's platform his intention to remain within the British Commonwealth. This would have been the view of virtually all Fine Gael supporters at the time and the minutes of Costello's report to the Cabinet on 11 October[1] read:

The Taoiseach reported on his recent visit to Canada and the United States of America and gave an account of discussions he had with the various people whom he had met and of the addresses and interviews he had given during the course of his journey through the two countries. The action taken by the Taoiseach during his visit to Canada and the United States of America was approved.

This minute is followed by a further note:

Repeal of Executive Authority (External Relations) Act 1936. Communication from British Government. The Taoiseach brought to the notice of the government a communication which was handed to him by the British representative in Dublin on 7 October 1948 on the subject of the proposed repeal of the Executive Authority (External Relations) Act 1936. A copy of the communication appears in the annexed schedule A. A reply in the terms of the annexed schedule B to be handed to the British representative by the minister for external affairs was approved.

Before Costello's visit to America, it was decided at the Cabinet meeting of 19 August 1948[2] not to accept an invitation to attend a forthcoming Commonwealth Conference in London 'as a member of the Commonwealth'. It was, however, decided to attend 'subject to Ireland's position in relation to the British Commonwealth of Nations being made clear . . .' This decision may have arisen because of conversations Costello claims were taking place with individual Cabinet colleagues about repealing of the External Relations Act 1936. The request to attend as an observer, rather than as a committed member of the Commonwealth, was refused by the British on the grounds that there was no precedent for such a special category of membership.[3] The Cabinet's proposal seemed an 'Irish' solution to the dilemma!

Subsequent to Costello's report of his visit to North America, there are several references in the Cabinet minutes to the negotiations which were conducted with the British and which led to an amicable settlement between the two countries.[4] The one contentious issue which was not resolved was the British guarantee to the North of Ireland that its relations with Britain would not change without the agreement of the majority of its people. This led to a strong note of protest from the Irish government and an outburst by Costello, which hardly seemed justified in view of the fact that implicit in the British guarantee was that the North's status was not deemed to be permanent.[5] Subsequently, the Cabinet sent a long aide-memoir objecting to the aspects regarding the North of Ireland in the 'Ireland Bill' presented to the House of Commons as a result of the repeal of the External Relations Act.[6]

Mulcahy mentions 'forces' behind the declaration of the Republic, where it is implied that it may have been based on legalistic motives possibly enhanced by irritation, rather than on motives of nationalism. My father did say to me once that, as a constitutional lawyer, Costello was unhappy with the anomalous relationship between Ireland (or 'Éire' as it was then called) and the United Kingdom and the Commonwealth which existed since the 1936 External Relations Act and that he was anxious to change the relationship to a more traditional model. He never suggested to me, or to anybody else to the best of my knowledge, that Seán MacBride was responsible for the decision; nor is there evidence, as far as I am aware, that MacBride had any hand in influencing Costello. Mulcahy's only reference to MacBride was that 'he was a weak person'.

Jack Costello had a valedictory interview with David Thornley on RTÉ 1 at the time of his retirement from politics in the early 1960s.[7] The interview presents Costello's account of the two Inter-Party Governments, of the Browne affair and of the declaration of the Republic. I believe that the most credible account of the declaration of the Republic was given by Costello himself during this interview. And I further believe that he makes a good case for the wisdom of the constitutional change. He said it was utter nonsense that he had made the declaration in Canada in angry response to the slights he received from the Canadians. He denied that MacBride had ever spoken to him about the matter but that both James Dillon and William Norton had recommended the repeal of the External Relations Act long before the change was announced. He stated categorically that the proposal had been discussed in Cabinet and that when the subject was broached by Norton in the Dáil, de Valera replied 'if you do it you will get no opposition from me'. He was unclear on whether the decision by the Cabinet was recorded in the minutes and added that the minutes 'were rather casually kept at those days', although, to me, the minutes of the two Inter-Party Governments seem to be quite comprehensive and detailed. I suspect that Costello is not entirely accurate that the subject was formally discussed in Cabinet; but it may have been discussed informally with individuals at the time of Cabinet meetings.

To those who knew him less well, Costello could appear rather humourless and gruff. And, indeed, urbanity was hardly part of his personality. He could be rather rigid in his opinions and the stances he might take. Although a man of few words to the casual observer, he could respond vigorously and trenchantly to criticisms or confrontations by his opponents, as is clear in his valedictory interview with Thornley on RTÉ at the time of his retirement. He and Cecil Lavery were the outstanding members of the bar in the 1940s and 1950s. He was a brilliant advocate and had the enviable reputation as a lawyer of believing implicitly in his client's case, no matter what the circumstances were, and of being totally committed to achieving a successful outcome, however unlikely the prospects. It used be said that his professional fees were so modest that other less successful barristers found it difficult to make a living because of the standards of remuneration set by him.

Another event requiring comment was Noel Browne's proposal to introduce a free mother and child scheme. Browne was one of the bright jewels of the new administration. He gained considerable public support and approval for his energetic public health measures, particularly in controlling the tuberculosis epidemic. The campaign against tuberculosis had been initially launched by his predecessor in the ministry, Dr Jim Ryan of Fianna Fáil, and fundamental advances in its treatment had coincided at the time. His free mother and child health scheme which had much to commend it but, as a measure of social progress, it might easily be perceived as ahead of its time; particularly in such a conservative community as predominately Roman Catholic Ireland. My father discusses this affair in some detail on tape.

The scheme was greeted with dismay by the medical profession and provoked their violent opposition. Later, members of the Catholic Hierarchy became involved. It was inevitable that the Cabinet, made up of mostly conservative members chosen from and representing a conservative electorate, would yield to the widespread pressure from the reactionary groups. Browne was asked to modify or to withdraw his proposal. When he refused to do so, after much misunderstanding between himself and the bishops and increasing disagreement with his Cabinet colleagues, he was asked to resign by the leader of his party, Seán MacBride. Whether his discussions with his colleagues were at an individual level or at Cabinet level is difficult to determine. For his part, my father was not aware of any Cabinet discussions on the Mother and Child scheme. The Health Bill 1949[8] was first mentioned in the Cabinet minutes on 4 November 1949 when it was approved for circulation to the Dáil. It was next mentioned at the Cabinet meeting of 14 November 1950[9] when a new section of the Bill was approved, but there was no mention of the details of this change or addition. The next and last mention of the scheme, now entitled the Mother and Child Health Service, was on 6 April 1951.[10] Browne was present at this meeting but resigned immediately afterwards. The text of the minute is as follows:

> Following consideration of a letter dated 4 April 1951 to the Taoiseach from his Grace, the Archbishop of Dublin, Primate of Ireland, on behalf of the Catholic Hierarchy of Ireland, intimating that the particular scheme called the Mother and Child Health Service proposed by the minister for health is opposed to Catholic teaching, it was decided (1) that the scheme referred to should not be further pursued; (2) that in the light of the government's conviction that mothers and children should not be deprived of the best available health care by reason of insufficient means, a scheme or schemes for a mother and child health service should, as soon as possible, be prepared and undertaken which would (a) provide the best modern facilities for those whose family wage or income does not permit them to obtain, of themselves, the health care that is necessary of mothers and children, and (b) be in conformity with Catholic social teaching; and (3) that consideration should be given to the question whether any amendments of the Health Act, 1947, additional to those proposed in the Health Bill, 1950, are necessary and desirable and, if so, that proposals for such amendments should be

submitted to the government.

We can conclude from this statement by the Cabinet, firstly, that Browne resigned because he would not accept a means test for those availing of the scheme. Secondly, that the Cabinet was reasonable in its decision to modify the Bill in the light of the Hierarchy and the medical profession's opposition. Thirdly that the Hierarchy's opposition was based on fatuous grounds, at least to those of us sixty years later, and fourthly that the medical profession opposed Browne's scheme because doctors feared the loss of private practice. We might also point out that, while Browne's scheme might have been perceived as being too radical by a conservative public, medical profession and Catholic Church, it was certainly less radical than the National Health Service introduced in Britain the year before.

As I recall, the main opposition to the Mother and Child scheme came from the medical profession, and particularly from the Irish Medical Association and the consultants. The latter included my own senior colleagues at the time at St Vincent's Hospital, Bob O'Connell and the Fitzgerald brothers, Paddy and Oliver, who were brothers of Alexis Fitzgerald, Costello's son-in-law and one of his closest advisors. Many of the consultants in Dublin had close social and professional relations with members of the Inter-Party Cabinet, including Mulcahy. I remember the strenuous lobbying of the members of the Cabinet, particularly by O'Connell who was as energetic as he was political, and who was a very prominent member of the Irish Medical Association. I believe that if the medical profession had not opposed Browne's scheme, the Cabinet and the Church would not have intervened.

The Browne affair was followed two months later by the dissolution of the Inter-Party Government after three years in office. It had too small a majority to continue without the support of Noel Browne and the one or two deputies who supported him, as well as a few independents who were disenchanted with the government's economic policies. The government was also under increasing pressure because of serious inflation and other economic problems.

The end of the three year administration of the first Inter-Party Government is generally attributed to Noel Browne's intransigence in relation to the Mother and Child scheme, and to his resignation and that of one or two supporters. However, Patrick Lynch, who was close to Jack Costello and aware of the affairs of the Cabinet and its members, told me in conversation that while the failure of the Cabinet to accept Browne's scheme was a dominant factor in the failure of the government, its early demise was inevitable because of increasing tensions within the Clann na Poblachta Party and particularly between Browne and MacBride. Their differences, which were bitter, were based on personal rather than political matters, according to Lynch.

Browne's scheme failed because it was revolutionary, at least in the sense that it provoked the opposition of an influential and reactionary medical profession. Throughout his political career he failed to learn two of the fundamental characteristics of a successful and effective politician – that politics is the art of the possible, and that the best should not be the enemy of the good. His subsequent political career was unsuccessful because he never had the capacity to understand these precepts or to compromise in matters of practice or principle. Surely only a very uncompromising individual would destroy what was a progressive piece of health legislation on the grounds of a means test. I often wondered about Browne's relations with others. He certainly could be bitter in a personal way toward some of his colleagues, and to his detriment could not compromise on many issues which required consensus.

There was much confusion about the Mother and Child affair and the resultant demise of the first Inter-Party Government due to different accounts of the proceedings leading up to Browne's resignation. Although a number of senior Cabinet ministers did try to influence Browne during the negotiations about the scheme, but some blame must be attributed to members of the Cabinet, particularly to the senior and more experienced members. Costello appears to have imposed little ministerial accountability on his colleagues, and clearly this must have been the case in the Browne episode. In Mulcahy's case, he had characteristically buried himself so thoroughly in the details of running the Department of Education, that he must have been little aware of the wider political aspects of the government; as Valiulis refers to his total and meticulous dedication to whatever responsibility or work he undertook. She notes this aspect of his personality and underlined the advantages and disadvantages of such an attribute. When he was army chief of staff, charged with organising the revolutionary army and subsequently the peacetime force, this trait proved to be of inestimable value, but as the senior member of the Inter-Party Cabinet, his remoteness and isolation in the Department of Education must have contributed, at least in part to the final dissolution of the government.

I cannot believe that even such a rugged individualist and political loner as Noel Browne could not have been influenced to modify his ambitions by more experienced colleagues, particularly if better ministerial accountability had been enforced and if he had not had such a disagreeable relationship with his own political leader. He also appears to have had little insight into the motives of his medical colleagues, who feared any changes in the health services which might threaten their livelihood. Costello, in discussing the episode in the Dáil after Browne's resignation, stated that Browne was incapable of taking advice and was impervious to reason or argument. Although the episode is described in some detail in Brian Maye's *Fine Gael – 1923-1987*,[11] the story is confused by the varying accounts of what transpired between Browne and the bishops and his ministerial colleagues during the development of the crisis.

After the repeal of the External Relations Act, the government extracted important concessions from the United Kingdom, which left the relations between the two countries little different from those which existed when Ireland was in the Commonwealth. The first Inter-Party Government achieved much with land reform and began the long and ultimately successful process of economic development. It established the IDA and an independent Central Statistics Office detached from the Department of Industry and Commerce, which has since provided comprehensive national, demographic and economic data essential to the functioning of a modern state. Mulcahy, according to Paddy Lynch, pushed the concept of an independent statistics office and recommended Roy Geary as its director. Geary was to prove a brilliant success as the first head of the CSO, and it continues to provide an excellent and necessary service to the government and community.

Cooperation with Northern Ireland was first initiated by the Inter-Party Government in relation to the Foyle Fisheries, the Erne hydroelectric scheme and the Irish transport system, when the latter was overhauled and modernised. However, the earlier break with the British Commonwealth cannot have furthered reconciliation with our countrymen in the North. I cannot recall speaking with my father in any great depth about the Northern situation or the possible reunification of Ireland. Although, I suspect he would have approved of the late John Kelly's view on the subject, which was essentially that reunification is entirely dependent on the wishes of a Northern, democratic majority; that now and in the foreseeable future the majority in the North will remain committed to Britain, and that a change to a united Ireland or a federal constitution can only be achieved by making the Republic more attractive than Westminster. The 1998 Good Friday Agreement would no doubt have been seen by him as a step towards the unity of the country. It was in the spirit of this belief that I attended the Sinn Féin Ard Fheis on 10 May 1998 as a visitor (introduced by the more radical Ulick O'Connor), and told Gerry Adams that I was representing my father, who would greatly approve of Sinn Féin's endorsement of the agreement as another stepping-stone following the ratification of the Treaty in 1922.

After the declaration of the Republic of Ireland, Britain gave formal assurances to the North that its relationship with the Britain would not change without the consent of the Northern people. Costello reacted to the British move by stating 'we would hit Britain in her pride and purse', but realistically there was little he could do. However, he then joined the Anti-Partition League, and thus began a national and international campaign to publicise the injustices of partition. The League lasted for a few years but gradually lapsed because of the indifference of the Irish Diaspora and the rest of the world and, indeed, most people in the Republic. Costello was supported by the Opposition, including de Valera, who travelled the world speaking on the subject. The Anti-Partition campaign did little but further antagonise the Northern majority and widen the gap between them and the rest of their countrymen. It was worse than futile and this opinion was shared by my father in later years.[12] But whether he believed it to be futile at the time is not clear. It entrenched the Northern loyalist intransigence, and had no effect on opinion among the Americans, Australians or any other world community, however powerful the Irish Diaspora in their midst. As one speaker said 'preaching against partition was like preaching against sin'.

The great hope for a lasting solution to the Northern question lies in the closer cooperation at economic, social, cultural and sporting levels between both parts of Ireland. And, of course, it would greatly help to solve the Northern problem if sectarian education were abolished at the primary and secondary levels in the North. It has taken almost ninety years since the Treaty to realise that the only approach to a real reconciliation and to a more cohesive answer to Ireland's problems is cooperation and mutual understanding between the two communities. Fundamental to the whole question is the fact that the North's economic, social and environmental problems are more like those of the South rather than Britain; and whatever Unionists may say, they will always be marginalised as long as they are controlled from Westminster.

Fine Gael won fifty seats in the 1954 election and was able to form the second Inter-Party Government with only two other parties, Labour and Clann na Talmhan. Jack Costello was again elected Taoiseach but it seems to me that the reasons my father was not elected Taoiseach in the first Inter-Party were no longer relevant in the second, particularly as Fine Gael now had a substantially larger number of deputies in the Dáil. It is also difficult to understand why Costello continued, after the two Inter-Party Governments, as leader of the Opposition. Unfortunately I cannot recall discussing these anomalies with my father. I would strongly suspect that he may have been responsible for maintaining the status quo of the leadership, perhaps because he was not encouraged by his colleagues to claim the leadership or, more likely, because he did not want the post. If he had any regrets, they were never expressed to his family or, I expect, to anyone else.

This second coalition had a majority in the Dáil and was clearly in a stronger position than the first one, depending as it did on five parties and a few independents. The prospects augured well for the new government but unfortunately it was faced with a major economic worldwide recession. The recession was caused in Ireland by serious balance-of-payment problems, leading to public expenditure cuts, increasing unemployment and heavy emigration. Despite setting up structures to restore the country's economy, which would pay dividends in later years, the government, yielding to increasing pressure and criticism and about to face a no confidence vote in the

Dáil, resigned and went into opposition after the election.

Mulcahy returned to his position as minister for education in the second Inter-Party Government, while remaining president of Fine Gael. The fifty seats won by Fine Gael in the 1954 election was a measure of how successful he was in reorganising the party and in proposing the concept of coalition governments. However, he must have been greatly disappointed in 1957 when the party was again reduced to forty seats. His tenure in the Department of Education during 1948-1951 and 1954-1957 took him entirely away from his organisational role in Fine Gael, which probably in part accounted for the deterioration in the party's fortunes in the 1957 election. Whatever about Costello's success as head of government, he certainly played no role in the organisation of the Fine Gael Party, which would face another sixteen years in opposition before the next Coalition government in 1973, led by Liam Cosgrave.

LATER YEARS AND LAST DAYS

During Mulcahy's years in parliament he was not much given to political talk and certainly not to reminiscing about the past. His later preoccupation with Dev's influence in provoking the Civil War lay dormant. However, after his retirement and as he become more occupied with his papers, he became greatly absorbed by the history of the foundation of the State and by his own experiences during these early years. While he was active in parliament and in the Fine Gael Party, he had an exceptional capacity to be totally absorbed in his work. This exceptional absorption in his day to day work was particularly evident from the start of his military and political careers, and continued when he was minister for education in both Inter-Party Governments. It left him with little time to be concerned with wider political issues. This trait certainly contributed to the decline of his public image and to his biographer's description as 'a forgotten hero'.

There were occasions when he appeared to be motivated by an unusual degree of stubbornness. Around 1955 a monument was erected on the road to Slane, near Ashbourne, where the successful battle against the RIC had taken place in 1916. Mulcahy was acknowledged by the survivors of that battle to have been the brains behind the successful assault on the police column and their ultimate defeat and capture. The unveiling was performed by Mulcahy's brother-in-law, Sean T. O'Kelly, the then-president of Ireland. Mulcahy refused to be present. He gave no reason for his refusal, but it may have been because he had little respect for O'Kelly as a man, and none as an activist during the War of Independence. My father never forgave him for his anti-Treaty stance, and his strong prejudice against de Valera and the Fianna Fáil Party would inevitably include O'Kelly. I suspect that he could not bear to be seen to be patronised on such an occasion by a man he deemed to be a political lightweight.

On the other hand, he may have had some regrets that he was partly responsible for the deaths of the nine policemen who were simply doing their duty in Ashbourne – a guilt which may have remained in his mind for many years. Nonetheless, it was surely very odd that the person whose widely acknowledged military reputation was initially based on his leadership and inspiration in 1916 at Ashbourne would refuse to be present at that important commemoration. What must the other survivors, who were present and who had such a high regard for Mulcahy, have thought of his unexplained absence?

During the War of Independence, Truce and pre-Civil War period, Mulcahy and Collins were equally acknowledged the leaders of the army and as the inspiration behind the Irish resistance to the British military and police. During the eighteen months from Collins's death in August 1922 to the Army Mutiny in March 1924, Mulcahy alone symbolised the leadership of the emerging peacetime Free State army. Despite his political appointment as minister for defence in January 1922, a position he held until the mutiny, he was widely thought of as an 'army man', and as such was widely admired by his supporters and respected, if not feared, by his opponents. Yet, despite his dedication to the advancement of the army as a highly professional peacetime force, well recounted in the Valiulis biography, and despite his palpable pride in its role in building a democratic state, he never allowed himself to be associated with the army or to be seen to have any connection with the force from the day he resigned as minister for defence. His complete break with the army and his distancing himself from its image and its progress must be reasons why the political and military reputation he acquired at the time of the State's foundation was eroded over time and the earlier biographies of many of his colleagues.

His post-mutiny attitude to the army was not an expression of loss of pride in its achievements. My mother remained chairman of the Army Benevolent Fund for many years and was obviously encouraged by my father to do so. I would put forward two reasons as likely to account for his self-imposed distance from the military – although I must admit that my views are somewhat speculative, for it was difficult to question him on his personal motives. He tended to be totally absorbed in whatever his current activity might be, to the exclusion of all other matters; a feature of his personality which I have already underlined. His future lay in politics, not the army, according to his own perception, and he threw himself into the life and work of the Dáil, his party and the task of chairing and writing a full report of the Gaeltacht Commission. He obviously wished to leave the army's future development to those who took over the Department of Defence. He was certainly the type who would be sensitive to accusations of interfering in areas which were not his concern. I cannot recall ever discussing his post-mutiny attitude to the army with him. It is unlikely he would have gone into his reasons and he certainly would not have in the years before his retirement. His answer would definitely have been brief, and he would probably end the conversation with a remark like 'Hadn't I enough things to do without meddling into other people's business.' One needs to look no further than the papers and tapes in the UCD archives to understand his lifetime pride in the army and in its non-political record.

On another occasion, perhaps in the early sixties, he was invited by Sean MacEntee, then a minister in the Fianna Fáil administration, to join an all-party committee to decide on of the design of the Garden of Remembrance, which was to be located in Parnell Square. My father mentions the invitation in a conversation with an old colleague, and gives the most tortuous and incomprehensible reason for his refusal to accept what was a perfectly ecumenical gesture. As far as one can tell from his remarks, his refusal was linked to his strong prejudice against MacEntee and his party.

Why was my father's military contribution to the foundation of the new State and subsequent political career largely forgotten by subsequent generations? Valiulis attributes it partly to the harsh decisions he made during the Civil War but if, through his conduct of the Civil War, he acquired many enemies, he also acquired at least as many devoted friends and admirers who appreciated his efforts to defend and uphold the democratic constitution of the country. His neglect in the collective memory is, I believe, largely the product of his own personality combined with his survival to old age. During his active years up to his retirement in 1961, he was reluctant to speak of past events, except perhaps in private and then only in response to the questions of family members and friends. His constant theme when discussions arose about the revolutionary period, and particularly the Civil War, was 'Haven't we enough to do with the country in the state it is, without worrying about what happened in the past.' He would never comment publicly on matters he would perceive to be historically inaccurate, particularly when they applied to himself. One example of his determination to avoid unnecessary controversy was his refusal to review Béaslaí's biography *Michael Collins and the Making of a New Ireland*, although after his retirement he was able to dictate a three hundred and ten-page critique of the book, which is replete with comments disagreeing with the author's facts, interpretations and omissions. His response to the publication of Béaslaí's book, when invited to review it, was characteristic of his unwillingness to get involved in what he deemed to be harmful controversy at the time.

He contributed to the eclipse of his own reputation for other reasons. While he gave numerous interviews to the media, historians and students of history during his retirement, he was a difficult and at times cantankerous interviewee, particularly in his declining years. He cannot have evoked the sympathy or understanding of some of his correspondents. He was also unpredictable in his responses to invitations to functions which were directly relevant to his own career, and which at times concerned him as the principal figure. He was a self-effacing person who lived to a good age. Most of his contemporaries who were aware of his military and political contribution to the foundation of the State, and who held him in high regard, predeceased him. In his last few years he showed the subtle signs of intellectual deterioration which affected his judgment and which distorted his opinions, and thus some of his critics judge him more by the writings of this time in his life, rather than by his earlier, sounder work. These are some of the reasons that led to the decline in Mulcahy's reputation, compelling Valiulis to describe him as 'the forgotten hero'. I feel sure that his seminal contribution to Irish history will be acknowledged, less through my efforts, but more through the publication of Valiulis's biography. He will be remembered because of the remarkable collection of War of Independence, Truce, Civil War and Cumann na nGaedheal papers he has left posterity.

I ponder at times Mulcahy's concept of nationalism. Michael Tierney, in his biography of Eoin MacNeill,[1] writes in detail about the conflict between nationalism as applied to the state and nationalism as applied to culture and race. Tierney is convincing about the divide between those whose national aspirations were based on the preservation of the Irish language and Celtic culture, and who were largely associated with the Gaelic League at the turn of the century; and those nationalists who were committed to the formation of an independent state and separatism, while generally ambivalent about the ancient Gaelic culture or language. It was quite clear that Mulcahy's concept of nationalism was based on the preservation of the Irish language and the Gaelic tradition, but I expect that he, like many others who thought that language and tradition were of crucial importance, saw their form of nationalism as an effective means of achieving independence. His concept of nationalism as applied to the state was a pragmatic one, and he would have been happy to remain part of the British Commonwealth, as long as we were free to counteract the pervading Anglicisation of Irish society. My father was close to MacNeill in many ways, in thought and action and, as MacNeill was described by Tierney, he was 'a tradionalist who saw that the essence of a nation was its history, not its aspiration to or achievement of statehood'. Is it possible that, had he not been drawn into fighting in the 1916 Rising, he might have had the confidence that a cultural movement would be preferable to military action? One can only admire the courage and martyrdom of the 1916 leaders, but – practically – did their actions really prove to be the best for Ireland?

Father Desmond McCarthy of Bray, Co Wicklow, wrote to my cousin, the Rev. Richard Mulcahy on 18 October 1992 after he had read Valiulis's biography. He was an old friend and admirer of my father's, and was familiar with the literature of the revolutionary period. He thought that the biography was the most accurate account of the Civil War and of the circumstances surrounding the foundation of the Irish Free State he had ever read. Fr McCarthy also had this to say:

> There was one aspect of the work in which I was disappointed. The public figure of Richard Mulcahy is excellently presented but . . . the man himself, his affability, his graciousness, his thoughts for others, his sense of humour would seem to have been passed over.

Padraig Colum, in his biography of Griffith[2] says of Mulcahy, comparing him to Sean MacEoin:

> He was a soldier of a different type, austere and intellectual, the presentment of a military monk. 'Every word,' writes an observer in *Free State or Republic?* . . . 'came slowly and earnestly, almost softly from the thin lips, the sharp jaws, with the thoughtful eyes above, and the meditative brow shadowing the whole countenance'.

Of course, opinions about people can differ widely. A Mr Boilbester, a journalist for the *Irish Times* in the late 1920s, refers to Ernest Blythe and Mulcahy in a letter to Lady Lavery, quoted in her biography.[3]

> Blythe and his cultural alter-ego [Richard] Mulcahy are sour-faced Puritans with all the zeal of that type and all its fanatical obstinacy. Blythe is a Lisburn Presbyterian. Mulcahy's grandparents are Quakers. Both he and Blythe are rabid teetotallers. So there you have the Free Staters' woes in a sentence. They are the sea green incorruptibles who will not be satisfied until the British connection – which bred both of them – has been snapped and until the jabber of the Gaeltacht echoes through a de-Anglicised countryside. Blythe and Mulcahy, the Orange convert and the soldier saint as poor Kevin O'Higgins used to call them . . .

Whatever about being a 'soldier-saint', he was never a person who exhibited the intolerance and the puritanical zeal attributed to him by Mr Boilbester. And I suspect that the latter's views were based on hearsay from casual acquaintances of my father. Mulcahy seconded the proposal in the Dáil that de Valera be elected President of the Republic in August 1921. A newspaper report of the proceedings went as follows:

> On the heels of Mr MacEoin, seconding his resolution came the second
> phrase maker and recaller of the past, Richard Mulcahy. I looked at him
> with surprise. Was this the redoubtable Mulcahy, 'Chief of staff', the
> planner far more than Michael Collins ever was on ambushes and raids,
> organiser of the flying columns? A little man in a blue coat, much too
> large for him, looking vaguely as if he had something to do with horses,
> and vaguely as if he had something to do with ideas. Well, the little
> man, with clear brow and fullish lips, was soon speaking and his words
> were the only real trial of the day. Downcast, looking at no one, his gaze
> deep in the realm of history, he began to speak of the threshold of Irish
> history, and heaven knows how far back that can have been, when 'The
> hosts of Connaught marshalled themselves against Ulster, when Ulster's
> leader, Cúchulann, was overcome by sickness' and he hesitated for a
> moment 'by magic and how the youths of Ulster were summoned and
> held the ford and saved the land.'[4]

LAST DAYS

My father had always been in good health, and lived to his eighty-sixth year.
His habits conformed to the best principles of modern health promotion.
(Although, he did make an unsuccessful attempt to pick up cigarette smoking
in the late 1930s.) He was mildly austere in his habits: he was a frugal eater,
and a lover of plain, simple food unadulterated by the garnishings of more
recent times. He drank little alcohol, and then only later in life. He was a
regular and brisk walker, and led a very regular life. He slept regularly and well,
and, unfortunately for my mother, was a heavy resonant snorer. No
circumstance in his life, however pressing or urgent, ever appeared to affect his
sleep pattern. Frank Holland questioned him about his good health and his
longevity, and got a straight, simple answer: 'Hard work, early rising, walking.'
Both he and Holland attribute their good health to not smoking and not
drinking alcohol. Holland and his two brothers took a lifetime pledge against
alcohol at the insistence of the commandant of their brigade, Con Colbert.

The latter, according to Holland, had a 'horror' of drink!

In his last few years his vision deteriorated, leaving him almost blind at the end of his days. He found it difficult to come to terms with his loss of vision. His chronic anxiety about his sight was aggravated by his doctor's failure to counsel him properly about the reality of his age and its inevitable consequences on his vital functions. It was not surprising that his regular and frequent visits to his eye specialist, believing that something could still be done to improve his sight, engendered a false hope of recovery. In June 1971 he complained of indigestion and he was admitted to the Pembroke Nursing Home, where a diagnosis of stomach cancer was confirmed by X-ray – a condition which had then, and still has, a very poor long-term outlook.

My father died on 16 December 1971. His death was marked by widespread press coverage and by a moving military funeral, attended by, among many others, his old foe Eamon de Valera. For a few days, he was no longer 'the forgotten hero', and his distant military exploits were remembered, as was his more recent, and more pedestrian, political career. I made a long tape recording encapsulating some of my immediate memories of him.

There were many tributes paid to Mulcahy after his death. From Eoin Coyle:

This was he / all men-at-arms should wish to be.[5]

Ulick O'Connor, referring to his speech over Collins's grave, said:

. . . [the speech] to my mind stands with Emmet and Pearse as one of the great pieces of valedictory oratory.[6]

From John Cusack:

History will record him as one of the Greats of all time.[7]

One old friend of his wrote to me after his death:

. . . he walked across the pages of history, leaving indelible prints . . . his utter indifference to his own fate, as a man of destiny, and his utter dedication towards us, for the right to decide our destiny through the ballot box.[8]

Professor John Murphy, in his review of the Valiulis biography,[9] described Mulcahy as a hero to his family. This was quite true. He was greatly admired and respected, particularly by his brothers and sisters and by his more intimate friends. My attitude to my father could be described as admiration compounded by curiosity. My admiration was not only based on his idealism, but also on his apparent lack of personal ambition and acquisitiveness. Nothing he ever did appeared to be motivated by self interest. His career testifies to his commitment to the cause of Ireland. When personal gain or self interest conflicted with the interest of his party or the State, he would give scarcely a thought to himself. His support and encouragement of Collins during the War of Independence and the Truce and his increasing admiration rather than resentment of Collins as the latter's military and political reputation soared; his toleration of the rebuffs of Cathal Brugha during the Truce and other difficulties he encountered during the Truce and the Civil War periods; and his resignation from the Department of Defence in 1924, were all important in the evolution of the army and his successful formation of a peacetime force.

His continued loyalty to and support of William Cosgrave and his party after the mutiny and his full-time attention to party and to parliament to the exclusion of any other gainful employment; his years of organisational work on behalf of Cumann na nGaedheal and Fine Gael, and his decision to accept the Ministry of Education in 1948 and 1954; his relinquishing the position of Taoiseach in the first Inter-Party Government, and his support of Jack Costello, all testify to a stable and mature political outlook and a personality of unusual idealism and self-abnegation.

He seemed to possess a sense of detachment which allowed him to accept, without resentment or concern, whatever might befall him – particularly any situation which he was unable to influence or control. He slept soundly whatever crisis was at hand and I never heard him complain about any aspect of his life, apart from his criticism of those whom he perceived to be opposed to the welfare of Ireland and its people. In private life, he was frugal and simple in his tastes, and limited in his demands and needs. While he may not have scorned such attention, he certainly did not seek publicity and notoriety, and, although he might respond to unjust criticisms, he never expressed regrets about his actions in defence of the army or of the State. I was aware that his public persona conveyed the impression of sternness, discipline and asceticism – O'Higgins's 'soldier saint' – but we need to be reminded that in private life he was very different. Father McCarthy had to remind Valiulis, after reading the biography, about his private profile: his affability, his graciousness, his thought for others and his sense of humour.

As I advanced in years and my relationship with my father matured, I realised he was most unusual in terms of his devotion to Ireland, its traditions and its culture. I was therefore determined to write about him as objectively as possible, and I had enough insight to realise that I could only portray an accurate picture of him by the strictest candour. I hope I have succeeded in this endeavour. It was because of his unusual career and his idealism that I felt we owed it to his memory and to posterity to add more details of his personal and family life to those recorded in Valiulis's biography – and more importantly to have him occupy his rightful place in the history of the country he loved.

It is said that the true revolutionary is one who succeeds in achieving freedom and who subsequently devotes his life to the well-being of his country. Apropos of this maxim, Maryann Valiulis published the only biography of Mulcahy in 1992. It received several reviews. The following are contrasting excerpts from two of them:

Eoghan Corry, in a review of the Valiulis biography in the *Irish Press* on 26 June 1992, wrote:

But it is a sobering thought that a general who won the admiration of friend and foe alike during the war had so little to offer the republic he helped found.

And in the *Phoenix* of 26 June 1992 we find:

Her book concentrates almost entirely on the twenties, which is just as well as Dick's career was one of those which peaked early and dragged along rather boringly thereafter.

From another reviewer:

It was he, with his close friend Michael Hayes, who did most to establish the dignity and authority of Dáil Éireann from 1923 until 1933. He gave the impression of having more respect for Dáil Éireann than any other of its members and he used it to considerable effect during the long years of his membership.

APPENDIX 1

MULCAHY'S HOMILY OVER MICHAEL COLLINS'S GRAVE, 28 SEPTEMBER 1922

Opening in Irish he said:

> That there was a burden of sorrow heavy on the hearts of our people to-day, that our minds, like the great Cathedral below after the last Mass had been said, and the coffin borne away and the great concourse of people emptied from it – our minds were dry, wordless, and empty, with nothing in them but the little light of faith.

And continuing in English:

> Our country is today bent under a sorrow such as it has not been bent under for many a year. Our minds are cold, empty, wordless and without sound. But it is only our weaknesses that are bent under this great sorrow that we meet today. All that is good in us, all that is strong in us, is strengthened by the memory of that great hero, and that great legend who is now laid to rest.
>
> We bend today over the grave of a man not more than thirty years of age, who took to himself the gospel of toil for Ireland, the gospel of

working for the people of Ireland, and of sacrifice for their good, and who has made himself a hero and a legend that will stand in the pages of our history with any bright page that was ever written there.

Pages have been written by him in the hearts of our people that will never find a place in print. But we lived, some of us, with these intimate pages; and those pages that will reach history, meagre though they be, will do good to our country and will inspire us through many a dark hour. Our weaknesses cry out to us, 'Michael Collins was too brave.'

Michael was not too brave. Every day and every hour he lived he lived it to the full extent of that bravery which God gave to him, and it is for us to be brave as he was – brave before danger, brave before those who lie, brave even to that very great bravery that our weakness complained of in him.

When we look over the pages of his diary for 22nd August, Started '6:15 AM Macroom to Ballineen, Bandon, Skibbereen, Roscarbery, Clonakilty,' our weakness says he tried to put too much into the day. Standing on the little mantel-piece of his office was a bronze plaque of President Roosevelt, of the United States, and the inscription on it ran: 'I wish to preach, not the doctrine of ignoble ease, but the doctrine of strenuous life, the life of toil and effort, of labour and strife; to preach that highest form of success that comes, not to the man who desires mere ease and peace, but to him who does not shrink from danger, hardship, or bitter toil, and who, out of these, wins the splendid ultimate triumph.'

Mura bhfuigheann an gráinne arbhair a theidheann sa talamh bás ni bhion ann ach e féin, ach ma gheibheann se bás tugan se toradh mór uaidh. (Unless the grain of corn that falls into the ground dies, there is nothing but itself in it, but if it dies it gives forth great fruit.)

And Michael Collins's passing will give us forth great fruit, and Michael Collins's dying will give us forth great fruit. Every bit of his small grain of corn died, and it died night and day during the last four or five years. We have seen him lying on a bed of sickness and struggling with infirmities, running from his bed to his work.

On Saturday, the day before he went on his last journey to Cork, he sat with me at breakfast writhing with pain from a cold all through his body, and yet he was facing his day's work for that Saturday, and facing his Sunday's journey and Monday's journey and his journey on Tuesday. So let us be brave, and let us not be afraid to do too much in the day. In all that great work, strenuous it was, comparatively it was intemperate, but it was the only thing that Michael Collins was intemperate in.

How often with a shout he used to get out of bed in the morning at 5 or 6 o'clock crying, 'All the time that is wasted in sleep,' and would dash around the room, or into some neighbouring room where some of us lay in the hope of an hour or two's sleep, and he would clear all the blankets off us, or would pound vigorously at the door which prudence had locked.

Crossing the square of the barracks on the Saturday morning that I mention, he told of his visit to one of the barracks in the South on his first trip there, and of finding most of the garrison in bed at 10 o'clock; and thinking of all the lack of order, lack of cleanliness, lack of moral strength and efficiency that goes with this particular type of sloth, and of all the demoralisation following on the dissatisfaction that one has with one's self all the day that one starts with an hour's disadvantage. 'Oh', he said, 'if our fellows would only get up at 6 o'clock in the morning.'

Yes, get up to read, to write; to think, to plan, to work, or, like Ard Riogh Éireann long ago, simply to greet the sun. The God given long day fully felt and fully seen would bring its own work and its own construction. Let us be brave, then, and let us work.

'Prophecy,' said Peter, who was the great rock, 'is a light shining in the darkness till the day dawn.'

And surely 'our great rock' was our prophet and our prophecy, a light held aloft along the road of 'danger or hardship or bitter toil'. And if our light is gone out it is only as the paling of a candle in the dawn of its own prophecy.

An act of his, a word of his, a look of his was day by day a prophecy to us that loose lying in us lay capabilities for toil, for bravery, for regularity, for joy in life; and in slowness and in hesitancy and in weariness half yielded to, his prophecies come true in us. And just as he as a person was a light and a prophecy to us individually, he looked to it and wished that this band of brothers, which is the Army, will be a prophecy to our people. Our Army has been the people, is the people, and will be the people. Our green uniform does not make us less the people. It is a cloak of service, a curtailer of our weaknesses, an amplifier of our strength.

We are jealous for his greatness. Words have been quoted as being his last words; Michael Collins is supposed to have said the fragile words, 'Forgive them.' Michael Collins never said these words, 'forgive them,' because his great big mind could not have entertained the obverse thought, and he knew those who sat around him and worked with him that they, too, were too big to harbour in their minds the obverse thought.

When Michael Collins met difficulties, met people who obstructed him, and worked against him, he did not turn aside to blame them, but facing steadily ahead, he worked bravely forward to the goal that he intended. He had that faith in the intensity of his own work that in its development and in its construction he would absorb into one homogeneous whole in the nation, without the necessity for blame or for forgiveness, all those who differed from him and those who fought against him.

He is supposed to have said, 'Let the Dublin Brigade bury me.' Michael Collins knows that we will never bury him. He lies here among the men of the Dublin Brigade. Around him there lie forty-eight comrades of his from our Dublin battalions. But Michael Collins never separated the men of Dublin from the men of Kerry, nor the men of Dublin from the men of Donegal, nor the men of Donegal from the men of Cork.

His great love embraced our whole people and our whole Army, and he was as close in spirit with our men in Kerry and Donegal as he was with our men in Dublin. Yes. And even those men in different districts in the country who sent us home here our dead Dublin men – we are sure he felt nothing but pity and sorrow for them for the tragic circumstances in which they find themselves, knowing that in fundamentals and ideals they were the same.

Michael Collins had only a few minutes to live and to speak after he received his death wound, and the only word he spoke in these few moments was 'Emmet'. He called to the comrade alongside him, the comrade of many fights and of many plans, and I am sure that he was calling around him the whole men of Ireland that he might speak the last word of comradeship and love.

We last looked at him in the City Hall and in the small church in Vincent's Hospital. And, studying his face with an eager gaze, we found there the same old smile that met us always in our work. And seeing it there in the first dark hour of our blow, the mind could not help travelling back to the dark storm-tossed Sea of Galilee and the frail barque tossed upon the waters there, and the strong, calm smile of the Great Sleeper in the stern of the boat.

Tom Ashe, Tomás MacCurtain, Traolach MacSuibhne, Dick McKee, Micheál O'Coileáin, and all you who lie buried here, disciples of our great Chief, those of us you leave behind are all, too, grain from the same handful, scattered by the hand of the Great Sower over the fruitful soil of Ireland. We, too, will bring forth our own fruit.

Men and women of Ireland, we are all mariners on the deep, bound for a port still seen only through storm and spray, sailing still on a sea full of dangers and hardships, and bitter toil. But the Great Sleeper lies smiling in the stern of the boat, and we shall be filled with that spirit which will walk bravely upon the waters.

Appendix 2

Mulcahy's homily over the graves of Thomas Ashe, Peadar Kearney and Piaras Béaslaí, 20 August 1967

We come here as pilgrims, not to raise our voices nor to travel prayerfully a path traced by many prayerful feet, to seek contemplation that will fill our hearts and help us find our purpose. The path we go is firm trod, other paths spread from it. Many figures and many voices from the past are around us while we go to mark another shrine along the way.

Some of us met this path at the spot where O'Donovan Rossa was laid to rest more than fifty years ago. There we met Pearse and Griffith and Eoin MacNeill. The Pearse of 1912 and the Barr Buadh had turned aside from the platform of argument and appeal to face and challenge, in the uniform of the Irish Volunteers, the force, deceit and false faith that would frustrate a nation's hopes. Griffith had acclaimed and appraised the spirit of Fenianism. From the front of Charlemont House which recalls the Volunteers of 1872, MacNeill had dismissed the armed parade which had honoured the grave of Rossa and given substance to the challenge of Pearse; he had dismissed them to an unknown morrow which was to lead to the days of 1919, 1920 and 1921, when in the hands of the men of the Dublin Brigade and the General Headquarters Staff, Parnell Square was to become Caisleán na hAiseirí, the Dublin Castle of Ireland's political resurrection.

Our high purpose here and the power upon which we rely will be manifest if we recall our Mass at Berkeley Road Church this morning. There, for the purpose of today and tomorrow, we remind ourselves that as the glories of the Creator are being day by day made more manifest by man's work in the world, the world's horrors and dangers increase. More and more resoundingly and in unison therefore we praise God's Providence and pray for greater strength to toll away the dangers and to do our part in creating the kingdom of peace on earth, and for light and understanding to recognise and realise the Kingdom of Heaven within us.

Ever more resoundingly now at Mass we dare to pray that to this end we may be given our daily bread, and that in the forgiveness of our offences and our mistakes we may be endowed with an increase of courage, strength and hope.

More humbly and no less daringly in the quiet of our hearts we pray also:

A dhia do chuir uaiseacht iongantach sa nádúr dhaona agus to a chrutú agus gurab iongantai ná san an athnuachaint a dheinis uirthe, tabhair dúinn tré rundiamhar an uisge agus an fhiona so go mbeimíd rann-pháirteach i ndiadhacht an té a dheonaigh bheith rann-pháirteach in ar ndaonacht, Iosa Chriost, do Mhac, ár d'Tiarna a mhaireann agus a rialann mar aon leatsa in aondacht leis an spiorad naomh ina Dhia ar feadh na siorraiochta.

We dare to ask that through the sacred mystery of the water and the wine of the Mass, we may be made partakers of the Divinity of Him Who partook of our humanity.

In that spirit we have come here to mark another shrine along the way – the grave where lie Tomás Aghas, Piaras Béaslaí, Peadar O Cearnaigh.

On the way we have stopped to pray by the grave of Michael Collins. Expanding around it many graves recall that even in many far-flung countries today struggling for peace, Irishmen are giving their services and their labours with a dedication marked by the sacrifice of their lives. We stopped to pray by the more isolated grave of Arthur Griffith, symbolic of the effacement and the retreat in which he laboured, freely offering every drop of his often wearied blood, and every day of his doubts and questioning to be our teacher and a pointer of our way.

Here we reach another shrine. We mark a grave of significance where the memory of three mingled lives will as the days pass enlighten our memories, enoble our emotions and inspire our doings.

We praise the Providence that brings the bodies of Tomás Aghas, Peadar O Cearnaigh and Piaras Béaslaí to a united grave and links their names on the one stone. Their mingled lives recall the basic gifts of Providence for man's sustenance, and the labour and faith in which Ireland received them gratefully and raised a nation.

Ashe's life and his traditions speak to us of the nature and of the quality of the basic gifts of Providence to us. *Or fé'n aitinn, airgead fé'n lúchair, gorta fé an bhfraoch'* – Gold under the furze, silver under the rushes, and famine under the heather; they tell of the tools our fathers fashioned to win the gold and silver and to banish the heather's famine, and the labour these tools involved. *An grafan, an suiste agus ag tomhas an talaimh to dornaibh* – The grafaun, the flail, the reaping hook, *an trí obair is cruaidh amuigh* – the three hardest labours ever; they tell of the companionship and society this labouring gathered, and of the song, the story, the prayer that in the passing centuries knit that society to a purpose and an achievement whose monument is Faith.

The story of Peadar Kearney epitomises for us the Dublin which in days of frustration and days of danger was our comfort and our sustenance and our protection. Its dedication to the gentle and gifted Tom Pugh marks the spirit of these days. The pages of Seamus de Burca's gracefully told story are crowded with the names of the writers, workers, artists, singers who made up Peadar's companionship. We know Peadar as the epitome of the appreciative and active citizenship of a capital which absorbed into its life and institutions everything of the grace, the culture, naturalness and gaiety that stemmed from the nation's roots.

His 'Soldier's Song' came to discipline our footsteps, lift our chins and enline our shoulders as we helped to guard and move a people through difficult times to triumph. In our marching it mixed with the 'Wearing of the Green', 'Sean O'Farrell', 'God Save Ireland', and marches which carried no words.

In 1916, in Knutsford Jail, it became linked with our prayers. In the company of 'Hail Glorious St Patrick', 'Faith of our Fathers' it helped to shake the roof and dash the walls and crash the foundation of a jail that is now gone.

Throughout the world its notes are the salute of the nations to the Irish Republic and the growing acknowledgment, a recognition of the existence of an Irish Nation. The tragic circumstances that surround it have caused the words to become a shy whisper in our own throats.

Piaras Béaslaí's youth introduced him to the life and literature of Europe. He came to Ireland to seek a climate in which to anchor his soul and face a worthy lifework. He found in Gougane the inspiration for a life that included long and daring service with those who manned and held the Parnell Square Caisleán. While we work and wait for the flowering of the Garden of Remembrance and for the echo of its walls to re-stimulate our voices, we will hear from this grave the murmuring of the Unsealing river '*ar eagla na habhann bheith doimhinn, a Rí na Foighne glac mo lámh, ar eagla na tuile bheith trean, a Mhuire, feach agus na fág*'.

And the thought will permeate all our work, *A Rí na bhFeart is agat atá Réiteach* – Oh, God of deeds, Thine is the settlement, Thine is the solution.[1]

Appendix 3
The Valiulis Biography

Mulcahy's biography by Maryann Gialanella Valiulis, *Portrait of a Revolutionary – General Richard Mulcahy and the Founding of the Irish Free State*, was published in 1992 in Dublin by the Irish Academic Press.[1] It deals with his military and political careers, mainly from 1916 to 1924. It contains little material about his personal and family life and only deals in summary in the epilogue with his subsequent career as a parliamentarian from 1924 to his retirement from politics in 1961. I have deliberately used little of her text in writing about my father, although our general views about his career do not differ greatly.

Valiulis's biography underlines the vital, if somewhat low, profile of the GHQ staff in the War of Independence. It underlines the more important aspects of Mulcahy's contribution to the foundation of the State. There are other aspects of GHQ and the chief of staff's role which are important and which are included in the biography, but my father's influence in guiding army policy and establishing a peace-time army to conform with the principles of a democratic state was his greatest single contribution.

Valiulis describes him as a forgotten hero, by which she maintains that his reputation as a soldier-politician and one of the major contributors to achieving Irish self-determination, widely appreciated during and immediately after the foundation of the State, but who was overshadowed by the exploits and reputation of Collins. His legacy was also adversely affected by the Army Mutiny. Valiulis puts forward these and other reasons for this decline in his reputation, a subject which is expanded in this text.

She writes about the gradual drift from the conservatism of his non-political family to his increasing attraction to nationalism and separatism, and to an exceptional commitment to the Irish language and Irish culture. She justifies her decision to dwell on the 1916-1924 period because this was the time in his life when he made his unique contribution to the foundation of the state and to the political nature and final structure of the independent nation. It was at this time his reputation as a soldier and leader reached its height.

The biography was originally conceived after she had written her earlier thesis on the Army Mutiny, *Almost a Rebellion – the Irish Army Mutiny of 1924*.[2] She thus became familiar with my father's prominent role in the army leading up to the mutiny, and later expressed an interest in the part he played in the foundation of the Irish Free State and the Irish Army. For many years my family had been under pressure from friends and colleagues of my father's to have a biography written, just as he had frequently been requested to prepare an autobiography while he was still living. Indeed, in the early sixties he was induced to cooperate with the late Mary Purcell to write his memoirs. He commenced to do so in his usual systematic way, but after preparing two chapters about his early years, which are available in UCD archives, his distaste for the task led to his neglect of the project. I have no idea how he managed to explain his lack of cooperation to Miss Purcell. After his death, we had always intended to approach a biographer, but failed to identify a suitable candidate – until Maryann Valiulis arrived.

The biography was published twenty-one years after his death. It was co-published by the Kentucky University Press for the American market. It is the product of ten years of research, if we include the four years devoted to researching Valiulis's first monograph, *Almost a Rebellion*. The bedrock of the research material used by her is the large Mulcahy collection of War of Independence, Truce, Civil War and Cumann na nGaedheal papers which are lodged in the UCD archives. She had access to other papers in the university archives and papers in the National Library, the military archives, the Royal Irish Academy and elsewhere. While I have no reason to be unhappy with Valiulis's perception of his military and political career or of her interpretation of his motives and actions, there are several reasons why I should add to her account of his life. Her biography is largely confined to the years 1916–1924, and there are certain insights into a man's character which can best be conveyed by those who knew him best. On the other hand, I am also conscious that familiarity and consanguinity can also lead to biases which can distort the truth.

Neither I nor my siblings were too concerned about the omission of the more personal aspects of our father's personality or family life from the biography. We thought it fulfilled an important purpose, which was to record the particular role he played in organising and directing an army, both in military and ethical terms, that could successfully stand up to British aggression, which would not alienate the local population, and which would play its role in establishing a free and democratically elected parliament.

I thought it an innovative idea to have a member of the subject's family review the biography in the capacity of a professional reviewer. It provides an opportunity of amplifying some of the aspects of his life and times that emerge in the text. Some additional information may be of interest, particularly in relation to Mulcahy's relationship with and recorded opinions of some of his contemporaries in the national movement. His public personality, portrayed with unusual clarity by Valiulis, and an appreciation of which provides an understanding of much of his career, naturally impinged much on his family through his characteristic austerity and self-discipline. While this was part of his public persona, his family and friends were aware of his other attributes: his graciousness, warmth, consideration and informality. An account of the family circumstances and background was included in my previous book, *Richard Mulcahy – A Family Memoir*.

Whatever views may have been expressed about the Valiulis biography by reviewers and by others, it was generally agreed that it was a most scholarly work, particularly rich in its use of documentary sources. It was its high academic standards that gave the greatest satisfaction to us. The integrity of the author was apparent from her objective account of his role and his personality, an assessment which was not free of criticism at times. By her objectivity and her frank interpretation of the events in which he was involved, she avoided the adulatory approach which can so often detract from a biography. At the same time she managed to encapsulate his personality in a remarkable manner, although some would – and did – say that the personality she portrayed was the one which was perceived by those who met him in his public life, and that his more affable personality attributes were only apparent to his family and friends.

While a few statements and conclusions in the book may require qualification from the vantage point of personal experience, the comments of some of the professional reviewers of the biography warrant examination. Anyone familiar with the art of reviewing books is only too aware of the temptations that afflict reviewers and of the irritations that can beset authors. The temptations afflicting reviewers can be based on failure to read the manuscript, on disagreement about facts with which the author may be more familiar than the reviewer, on indulging in 'ego trips' which distract from the purpose of a review and which may be based on the reviewer's own fixed ideas and prejudices, and on preoccupation with trivial or anecdotal details.

As a frequent reviewer of medical papers and books, and as the author of papers and books subjected to review, I am well aware of the reviewer's foibles, and of the sensitivity and limited insights of authors. So I found most of the reviews to be disappointing in that they missed the chief messages in Valiulis's scholarship. It was clear that some of the reviewers had not read the book, or at least had not sufficiently acquainted themselves with it to grasp its main substance. In other cases, the reviewer seemed to be on some kind of ego trip, leaving the review largely irrelevant or too preoccupied with the unnecessary, trivial details of my father's life.

Valiulis's biography is an important contribution to recent Irish history. It emphasises the role of the GHQ staff in organising the Irish forces in the War of Independence and in achieving such military success. The role of the GHQ staff has been neglected by historians and writers of the times. This is almost certainly because the early Béaslaí biography of Michael Collins became an important source document about the War of Independence for subsequent writers and historians, but it makes no mention of the GHQ staff as such, and deals almost entirely with Collins's exploits. It leaves a gaping lacuna in the military history of the revolution.

The biography refers to some aspects of Mulcahy's career between 1916 and 1924 which have also been neglected by reviewers and historians, and which had an impact on subsequent Irish history. These were his insistence that the army should maintain high ethical standards, even under the stresses of increasing British harassment and atrocities and a bitter civil war; and that the army should remain subservient to the Dáil and the will of the people. He could not ensure that all his soldiers conformed to his standards of conduct, but history tells us that civil wars are the most brutal form of human conflict and, as in the Irish Civil War, neither side truly wins. It is a loss to the whole nation, to its self-esteem, and to its reputation.

Mulcahy's devotion to democracy ensured that his primary motivation during his time in the army and his many years in politics was based on a deep commitment to the supremacy of the people's will. This is apparent from the following excerpt, written by him many years later when proportional representation was under threat by Fianna Fáil.

> I think it could be said that even today, democracy, as we understood it from Griffith's dream and teaching back in 1908 etc, has its work cut out for it to maintain the concept it had then for us, of freedom and dignity and the sense of personal responsibility and worth, and the understanding of communal or society power that we associated with the idea of a parliament based on proportional representation.[3]

Throughout his military career from March 1918, when he became chief of staff, to March 1924, when he resigned from the Department of Defence, he was always committed to the philosophy that the army must remain subservient to parliament and the people. This philosophy, which I believe is the imporant message to be derived from Valiulis's biography, is clearly apparent from his papers and tape recordings, and from his subsequent history. It is encapsulated in the phrase he used in his homily over Michael Collins's grave:

> Our army has been the people, is the people, and will be the people.

Appendix 4

The 1999 Memoir, the Mulcahy Papers, Annotation and Tapes

I have used four documentary sources in writing about my father. They are my previous book, *Richard Mulcahy – a Family Memoir*, his papers lodged in the archives of University College Dublin, his three hundred and fifty page annotation of Béaslaí's *Michael Collins and the Making of a New Ireland*, and his tape recordings made between 1961 and 1970.

The Memoir: Richard Mulcahy – a Family Memoir

Richard Mulcahy – a Family Memoir was published by me in 1999. It was a memoir about the extended families of my father and mother, the Mulcahys and the Ryans, and about our home while I and my five siblings were living in Lissenfield House in the inner suburb of Rathmines in Dublin. It was first published privately and dedicated to my six children as a source of information about their family background. It was subsequently published for public distribution after it had been reviewed by the *Irish Times* in summer 1999.

The Mulcahy family were prominent in the army, in the Church and in education. Patrick and Elizabeth Mulcahy had eight children. Patrick Mulcahy was a post office official in Waterford, and later postmaster in Thurles and finally in Ennis. Four of his five daughters were nuns, three in teaching Orders and one in the Sisters of Charity. The fifth sister was a teacher, who eventually married and had six children of her own. All of the sisters received a third level university education in Dublin. The three boys were expected to fend for themselves from the age of sixteen.

My father's brother Patrick fought with the British sappers in the Great War and afterwards joined the Irish Volunteers during the War of Independence. He remained in the Free State army after the Treaty and was chief of staff in the 1950s, succeeding his elder brother in the position by more than thirty years. The youngest boy, Sam, joined the Cistercians in Roscrea and later, as Abbot Dom Columban, he established the first post-Reformation monastery in Mid-Lothian in the heart of Presbyterian Scotland where he played a crucial part in the ecumenical movement.

There were twelve Ryan children born to John and Elizabeth Ryan of Tomcoole, near Taghmon in County Wexford. The family had been farmers in the area for many generations. My mother, Mary Josephine or 'Min', was the sixth. Eleven of the twelve siblings had a third level education at the Royal University or later at University College, Dublin, or at an agricultural college. Six of the eight sisters were trained as teachers and one as a scientist. As a family they were dedicated to education and they were politically and nationally minded, first after the centenary celebrations of 1798 and later more radically, after the 1916 Rising.

The Ryan family was divided on the Treaty. James Ryan was aide de camp to Joseph McDonagh in the GPO in 1916. He later opposed the Treaty and was for many years a minister in Fianna Fáil administrations. Kate Ryan married Seán T. O'Kelly, who was also anti-Treaty and prominent in Fianna Fáil and later president of Ireland from 1954-1968. After Kate's death in 1934, O'Kelly married my mother's youngest sister, Phyllis.

Agnes Ryan married Denis McCullough, who was president of the IRB before the Rising and who established the radical nationalist Dungannon Clubs in the North. McCullough supported the Treaty and was for some time a Cumann na nGaedheal deputy. Those who remained in Wexford were anti-Treaty, but after some years there was a reconciliation thanks to the good sense of our various parents on both sides. The next Ryan generation was unaffected by the family's political divisions.

My memoirs provided considerable details about both families. I also wrote about my father, but I was mainly concerned with his opinions about other military and political leaders and about some of the important events with which he was associated during the revolutionary period. This current memoir deals only with my father's life from his early years up to his retirement from politicas and the Dáil in 1961. It contains a considerable amount of fresh material which I have added since my memoir of ten years ago.

THE MULCAHY PAPERS

I have included additional material which will confirm the view expressed by many of Mulcahy's contemporaries that, through his intimate contact with the leading politicians and military figures from 1916-1924, and his large collection of War of Independence, Truce, Civil War and Cumann na nGaedheal papers; he was probably the best qualified surviving participant to write about these historic times. One of his correspondents writes 'as well as being the maker you will also be the narrator of modern Irish history'. Páidín O'Keefe, secretary of Sinn Féin during the revolution, exclaims 'that the people of Ireland know that some day the truth will be written, and this can be by only one man, that is, Mulcahy', and, perhaps seeking divine support for his opinion, he adds 'God help us!' The same views were expressed by Col Gerry Ryan, the IRA leader in Tipperary.

Having been trained in the postal service, as part of his organisational skills he was a stickler for detail. He was also an assiduous collector of papers. His papers were presented to the UCD Archives in 1970–1971, where they form a substantial part of the university's collection of early twentieth century material. His earlier War of Independence papers were captured by the British in November 1920 and were later destroyed by fire during a doodle bomb attack on a British army installation in London during the Second World War.

The index of his papers is divided into sections and runs to ninety-three pages of typed A4 paper. The earlier papers dealing with strictly military matters were originally lodged in Portobello Barracks when he retired from the army after the Civil War in May 1923. They were removed by him when he was preparing his submission to the Army Mutiny enquiry. They were never returned to the army but were carefully maintained by him at his home, Lissenfield House, until they were presented to UCD. They were in excellent order and fully archived, in his style, so that the task of the staff in the Archives Department was made substantially easier than usual in such situations.

When he retired from politics in 1961 at the age of seventy-five he was a little disconsolate and unhappy out of the corridors of Fine Gael and Dáil Éireann. He had retired reluctantly and partly due to family pressure. He found himself at an unfamiliar and unwelcome loose end. His dilemma was my reason for suggesting that he consider putting his large collection of papers in order, and that he should write his autobiography or at least put on paper an account of his career in the army and in politics.

His memory of events was remarkable, as was his recall of people. No doubt in this regard he was greatly assisted by his huge archive. However, during his active years in politics, he did not concern himself with past events and constantly expressed the view that, rather than waste time and energy in recalling the past, the problems of the present were more than enough to occupy his time and his talents.

With a part-time secretary, a typewriter, and an inexhaustible supply of tapes of every size and description, all this was to change. He threw himself enthusiastically into the task of recording and archiving his collection of papers, and of recounting the background of his early military and political career.

THE ANNOTATION

His annotation on Béaslaí's *Michael Collins and the Making of a New Ireland* was dictated in 1961 and 1962. The annotation runs to 310 pages of A4 typescript. It was done at my suggestion, because I was aware of the heavily blue-pencilled volumes of the Collins biography in his library and of his dissatisfaction with many of Béaslaí's opinions and accounts. The index of this annotation was completed by me in 1995. Each quotation I have included is referenced by Béaslaí's volume number and the annotation page number. The annotation was dictated initially on tape and subsequently transcribed by his secretary, Chriss O'Doherty. His comments have not been edited in any way, nor have any changes been made in punctuation or syntax (which may have been influenced by the Irish idiom) apart from an occasional change to clarify meaning. The style and syntax is distinctly that of the spoken, not written, word, but is no less readable for that.

The annotation with its index is available in the UCD archives. Mulcahy's comments in the annotation will complement the information available on his tapes. Information from the annotation can also be sought indirectly by consulting the index of the Béaslaí biography and referring to the appropriate page in the annotation, although Béaslaí's index is incomplete. I have included some extracts from Mulcahy's annotation in my summaries of the tape material where these extracts are relevant to the recordings.

The index of the annotation includes the names of participants, key subjects and events. The subjects chosen are those of principal interest. There is inevitably some overlapping between some of these. Some subjects might appear to be incompletely indexed because of the use of different headings. An example is 'IRA, including Volunteers'. Some references to the IRA/Volunteers appear under other army headings. This may apply to other subjects as well.

The names of all participants are included, except for casual references to individuals who would be of little interest to the researcher. References to the names of people who are included are infrequently omitted when they appear in a context which is irrelevant to them or which adds no useful information to their roles. Sections of particular interest or of a comprehensive nature are included in bold type and underlined in the index.

Mulcahy's military career and the role of the GHQ staff were overshadowed by the publication of Béaslaí's biography of Collins in 1927. While he was writing the biography, Béaslaí never consulted Mulcahy. This was surely remarkable in view of Mulcahy's intimate association with Collins from 1917 onwards, and without the Mulcahy papers Béaslaí could not have had access to information about the GHQ and many aspects of the army's organisation. Nor did Béaslaí consult the senior members of the Irish Free State army who had been attached to GHQ and to Collins's group during the War of Independence, including Sean McMahon and Sean O'Muirhile. Despite

Béaslaí's failure to consult with several important figures who worked with Collins and despite the incomplete research material available so soon after Collins's death, his book was perceived to be a history of the War of Independence and became the main source material about the war for other writers and historians.

Reference to the annotation bears testimony to the many errors of fact and omission which Mulcahy perceived the biography to contain and which could only be attributed to Béaslaí's failure to exhaustively research his subject, at least if one is to accept his biography as a comprehensive account of the War of Independence.

A history of the Collins biographies by Béaslaí and Rex Taylor has been published by Déirdre McMahon.[1] From her detailed account of the commissioning of the Béaslaí biography, it is clear that the work was undertaken in the midst of considerable controversy. Some of Béaslaí's closest colleagues thought him unfit as Collins's biographer, and the Cabinet was opposed to its publication at such an early date. If it had not been for the pressure exerted by the Collins family, it is unlikely that the biography would have been written at such an early stage in the evolution of the Irish Free State.

The biography's limitations as a history of the war are clear in that it was largely devoted to Collins's military and political contributions, and made only casual reference to other members of the GHQ staff, and their considerable routine work during the War. Béaslaí fails to mention the setting up of the Volunteer Executive in October 1917 and the GHQ staff at the time of the conscription threat in March 1918. He does not identify the leaders of the Dublin Brigade after its re-establishment in August 1917. Béaslaí had no idea of the membership of these three bodies. It might be construed from his account (and of course from Neil Jordan's 1996 film) that, from October 1917 to the end of the war in July 1921, Collins was the prime influence in organising the army leading the resistance. GHQ is not included in the index of the book, although some of the members are, but then generally only in the context of Collins's role.

The Béaslaí biography was influential in leading to certain misconceptions about the War of Independence, such as the chief of staff position, where my father is described as the assistant chief of staff and Brugha as the chief of staff. On the occasion of the anniversary of the first meeting of Dáil Éireann in 1974, a government publication describes Cathal Brugha as chief of staff, confirming Béaslaí's error, and Mr Albert Reynolds in 1994, in his address on the same occasion, stated that Michael Collins and Cathal Brugha directed the War of Independence. Brugha was never chief of staff, nor did he ever attend staff meetings. The biography led to other inaccuracies such as in the army's 2006 brochure commemorating the ninetieth anniversary of the Rising when Collins is described as 'our great chief of staff'. I have in the recent past brought this misleading statement to the notice of the army authorities.

Apart from the tape recordings, perhaps Mulcahy's single most important contribution was to dictate the annotation. It is a valuable critique of the Béaslaí biography and goes a long way to clarify the Collins story, as well as qualifying or even contradicting many aspects of Béaslaí's account. He is highly critical of Béaslaí's account of the War of Independence, not only because of his many errors of fact, but also because he maintained that Béaslaí's experience was confined to the Collins intelligence group, 'the Squad', and the Vaughan's Hotel area. He goes on to say:

> If this work of Béaslaí's were carefully examined to see what particular parts of the country he deals with, it would be found that he had little general picture of the country as a whole. To some extent, or perhaps to a large extent, this restriction in outlook is related to his rather concentrated connection with the Vaughan's Hotel citadel and . . .[2]

> Except for the fact that we probably will find in the Murthuile papers, that some of those people who congregated at Vaughan's Hotel or at Devlin's had their minds working rather in an IRB enclosure of a very limited and personal group kind, and didn't see the work of those outside that group.[3]

Mulcahy refused to review the biography when invited to do so by the publishers in 1926, as did my mother. His reasons for doing so were clear. He did not wish to rekindle any fresh controversy after the bitterness of the Civil War and the subsequent mutiny, and he was consistent in avoiding any public reference to the personalities involved in the struggle and to the many conflicts which arose. He stated that a comprehensive commentary by him would not be much shorter than the biography itself. He also refused to review the second abridged edition which was published in 1937.

> One of my deficiencies may be that I find it easier to do things with a shut mouth, and that it would be very difficult even with a natural or developed sense of publicity, to note what things ought to be publicised in the days of '22, '23 and '24.[4]

Béaslaí was one of the thirteen members of the GHQ staff portrayed in the painting by Leo Whelan which now hangs in McKee Barracks. He had no military function during the War of Independence but was the editor of the clandestine paper of the army, *An tÓglach*. Despite Mulcahy's criticism of Béaslaí's biography and his views about the author's limited knowledge of the work of the Volunteers during the War of Independence, it was characteristic of his loyalty to his colleagues in the army that he gave the homily at Béaslaí's graveside and paid him a most gracious tribute for his sterling work as editor of *An tÓglach*.

THE TAPES

I completed an abstract of the one hundred and sixty tapes which Mulcahy recorded during his retirement. I did this for the convenience of research students and others, but the abstracts are not sufficiently detailed to provide a comprehensive word search nor are they available online. The text is available in the UCD and Military Archives. The tapes are currently being digitised and will be available on CD by the mid-summer of 2009. Hopefully an index of the tapes will be provided in the future. The tapes are of particular interest because of his interviews with my mother, myself, a number of historians and media correspondents, and with a few of his contemporaries who lived through the revolutionary period. I have added a number of my own observations at various stages in the summary of the tapes which were relevant to his interviews. This document runs to 147 pages and might be of interest because of the comments derived from conversations I had with my father.

When I began medical practice as a physician in Dublin in October 1950, I started using a tape recorder to dictate letters and papers which were then transcribed by my secretary. I would dictate directly to tape, although conceptualising and dictating at the same time requires some experience and practice. I was something of a pioneer in using a tape recorder, at least among my colleagues in the medical profession, and indeed many of my colleagues continued to dictate directly to their secretaries for decades after this time.

My interest in using tape recorders must have been derived from my father's long interest in this form of communication. His interest in the early years started in 1925 when he attended the Inter-Parliamentary Union Meeting in New York, where he first saw the dictaphone. He refers to this visit on tape. He had a machine imported for his own use and he proceeded to record documents and speeches, and had some contact with Delargey of the Folklore Commission. I have a photograph of a group using the dictaphone to collect songs and stories from a *seanachaoidhe* in the Aran Islands. He also recorded songs and stories for *An Fear Mór* at Ring College in County Waterford. In the late 1930s he was using a wire recorder which had been manufactured in Chicago. There is a reference to his first contact with a recording machine, a phonograph in the possession of Father O'Flynn in Ballingeary, which was a primitive forerunner of the modern dictaphone. According to the dates of the various tapes, they were recorded between 1963 and 1970. However, Mulcahy was using a tape recorder as early as 1961 just after retirement, but he probably did not start recording conversations until after he had dictated the annotation about the Béaslaí biography in 1961 and 1962. He also did some earlier recordings but, like the annotation recordings, these tapes may have been destroyed after they were transcribed by his secretary. These transcriptions are available in the UCD archives.

The tapes which were recorded in the earlier years contain the most important material dealt with in the discussions. In the earlier stages he retained the sharpness of mind and the occasional terse sentence which were attributes of his during his more active years. However in the later tapes, during his last years, his speech and his thought reactions are slower, his speech is more hesitant and inclined to slurring and he often becomes preoccupied by certain themes about which he becomes repetitious and almost obsessive. By this time he was almost blind and was showing early signs of intellectual deterioration as part of the ageing process. The themes which preoccupied him include, among others, de Valera's perceived failure of leadership during the War of Independence, the shortcomings of the Fianna Fáil regime, the shortcomings of the historians who wrote about the 1916-1924 period, and his sensitivity to criticism of Collins and Griffith. While my father might occasionally in his earlier years and in private be encouraged by visitors to talk about some of his exploits during the War of Independence, particularly his numerous escapes from the British forces while he was on the run, he had little inclination to talk about the past, at least until I became his confidante after his retirement. His reluctance to talk about the past is well summed-up in the letter he wrote to the publishers of Béaslaí's biography when he, and later my mother, refused to review the publication, making a remark made by him on more than one occasion: 'Haven't we enough to do with the country in the state it is without the futility of going back over the past!'

He expressed strong and trenchant views about historians in general and Desmond Williams in particular.[5] His views of the shortcomings of historians are scattered about in several places in the later tapes, and were based on the historians' interpretation of certain aspects of the history of the War of Independence and its aftermath which conflicted with his own experience and opinions. His criticism of Williams was largely based, I believe, on the latter's view, expressed in a Thomas Davis lecture at the time of the fiftieth anniversary of the Civil War, that de Valera and Collins were equally responsible for the Civil War. There is little doubt that Williams had a point in implicating Collins, but this view grated on Mulcahy's sensitivity about Collins and his apparent view that Collins could do no wrong.

During the recordings Dad showed himself to be a good listener, to have the patience of Job, and to have a terrier-like persistence when seeking the information he desired. He also maintained his sense of humour, and of all the speakers on the tapes, he is probably the most articulate, if one allows for his circumlocutions and fondness for metaphor. The best tapes are those which were recorded in the early sixties and those which were recorded by him on his own, or in conversation with myself, Prof. Kevin Nowlan and a few others who spoke as clearly as he and who were as articulate as he was.

Because my father recorded a great number of interviews with many different people, it is inevitable that there is a considerable amount of repetition, particularly when he is describing his own participation in the events of the time.

The tapes were a miscellaneous lot of different sizes and manufacture. Because of the difficulties of having them duplicated on to better quality tape in Ireland, they were brought to the United States by Maryann Valiulis where two copies were made. Shortly after they were duplicated, the original tapes, with the indexes prepared by Mulcahy, were accidentally destroyed. The two duplicate sets were returned to me in 1992 about the time of the publication of Mulcahy's biography. During 1993 and 1994 I made a summary of their contents and added further material about my father and the revolutionary period. Most of this added material was derived from conversations with him or from his annotation. In the latter case the appropriate page of the annotation is referenced. Many of the tapes have been transcribed and the transcriptions will be found in the university archives, particularly in the section marked P7b/176-200. Reference to the tapes in the text of the memoir shows the tape number and side.

The tapes' quality of reproduction is mixed. Relatively few are sufficiently well recorded to be suitable for direct transmission by radio, although excerpts, suitably edited, would be satisfactory for this purpose. There are substantial problems created by the absence of information about the identity of some of the people interviewed by Mulcahy, a problem compounded by the loss of the original tapes and his detailed index. There is also the problem of the poor delivery of some of the interviewees, and the unstructured arrangements when three or more people are taking part in a conversation. In the latter case, the conversations are difficult or impossible to interpret because of repeated interruptions or when two or more participants speak at the same time. During some conversations the speakers may have been badly seated in relation to the microphone, and are therefore difficult to understand. Unfortunately, because I did not listen to the tapes when they were initially recorded, it did not occur to me at the time to supervise their production.

Because of the considerable amount of work involved in the preparation of the tape abstracts, and of the tedium of the work, some details of value may have been omitted. I have, where possible, provided information about the dates when the recordings were made. This is important, if only because my father became unduly prolix, repetitive, and sometimes slightly irrelevant in his last few years.

REFERENCES

Annotation references: eg V1 26, volume number of Piaras Béaslaí's biography of Michael Collins and page number of Mulcahy's annotation.

References to Mulcahy papers: eg P7b/182.

References to Cabinet papers, 1919-1922 & 1948-1952: eg CPs 9/1/21.

The tapes, annotation and papers are available in the University College Dublin Archives. The Cabinet papers are available in the National Archives.

INTRODUCTION

1   Maryann G. Valiulis. *Portrait of a Revolutionary: General Richard Mulcahy and the Founding of the Irish Free State.* Dublin: Irish Academic Press, 1992.
2   Piaras Béaslaí. *Michael Collins and the Making of a new Ireland.* Dublin: Phoenix, 1926.

CHAPTER 1: RICHARD MULCAHY: A SUMMARY OF HIS CAREER

1   P7a&b 182
2   Maryann G. Valiulis. *Almost a Rebellion: The Irish Army Mutiny of 1924.* Cork: Tower Books, 1985.
3   P7b/182, pp 27-46

Chapter 2: The Years 1916-1924

The Rising, Knutsford and Frongoch

1   V1 8
2   Joseph Lawless, *The Capuchin Annual*, 1966, p 309
3   Joseph Lawless, *An t'Oglach*, July 1926, p 4
4   V1 15 (*The Constabulary Gazette*)
5   *An t'Oglach*, April 1961
6   V1 25
7   Michael Tierney, *Eoin MacNeill: Scholar and Man of Action, 1867-1945*. Ed. F. X. Martin. Oxford: Clarendon Press, 1980. p 266
8   V1 20
9   V1 16

Return from Frongoch and Army Leadership

1   V1 95-100
2   V2 15-16 includes O'Muirthile's memoirs
3   V2 41
4   V1 95-100 and V1 126
5   V1 48,49
6   V2 173
7   *An Cosantoir*. Vol. 40, 1980. pp 35-39, 67-71, 99-102
8   C. C.Trench, *Irish Independent*, 8 August 1992
9   V2 89, 103, 117
10   V2 43
11   V2 32

The War of Independence: Army Policy

1   *Irish Indiscretions*. London: Allen and Unwin, 1922.
2   P. S. O'Hegarty. *The Victory of Sinn Féin*. Dublin: The Talbot Press, 1924. p 166
3   V1 130
4   V1 69
5   V1 29
6   Michael Collins. *The Path to Freedom*. Dublin: The Talbot Press, 1922. p 61
7   V1 33

8   V1 30

9   V1 102

10   P7a/196

11   Desmond Ryan. 'Sean Treacy and the Third Tipperary Brigade.' *Kerryman*. Tralee, 1925.

12   V1 89

13   V1 103, 104

14   V1 123

15   V2 36, 37

16   V2 161

17   V1 92

18   David Fitzpatrick. *Politics and Irish Life, 1913-1921: Provincial Experience of War and Revolution*. Dublin: Gill and Macmillan, 1993. p 93

19   Ibid p 206

20   Ibid p 208

21   V2 96

22   V2 288

23   CPs 10/6/1920

24   V1 32

25   P7v/182

26   P. S. O'Hegarty, op cit

27   Ibid p 171

28   V1 24

THE FIRST DÁIL AND SINN FÉIN

1   V1 61

2   V1 85, 86

3   Michael Laffan. *The Resurrection of Ireland: The Sinn Féin Party 1916-1923*. Cambridge: Cambridge University Press, 1999.

4   V2 133

5   CPs 15/9/21 and CPs 4/11/21

6   Cps 29/9/21

7   P. S. O'Hegarty, Op cit

8   CPs 24/1/1922
9   V2 28

THE TRUCE

1   P7a/5
2   CPs 24/11/21
3   P7b/182
4   CPs 29/9/21
5   V2 166
6   V2 165

CHAPTER 3: THE LEADERS

MICHAEL COLLINS

1   V2 256
2   V1 35
3   V2 113
4   V1 94
5   V2 73
6   V1 7
7   V2 164
8   V1 118
9   V2 45
10 V1 33
11 V2 80
12 V1 134
13 V1 135
14 V1 38
15 V2 36-37
16 V1 39
17 V1 43
18 V2 20 and V2 175
19 V1 95
20 V2 239

21   V1 117

22   V2 176

23   V2 147

24   V2 174

25   V2 162

26   V2 72

27   V2 159

28   John Regan. 'Looking at Mick again: Demilitarising Michael Collins.' *History Ireland*. Vol. 3, No. 3. pp 17-22

29   P7b/189, pp 51-54

30   Calton Younger. *Ireland's Civil War*. London: Muller, 1968. p 435

31   Piaras Béaslaí, Op cit

32   Ulick O'Connor. *Oliver St. John Gogarty*. London: Mandarin, 1990. p 1900

33   *An t'Oglach*. Winter 1967

34   P7a/178

35   P7a/196

Arthur Griffith

1   V2 108

2   Padraic Colum. *Arthur Griffith*. Dublin: Browne and Nolan, 1959. p 53

3   V2 159

4   V2 159

5   M. J. McManus. *Eamon de Valera*. Dublin: Talbot Press, 1944. p161

6   Lord Pakenham, Earl of Longford and Thomas P. O'Neill. *Eamon de Valera*. Gill and Macmillan, 1970.

7   Max Beaverbrook *The Decline and Fall of Lloyd George*. London: Collins, 1963. pp 82-123

8   V2 163

9   V2 164

10   V2 147

11   V1 108

12   V2 6

13   Oliver St. John Gogarty. *Arthur Griffith and Michael Collins Memorial Issue*. Dublin: Martin Lester, 1924. p 54

EAMON DE VALERA

1 V2 4
2 V2 108
3 V2 124
4 V2 139
5 V1 49
6 V2 171-2
7 V2 173
8 V2 190-191
9 V2 138
10 V2 1
11 V2 3
12 V2 6
13 V2 67
14 V2 74
15 Ibid
16 Ibid
17 V2 109
18 V2 108
19 V2 6-8
20 Michael Collins, Op cit p 33
21 CPs 30/11/20
22 CPs 13/12/20

CATHAL BRUGHA

1 V1 132-133
2 V1 94
3 V2 41
4 V1 77
5 V2 56-57
6 V2 7
7 V122

ERNIE O'MALLEY, DICK MCKEE, LIAM LYNCH AND OTHERS

1   V2 85
2   V2 87
3   Ernie O'Malley. *On Another Man's Wound*. London: Rich and Cowan, 1936.
4   V1 44
5   V2 81
6   V2 233
7   V2 123

CHAPTER 4: FURTHER FACTORS IN GENESIS OF CIVIL WAR

1   *The Last Days of Dublin Castle: The Diaries of Mark Sturgis*. Ed. Michael Hopkinson. Irish Academic Press, 1999.
2   V2 220
3   V2 248
4   V2 250
5   V2 244-246
6   Tom Garvin. *1992: The Birth of Irish Democracy*. Dublin: Gill and Macmillan, 1996.
7   J. J. Lee. *Ireland 1912-1985. Politics and Society*. Cambridge: Cambridge University Press, 1989.
8   Michael Tierney. Op cit, p 266
9   V1 61
10   Tom Garvin. 'The Anatomy of a Nationalistic Revolution: Ireland 1858-1928.' *Comparative Studies in Society and History*. Vol. 28. Cambridge University Press, 1986.
11   *Irish Independent*, 9 December 1921

CHAPTER 5: POST-TREATY AND THE ARMY MUTINY

1   P7b/182. See John F. Larchet. *The Army School of Music*. Dublin: Corrigan and Wilson, 1923.
2   P7a/201
3   *The Kilkenny People*, 6 October 1923, quoting an article from *Collier's Magazine*.

4   P7a/196

5   Pb7/182/27-46

6   Terence de Vere White. *Business and Finance*, 7 July 1967. pp 28-29

7   Paddy O'Connor, personal correspondence in author's possession.

8   Maryann G. Valiulis. *Almost a Rebellion : The Irish Army Mutiny of 1924*. Cork: Tower Books, 1985.

9   V1 46

10   Michael Tierney. Op cit, p266

CHAPTER 6: THE YEARS 1924-1932

POLITICAL WILDERNESS

1   P7B/12

2   P7B/35-50

3   P7b/182/27-46

CUMANN NA NGAEDHEAL

1   Maryann G. Valiulis. *After The Revolution: The formative Years of Cumann na nGaedheal.* (personal communication)

2   Michael Tierney. Op cit, p 355

3   P7b/23

4   *Clonmel Nationalist*, 28 November 1959

THE IRISH LANGUAGE

1   Michael Tierney. *Studies*, March 1926

2   Richard Mulcahy. *Studies*, March 1926

3   CPs 9/1/21

4   CPs 20/2/20

5   John Coolahan. *Irish Education: Its History and Structure*. Dublin: IPA, 1981. p 45

6   Ibid p 81

7   *Claidheamh Soluis*, 29 November 1902, quoted in Michael Tierney (1980)

Chapter 7: 1932 and After: Opposition and the Inter-Party Governments

1   CPs 11/10/48

2   CPs 19/8/48

3   Patrick Lynch, personal communication

4   CPs 9/11/48, CPs 12/11/48/ and CPs 14/11/48

5   CPs 7/1/49

6   CPs 3/5/49

7   Prof. John Murphy. *Sunday Independent*, 17 August 1992

8   CPs 4/11/49

9   CPs 14/11/50

10   CPs 6/4/51

11   Brian Maye. *Fine Gael – 1923-1987*. Dublin: Blackwater Press, 1993.

12   Ibid

Chapter 8: Later Years and Last Days

1   Michael Tierney. Op cit

2   Padraic Colum. Op cit

3   Boilbester, *Lady Lavery's biography*. p 151

4   P7b/27

5   P7b/17/13

6   P7b/17/15

7   P7a/201

8   P7b/17/6

9   Prof. John Murphy. *Sunday Independent,* 17 August 1992

Appendix 2: Mulcahy's homily over the graves of Thomas Ashe, Peadar Kearney and Piaras Béaslaí, 20 August 1967

1   *An t'Oglach*, Winter 1967. pp 4-5

Appendix 3: The Valiulis Biography

1   Maryann G. Valiulis. *Portrait of a Revolutionary: General Richard Mulcahy and the Founding of the Irish Free State.* Dublin: Irish Academic Press, 1992.

2   Maryann G. Valiulis. *Almost a Rebellion: The Irish Army Mutiny of 1924.* Cork: Tower Books, 1985.

3   V2 114

Appendix 4: The 1999 Memoir, the Mulcahy Papers, Annotation and Tapes

1   Déirdre McMahon. 'Michael Collins and his Biographers: Piaras Béaslaí and Rex Taylor'. *Bullan.* Vol. 2, No. 2. Oxford, 1996. pp 55-66

2   V2 81

3   V2 35

4   V1 46

5   V2 262

Index